Old Market, Halifax

North Side.)

Heritage Shell Guide

West Yorkshire

William (Bill) Glossop was born in Yorkshire where his grandparents were all engaged in local trades. He attended a Butler Act Technical School in Sheffield run by a redoubtable Methodist head and went on to read English literature and politics at Keele. After a spell teaching in further education he was called to the Bar by Lincoln's Inn and developed a career at the criminal bar. He now sits as an Immigration Judge in London.

He continued to live in and around Yorkshire until recently. He is married with two children and lives in the West Country. His interests are church music, architecture, politics and defence.

Heritage Shell Guide

West Yorkshire

William Glossop

CANTERBURY
PRESS
Norwich

First published in 2012 by the Canterbury Press Norwich
Editorial office
Invicta House,
108–114 Golden Lane
London, EC1Y 0TG, UK

Canterbury Press is an imprint of Hymns Ancient & Modern Ltd (a registered
charity)
13A Hellesdon Park Road, Norwich,
Norfolk, NR6 5DR, UK

www.canterburypress.co.uk

Sponsored by the Heritage Shell Guide Trust
www.heritageshellguidetrust.org.uk

British Library Cataloguing in Publication data

A catalogue record for this book is available
from the British Library

978 1 84825 127 4

Typeset by Regent Typesetting, London
Printed and bound in Great Britain by
Ashford Colour Press, Gosport, Hants

Photo on p. vi   KIRKSTALL ABBEY, LEEDS.
Photo on p. vii PENNINE WAY.
Photo on p. ix   HAREWOOD HOUSE, LEEDS.

Contents

To Frank and Lilian

Foreword

This book was originally commissioned by Faber & Faber in 1974 when John Piper was the editor of the Shell Guide Series. It was to have been South and West Yorkshire because of the reorganization of local government into new counties. This swept from the West Riding a swathe of country north of the River Wharfe which went to North Yorkshire. Nonetheless the large urban and industrial area which remained, with three major cities and six large towns, was an unwieldy task and was still not complete when Shell withdrew funding from the project. Fresh impetus, however, came from the publication of another of the originally commissioned manuscripts, *North Yorkshire*, by Peter Burton in 2001 with help from the Millennium Fund. Encouraged by Stephen Platten, Bishop of Wakefield – a dedicated Shell Guide enthusiast – a group was formed under his chairmanship to continue the guides. The project became a charitable trust: the Heritage Shell Guide Trust. The guides had never made money and used to be subsidized by Shell to the extent of £30,000 per book even 30 years ago. Publishing has developed since then and although still requiring help from the Trust we have found a way to produce the present book with rather less subsidy.

This guide has over 200 black and white photographs, in line with past practice for buildings and places. The Trust feels it important to continue this tradition, and to promote the art of black and white photography is one of the Trust's objectives. We have also included colour photographs to depict items that are not at their best in black and white: stained glass; oil paintings of places or viewpoints which have been lost; subtle colour in room design, as in Adam's schemes at Harewood and Nostell; and locations brought alive by colour, such as Roberts, Dyers and Finishers Mill in Keighley.

We have also furnished information about markets in the county and addresses for the major houses, gardens and museums.

A fourth innovation is the provision of plans to assist in finding the way around urban areas by foot, bike or car. Looking at Warwickshire, for example, I was baffled by the seemingly endless lists of roads. It was felt that this was a particular difficulty in West Yorkshire where the townscape amounts to perhaps half the county. I hope the organization of relevant text into walking and car routes will be welcomed. Some places have been forgone, but the Guides do not claim to be comprehensive. Some information is locally acquired and I should be pleased to learn of competing views via the Trust website.

The semi-stiff cover is also new; this is to encourage the reader to leave the book in the car and treat it more casually than was the case with paper covers and hard back. Finally, after much debate, we have elected for two columns of print rather than three on the basis that it is easier to read. Over the years, the note style of entry has been forgone in favour of lucidity. Italics indicate places, buildings or people of particular interest.

I have revisited every part of West Yorkshire for this edition, leaving South Yorkshire for a separate book. The differences found in this close survey over a period of 30 years are tremendous. The smell and grittiness of West Yorkshire has subsided. Thirty years ago there remained many collieries with associated spoil heaps. Nostell Priory looked out over slag and gantries of winking lights. In mining towns like Normanton the round whirling eyes of the pithead looked out over black terrace roofs into the churchyard. Steam still powered some engines in the mines and mills. Though not thick with sulphur, the air had that tang of poisonous metal imagined by Keats in Satan's Den. That has all gone now. At Caphouse Colliery, open for visits, you may catch the smell of coal burning in the furnace of its steam winding engine but the cage is lowered for visitors by an electric motor. The sound of miners singing in the white tiled baths brings the place alive, but it is a tape. The familiar routine and sounds belong to another age. A hundred mines have closed and their spoil removed in an operation that has brought light and air to the county. Pontefract, for example, is a wonderful Georgian town for long resting under the pall of coal dust from three collieries. Mining inhibited development so that a lovely old market town has been preserved.

At the heart of West Yorkshire was also the wool industry; its legacy has been more enduring. Huge stone-built Italianate palaces housed spinning and weaving machinery as long as many football fields and they still remain objects of wonder in the landscape. At Elland and Ludden-den massive mills stand alone in the fields; their workers' cottages randomly perched on hills. At Saltaire Titus Salt created an organic development of mills, cottages and community facilities where every need was catered for. Only recently out of production, Saltaire now has a Hockney Gallery, bookshops and exhibitions making good use of the vast mill floors. At Huddersfield new buildings copy large mill structures which have a gaunt familiarity in the valleys. Surprising is the fact that 5,000 people still work in textiles in Yorkshire, though many now in modern factories. Leeds provides the best of the industrial archaeology with water power, steam power and historic equipment like the 'Slubbing Billy' – the Leeds version of a Spinning Jenny. Bradford ought to be pre-eminent showing how its famous worsted was woven, it has an industrial museum which could achieve so much more.

John Piper was keen to have a Shell Guide for an industrial county with mills and industrial archaeology; his plan was a 'coal and wool' emblem for West Yorkshire and 'coal and steel' for South Yorkshire. Much has changed over 30 years, however, and the remnants of industry now have to fight for funding lest even the few slender relics be lost. I have given equal prominence to industrial archaeology with the county's medieval, Georgian and Victorian buildings. I hope John Piper would be pleased with the mix. He and *Myfanwy* used to invite me to dinner annually in the 1970s. I usually attended with some foreboding, having failed to make sufficient progress on the book. The editor was completely relaxed: 'Take your time,' he would say. 'Make sure you enjoy it!' He was the kindest editor you could have with a huge interest in all kinds of buildings and all kinds of people. He was delighted to learn that a well-known restaurant was being used by miners.

The task of getting into houses, factories and churches is not easy but how rewarding it has been to visit so many unpublicized corners of England. I am extremely grateful for all the kindness shown to me by the guardians of this heritage. When taking a rest from exploring I would head up to the moors for large views of the valleys below. Little pubs bustle with activity at Sunday lunch and many a kind landlord has exceeded his 'full today' sign to replenish and send me off exploring again. I share with you a particular few experiences and places: Jacobean Scout Hall near Halifax, its windows unglazed for decades and surrounded by long grass, looks down over unspoiled Shibden Dale. Haworth Parsonage in the grip of snow, icicles clinging to gutters, the silent wooded churchyard listening to stories from the past. The crazy over-elevated Victorian Memorial Tower at Castle Hill, Almondbury, built on the remains of an ancient British fort, itself perched high above the Holme Valley – where it is always windy and the location can make you feel giddy. The blackened medieval shape of Halifax Minster against the green of Signal Hill; the stunning colours of Adam's interior design scheme for Harewood rediscovered by the late Earl; one's first sight of Halifax by night with car headlamps seeming to ride through the sky; the myriad coloured fibres streaming into newly woven cloth on a Jacquard loom; the basement of Armley Mills where the rush of water can be heard from the old waterwheel and the warm smell of oil emanating from *Fiona*, the factory engine. I could go on but it is best that you explore yourself.

W. Glossop
www.heritageshellguidetrust.org.uk

Acknowledgements

I express particular thanks to John Piper, who guided the unpublished first edition of this book. Peter Burton was my colleague in that venture and has remained on board for the present volume. Some of his photographs for the original text are reproduced here – that is because they cannot be bettered. Peter and Harland Walshaw have accompanied me on many expeditions over the last three years, revising entries and taking photographs. I shall always be grateful for their advice and companionship. I am also grateful to the trustees of the Heritage Shell Guide Trust: Stephen Platten, Charlotte Scott, my brother Roger Glossop, who together with Peter and Harland have helped forge this revised publication. I express my thanks also to my publisher, Canterbury Press, and in particular to Christine Smith and Mary Matthews. The Trust is grateful to Veronica Davies, archivist at Shell, for her help and encouragement. I acknowledge gratefully the assistance I have had from Richard Taylor and Leeds City Council; Christopher Hammond in Bradford; Francis Guy and Louise Richardson of Wakefield Council and The Hepworth Wakefield; Chris Edwards; Franne Wills and Richard Macfarlane of Caldersdale Council; Joanne Balmforth of Kirklees Council; Malcolm Swift and George England of the Yorkshire Bar; Stephen McClarence and the Yorkshire Post; the late Earl of Harewood; the present Earl and Countess, and the Harewood Trust; David Slater of Roberts Dyers and Finishers; and last but by no means least Lois Moretti who typed the manuscript and guided my pen in sensible ways.

List of Photographs

Introduction to West Yorkshire

The county dates from the splitting of the old West Riding into North, South and West Yorkshire in 1973. The old West Riding was the largest of the Yorkshire Ridings and ran from Rotherham in the south to Cumberland in the north – its northernmost parts are now in North Yorkshire. Today's West Yorkshire is a metropolitan county of unitary authorities – Bradford, Halifax, Huddersfield, Leeds and Wakefield – which have county services for fire, police and ambulance. Its identity comes from the towns that grew so rapidly from the manufacture of wool and textiles powered by locally mined coal. Despite the downturn in wool manufacturing a strong community remains between the wool towns. They are gathered behind the bulwark of the Pennines to the west and to the south. From these hills rise three rivers – the Wharfe, the Calder and the Aire – whose valleys now define the county and form corridors of settlement and commerce leading towards the Humber. Their high, fast-flowing streams were captured to power the early mills. The growing, spinning and weaving of wool has endured from medieval times, giving a wealth disproportionate to the bare and inhospitable hills.

Leeds apart, West Yorkshire is a stone-built county from its high Pennine valleys to the borders of the Vale of York. The Pennines are predominantly millstone grit – a coarse, pebbly material named for its importance as grinding wheel stone. The south and west fringes of the county are high gritstone moors, hectare upon hectare of desolate peat waste from millennia of rotted sphagnum. Coarse grasses bend the way of the wind and give life to these billowing upland seas. Even on the lower hills the grass only flushes green on the hilltops by the end of June, but in July and August some hills have purple heather crowns. The western edge of the county is traversed by the Pennine Way along the watershed of the Irish and North Seas, granting immense views now to the east and now to the west. The Wharfe rises in part on Rombalds Moor which shows gritstone teeth to the gentle river valley below. Ilkley on the Wharfe became prosperous from proximity to its windy moor (but also its tepid spa). Headstreams of the Worth and Aire gather below the bleak charms of Howarth and Oxenhope, but the chasmed defiles of the Calder Valley are the steepest and most charming. Here narrow valleys filled with trees are overlooked by crags of millstone grit. West of Halifax picturesque villages cling to the valley sides at Heptonstall, Luddenden and Cragg, where houses jostle for space as in Cornish fishing villages. At Heptonstall old cottages perch high on the hillside around an abandoned sixteenth-century church (replaced by a wealthier nineteenth-century one). At Ludden-den houses cluster in the steep valley. Here the stream rushes through the churchyard below a

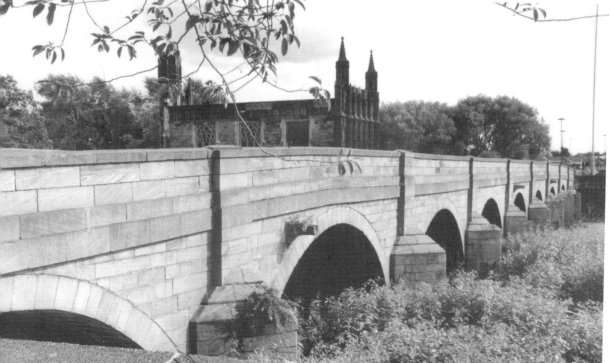

cliff. There is too little space in the village for cars to pass. Above Hebden Bridge where Hardcastle Crags look out over tree-girt Hebden Water, you might be in Scotland. South of the Calder a tributary of the River Ryburn falls from a high Pennine pass via little reservoirs that seethe under the whisking of westerly winds. Lower down in Ripponden a stream rushes through the old town under a high arched bridge formerly part of an important cross-Pennine packhorse route.

Further east undulating valleys become softer where gritstone is overlaid by the Coal Measures which include shales, mud and sandstones. These yield the glorious golden stones of Bradford, Halifax and Huddersfield. The most famous quarries are Bramley Fall and Bolton Woods in Bradford, the source of stone for many public buildings both in Yorkshire, London and overseas. They are from the youngest geological age and light up brilliantly in sunshine, granting newly cleaned towns like Dewsbury and Halifax illumination of their architecture not seen for 150 years. Horbury near Wakefield grew from the quarries there and its most famous son, master builder John Carr, returned a gift to his town in 1793: the exquisitely designed sandstone church of St Peter and St Leonard.

Sandstone and Coal Measures cover two-thirds of the county, providing rolling tree-clad hills – an unexpected pleasure entering the county from the south. In these hilly locations with prospects of woods and water are the mansions of the Earl of Harewood, Lord Darcy at Temple Newsam, Lord St Oswald at Nostell Priory and Sir William Wentworth at Bretton. Further east the county quietens to a land of Permian limestone along its border with North Yorkshire. All along this boundary south from Wetherby to Wentbridge is the beginning of the Vale of York where rich, flatter farmland sits on the most recent rock. Unlike carboniferous limestone in the higher Aire Valley, such as around Malham, there are few outcrops. It does, however, make attractive cottages of grey, cream or even pink limestone often roofed with red pantiles. These signal a 'wolds' area extending down the A1 into South Yorkshire. Just over the boundary at Tadcaster the limestone is particularly pure and was used for the chimneys at Temple Newsam. The Permian limestone of Jacobean Ledstone Hall gleams pink in the setting sun across its valley with a myriad of sparkling windows. The once massive and terrible castle of Pontefract, named the 'White Castle' by Chaucer, had seven limestone towers surrounding its keep and doubtless glowed blood red in its day.

The underlying rocks of West Yorkshire still set the scene for the buildings of today – every part of it reflects what lies beneath. In the very west inhospitable moor and crag is virtually bare of homes. Lower down in the valleys are gritstone farms and weavers' cottages with strings of mullioned windows to capture most light for the production of wool. These illustrate work in the sixteenth to eighteenth centuries at upland sheep farms. Early commercial success shows in mansions whose big hall

Opposite, above: St John Baptist, Norman chancel arch, Adel; below: St John Baptist, arch capitals, Baptism of Christ, Adel.

Overleaf, left: Assize Court, 1810; right: West Riding County Hall, 1894, Wakefield.

windows were carved by sections – in the richest cases comprising 20–30 separate lights as at Barkisland and Wood Lane Halls. They extend along the western part of the county, particularly around Halifax, where timber-framed and many gabled mansions survive. There are a surprising number of timber-framed houses in West Yorkshire – given its bareness in the west and the availability of stone. The grandest is Shibden Hall near Halifax which has diagonal strutting in two gables, timber mullions and a fine aisled barn. In Halifax itself at Woolshops one timbered house remains. From the evidence of surviving timber houses one infers a greater number. Medieval Halifax may have been of strikingly Alpine appearance. At Sharleston near Nostell Priory is an Elizabethan part-timbered hall with a gable of cross-strutting. At Kirklees are the ruinous remains of the priory's timber Elizabethan gatehouse; and at Thornhill Lees is a worthy Tudor survivor once written off by the council that sought its demolition. Despite an industrial location in the shadow of cooling towers (now demolished) it remains standing and in the care of the same family who saved it.

The early cottage industry was performed by carrying wool pieces from process to process and eventually to market. A survivor of

Opposite: LUDDENDEN MILLS;
below, left: SOWERBY BRIDGE, WOOD LANE HALL;
right: WEAVERS' COTTAGES. OLDFIELD.

those days is the Piece Hall in Halifax, a magnificent Georgian market where handmade goods were sold. Weaving on old hand looms was described by J. K. Snowden (*Web of an Old Weaver*, 1896) as 'horse-work':

It was all good-paying stuff, but heavy to weave – a camlet cloth, needing weighted slay-boards. I gat a share of it, in place of one that was laid at home badly, I know not that I ever devoured work with such gluttony as I did that. After the first two days it seemed as if I could not tire. When we went to it of a morning, the smell of the shop made me keen; and all day the din of the looms clacking and bumping set me merry. They faced all one way, the length of a narrow chamber, and I could look along and see the others belting it. But to my thinking we were never fairly agate till after dark, when we had lighted candles, and the shop was throng with great, dithering shadows. By that time we had done talking, and no matter what weather it was, steam ran down the windows.

In the nineteenth century tall mills became an icon of the age, some isolated on the valley floor and some standing on hillsides. Almost every mill was carved from stone on a large Georgian scale, some as massive Italianate palaces, their chimneys built to resemble Florentine campaniles, and the most modest with an eye-catching corona. Today the rhythm of industrial life has been lost. It was well described by writer and artist William Holt even as late as 1939:

In the morning, at dinner-time, and in the evening weavers, spinners, and other workers clatter along the street in their iron-shod clogs. Six days of the week smoke rises from the factory chimneys and steam rises from the neighbouring grates in the streets, where weft-skips, boxes, and wooden beams with iron flanges are stacked high, and all the time warm water flows from the factories into the canal. On Saturday morning at half-past eleven the droning note of machinery in the town sinks gradually into silence and the working folk go home to wash and dress up for the week-end. The womenfolk come out in the afternoon with shopping-baskets covered with white crochet-work cloths to visit shops and the pagoda-like stalls on the little market ground, while most of the men go to football or cricket matches. On Sunday the shops are closed and the town enjoys a quiet Sabbath, silent save for the pealing of church-bells and the organ-led singing in the chapels.

In the eighteenth century the valleys provided routes for canals through the Pennines to Liverpool via the longest tunnels in the country, and also to the West Riding port of Goole. In the late eighteenth century coal began to be abstracted in earnest from hundreds of mines which grew like barnacles clinging to the hillsides as well as in the valleys. Tortuous railways were built to ascend hills to carry off the spoil; but even under industrial necessity houses were still built of stone. Coal and steam enabled mills to take over domestic weavers' tasks. Examples of these engines remain and can still be seen working at Armley Mills in Leeds (which retains carding, spinning and weaving machines) and Caphouse Colliery. Other historic textile machinery can be seen working in Bradford at Undercliffe.

Coal was once such a pervading factor that many believed the county irremediably despoiled by the massive waste heaps, fumes and ugly gantries. Even in the 1980s no-one would have believed how complete could be the removal of mines and tips. Now many villages have returned to rurality, such as South Kirby with its handsome Perp church and tower which looks today as if it was for ever in the cornfields of rural England (but its miners' memorial gives the true history). Enthusiasts of mining will find remnants of the industry at Scissett where a private coalmine eats into the hillside. At Caphouse Colliery a hillside mine is preserved as a museum complete with lamp room and steam-powered winding engine. Life below ground can also be seen. On the boundary of the very east of West Yorkshire, in an unreformed zone of coal power stations, glass manufacture and chemical works, remains a large deep mine at Knottingley.

Evidence of very early human occupation abounds on the moors of West Yorkshire. A spectacular Iron Age camp is conspicuous at Almondbury where a hilly ridge end was artificially raised about 300 BC; it was fortified with a stone rampart, ditch and a huge outer barricade. Its occupants, the Brigantes, made this their regional centre – so it may be inferred, as they left no words behind. The Romans regarded them as the largest native tribe in Britain and their fortresses were opposed to the colonizing Romans. By AD 60 the Romans had the upper hand against the British. Roads were built from Mancunium over Blackstone Edge to Ilkley and Tadcaster; from Danum (Doncaster) to Castleford and north via Catterick; from Ribchester through Ilkley and Adel to York. The two-acre fortress at Ilkley, *Olicana*, was built under Agricola, now the site of the parish church, and many relics are in the manor house museum. For visible remnants go to Blackstone Edge near Ripponden where there is a stone road, 16ft wide between deep stone kerbs. Doubtless the tepid wells at Ilkley were a further attraction for the Romans.

After the Romans, architectural activity dwindled until the Saxons established churches – their sites still marked by crosses carved with emblems of faith and superstition; once set in churchyards they are increasingly taken into churches to protect them from harm. A Saxon cross at Leeds was 'preserved' as infill material and found during the rebuilding of St Peter's; it is now once more on show. Saxon buildings are at Bardsey where a Saxon tower has twin-arched windows and at Ledsham where a Saxon tower has an arched window and a finely carved doorway. There are Norman chapels at Lotherton and Adel which has a magnificently carved chancel arch and South doorway, and quite spectacular herringbone masonry at Kippax. Norman towers can be seen at Hartshead and Birstall. A magnificent Romanesque building, however, exists at Kirkstall Abbey, set in a tranquil location by the River Aire, west of Leeds. Here Cistercians built a sister abbey to Fountains in about 1175 spreading design and knowledge from Burgundy on a dramatic scale. The round-arched West door has five orders including zigzag; there is a great Norman crossing tower and long nave of round piers. Kirkstall is almost as it was when its roofs were removed by Henry VIII and is the best preserved of English Cistercian abbeys. This led to an elaborate plan in the nineteenth century by Sir George Gilbert Scott to restore it. Its proponents were defeated by lovers of romantic ruins, yet recently limited restoration under English Heritage has taken place: new

Overleaf, left: JACOBEAN ROOD SCREEN, CATHEDRAL OF ALL SAINTS, 1635, WAKEFIELD; *right*: TEMPLE NEWSAM.

oak timbers and roofing to the aisles and chancel chapels has occurred to preserve the stonework below.

Little can be seen of EE or geometric Gothic in West Yorkshire, that is, between 1200 and 1300, so that the East transept at Guiseley with its model geometry is something of a surprise. Unusual semi-shafted piers like roll-mouldings will be found in aisle arcades at Bradford, Guiseley and Sandal Magna; but at Dewsbury the shafting is free of the piers. There is little from the Dec period save for the elaborate recarved bridge chapel at Wakefield. The glory of West Yorkshire in churches is the Perpendicular, reflecting the prosperity of towns in the centre of the medieval wool trade, for example Wakefield, Halifax and Bradford. Two of these churches are now cathedrals and the third, Halifax, remains a warm and gloomy cavern where aisles, chapels and the trophies of past ages meld into an agreeable whole; its dark and craggy exterior, embattled with acanthus leaf, contrasts with warmth within.

In domestic architecture new ideas show at Bramham House, with tall Queen Anne windows, prominent cornice and balustrade. Its hall is built as a cube of stone with flamboyant giant pilasters and carved stone frieze. Lord Bingley (Queen Anne's Minister) surrounded his house with a spectacular garden in Louis XIV style with avenues radiating through star-cut shapes in woodland to temples and obelisks. Also representing the early eighteenth century are two particular houses, Kettlethorpe Hall, 1727, in Wakefield, and Farfield Hall, 1728, between Addingham and Bolton Abbey – whose florid baroque seems to have a continental air. Kettlethorpe is easily accessible but Farfield can only be glimpsed through trees. Of this period too is the sadly demolished Parlington Park at Aberford which was Italianized after Sir Edward Gascoigne returned from his Grand Tour in 1726. Here he installed figures

from mythology in his hall and drawing room, and decorations by Francesco Vassall. Bretton Hall, 1720, was designed by its owner Sir William Wentworth in collaboration with Colonel Moyser, a friend of Lord Burlington. It remains in its own huge park but is rather a plain house. Roughly the same size as Bramham, Bretton is two and a half storeys with balustrade but Bramham has a piano nobile between half storeys.

Colonel Moyser also lent a hand in the design of Nostell Priory which the Wynn baronets had owned since the seventeenth century. He seems to have taken ideas to Nostell (1733) from Bretton, for example a symmetrical plan for rooms leading off twin staircases and which rise from a central hall. At Nostell some 'movement' was achieved by the curved external staircase ascending to the first-floor terrace and state rooms: a good design for living which affords distant views through parkland. Nostell also has a hipped roof but its front is livelier than Bretton with attached Ionic columns below a pediment. An idea from Palladio via Lord Burlington was for four corner pavilions to be attached by curved colonnades – but only one was built. James Paine began here as building supervisor in 1733, later taking on much of the design despite his young age. He went on to design Heath House at Wakefield in 1744 which is a complete essay in the Palladian style.

These Georgian houses are the architectural gems of West Yorkshire. It is, however, the exquisite decorative skill of Robert Adam which converted Nostell and Harewood from country houses to palaces. Adam designed the Top Hall on the first floor of Nostell in a Roman style with apses connecting the Saloon 'back-

to-back'. The Georgian Adam work contrasts with Paine's earlier Rococo, but Adam, the plasterer Rose and classical painter Zucchi predominate. The same team operated at Harewood joined by Angelica Kauffman and Chippendale. Research at Harewood has enabled the rooms there to be decorated precisely as originally painted. The multitude of balanced crisp designs rendered in delicate but firm colours is truly wonderful and renders Harewood another five-star destination. John Carr in following the fashion for Adam's Etruscan style applied it at Bretton Hall and Bolling Hall (Bradford). All these important houses miraculously escaped from industrialization. Nostell was overlooked by mining gantries, spoil heaps and railways; Temple Newsam was mined in its own garden; Bretton kept company with hillside mines; and Bolling was actually situated within an ironworks.

The eighteenth-century classical revolution influenced church building just as radically as houses. The earliest is Holy Trinity, 1721, in Leeds. A slightly dour Roman temple with apse and arched aisles of Corinthian columns, it copied features of St Martin-in-the-Fields. It was then itself copied in an unlikely location at Sowerby – on top of a windy hill in a sparsely populated village in 1763. This largely untouched classical monument with plaster Royal Arms over the East Venetian window remains to this day. The architect was the local stonemason, John Wilson. It might have been in the thoughts of Revd Titus Knight (rather than Square Chapel) when the new classicism erupted:

What is this Building, so magnificent . . .
'Tis sure a Pantheon of the present Age,
Or pompous Theatre, to set off the Stage.
Forbear your Taunts, this Structure is
  design'd
An Habitation for th' eternal Mind.

Slightly unusual churches of these times will be seen at Rastrick (1796) where the thick tower is gabled before rising to a tall lantern and cupola. It could be an ornament for a stable yard. At Tong in an almost preserved village is St James, 1727, with arched windows in a traditional tower: three-decker pulpit, squire's pew (for Sir Geo. Tempest), box pews and gallery. Many churches simply followed the fashion for storeys of Georgian windows, such as St Bartholomew at Meltham and St James at Slaithwaite.

The gabled brick Unitarian chapel at Westgate, Wakefield, 1752, has two balanced pedimented doorways with a Venetian window between them, believed to be by Carr. Its pulpit, rescued from another chapel by the river, has the character of a seventeenth-century baroque doorway. But the Queen of all churches is Carr's St Peter and St Leonard at Horbury. It was paid for by the hugely successful Carr who spared no expense or effort on it. The opposite of plain, its South front is a large Ionic portico, the aisles within are screened by Corinthian arcades and there is an octagonal apse. Built of finely grained honey-coloured sandstone, the exterior gleams in the sun with rare beauty. Its tower rises through five carefully proportioned stages before the sixth, a fluted spire. Exquisite is the only possible adjective. Carr's balanced proportions follow Wren's advice to choose a site, in the thick of population and 'where most open to View adorned Porticoes . . . which with handsome Spires or Lanterns rise in good proportion above the neighbouring houses'.

The gentlemen of the West Riding favoured Pontefract, Leeds and Wakefield in the eighteenth century for their townhouses. Wakefield's Westgate still has many palatial Georgian houses, although those nearer the centre have had shops cut into them. Fine new terraced houses were built in estates for professionals. The St John's area remains largely as built with an eighteenth-century church – round-headed windows, balustraded roof and tower with octagon and cupola – in the middle of St John's Square. Another corner for contemplation from this period is South Parade, 1775, in the centre of the town where a quiet terrace of large houses looks over extensive gardens. In Leeds eighteenth-century Park Square lost its church, St Paul's, in 1905 but the square remains. It does not, however, have the discipline and height of the Wakefield houses. The market town of Pontefract, long hibernating under a pall from coalmining, has a cobbled market place with dignified eighteenth-century town mansions; the pretty Buttercross, 1734 (a Georgian trading shed). Paine's Town Hall, 1785, presides over the Market standing on an open arcade and rising with pilasters to a pediment and cupola. The apparently Georgian church of St Giles in the Market has seven Gibb's arches and classical tower but hides a thirteenth-century core exposed when the walls were blown off by cannon fire in the Civil War.

The nineteenth century saw a huge increase in the population of Yorkshire's towns from the country. Much of their housing remains, especially in Leeds, where estates of tight back-to-back houses have more recently been colonized by immigrant labour. The areas around St James's Hospital or Hyde Park make a fascinating window into social and economic history. At Hyde Park a cinema with Arts and Crafts staircase and extant gas lighting remains. The reason for creating these

estates has now largely evaporated with the lost industry. Leeds has proved resilient from its other economic streams, but others like Bradford and Batley have suffered greatly. A sad and telling contrast is provided by Batley's richly carved Italianate wool warehouses by the station, some with disused half-abandoned shells. Bradford had tried for success by demolishing half of the glorious Victorian buildings in its centre but still cannot make a go of modern commerce. It has now demolished half the town centre for the second time since the Second World War and cannot afford to rebuild. Although the glorious mills of Manningham and Saltaire remain, much of Bradford is down at heel – its former source of wealth, the mills, abandoned. There is scarcely a more desolate experience than a walk from the thriving National Media Museum in Bradford, past the abandoned Odeon, up Tetley Street with split-open warehouses and truncated chimneys to City Road where, going west, you pass semi-derelict mills with their stone-and-brick factory chimneys. Unusual structures required by the trade remain, such as a water tank atop a chimney-like tower at H. Hey & Co.; and an Italianate towered entrance-gate with arched windows and louvres at the abandoned Oakwood Dye Works.

Visitors will wish to see the nineteenth-century model towns created by benevolent manufacturers. Sir Titus Salt was a successful Congregationalist manufacturer whose mills at Saltaire present a mighty aspect in stone. Tiers of windows are interrupted only by lanterned towers like Italian belvederes. The

Overleaf, left: HARDCASTLE CRAGGS, HEBDEN WATER;
right, above: BEESTON, 2011;
below: HOLME, MOORLAND.

richer façades of nearby Manningham Mills rise six storeys to a large cornice and attic storey. Its stupendous mass needs to be seen and felt. Saltaire is open as a multi-floored gallery and trading establishment with restaurants, and it is possible to enter and see how the place was constructed. Of course Saltaire was a complete town with laundries, schools, church and cookhouses for the workers, whose Italianate houses each had some open space. At Halifax Colonel Akroyd and the Crossleys also provided lavishly for their workers on paternalistic estates. Akroydon workers had Gothic or Tudoresque houses, a park and what G. G. Scott thought was his best church. More could be made of the history of these places and it is sad to see Scott's church becoming unkempt once again. More too could be made of Bradford's industrial museum. To celebrate the glory and prosperity of Bradford, famous throughout the world for its worsteds, a working line of worsted manufacture would be of considerable tourist interest and its product a marketable item. The museum does have period machinery which is run; so too does Armley Mills in Leeds. Another museum of manufacture, Thwaites Mill at Leeds, demonstrates how factories were worked by water power in pre-steam engine days.

The industrial trail for tourists must include a walk over the iron bridge at Halifax from where Dean Mills in all its massive splendour can be seen below. Crossley carpets were once made here by the acre. To the east stands the magnificent spire of the Crossley-sponsored Congregational church and to the west, Scott's spire of All Souls. In Huddersfield not all mills are silent. The best walk is down Queen Street South to follow the canal and thence east perhaps as far as the lifting canal bridge. In Leeds visit the warehouses along Wellington Street, and from Leeds Bridge contemplate the River Aire with its cluster of tall warehouses gathered around a miniature Pool of London. Less than a hundred years ago prints show the river busy with steam vessels, tugs and barges. Today the scene is cleansed by conversion to apartments but it is still easy to imagine the Victorian industry that created it. In Bradford, Little Germany is a largely undisturbed area of tall warehouses built for the German trade from 1850 onwards; the streets are narrow, the decorative frontispieces tremendous and the atmosphere entirely Dickensian. The keen student of industry will find remnants of earlier warehouses on the opposite hill of Bradford, for example Piccadilly, where the flavour of earlier nineteenth-century Grecian architecture can be detected. But scattered all over the west of the county are mills in little towns, isolated in fields or seemingly stranded halfway up hills.

A special delight in West Yorkshire is the incidence of Victorian churches. The tours described in the Gazetteer for Leeds, Bradford and Halifax show where to find buildings by G. G. Scott, G. F. Bodley, J. L. Pearson, William Butterfield and A. W. Pugin. Inevitably some churches have been lost; there was no greater contrast than between Norman Shaw's demolished Holy Trinity at Bingley with its austere spire rocket to the heavens and his warm, low and expensive St Margaret's at Ilkley – built only 12 years later. The former

Overleaf, *left*: BRADFORD TOWN HALL; *right*: CORN EXCHANGE, LEEDS.

reflects bleakness in blunt architecture and the poverty of industrial life; the latter celebrates a comfortable gentleman's existence in a spa town with a pretty Perp design. The forceful Dr Hook, Vicar of Leeds, was a great proselytizer and opponent of non-conformists. He organized the building of no fewer than 43 churches for Leeds. Another contribution by him was the promotion of surpliced choral services with proper-proportioned Choir and Chancel as in the rebuilt Leeds Parish Church. His determination is evident from his sentiment, 'I shall have a good choral service even if I go to prison for it.' The desire to best the Non-conformists was matched by (and perhaps accomplished with) a move to the liturgical right. Dr Pewsey secretly put up money for a 'proper' church in the east of Leeds. It has transepts, crossing tower and lambent stained glass by Pugin and Morris & Co.; all projected in thirteenth-century style but, alas, the steeple and pinnacles (to be copied from St Mary's, Oxford) did not come about. It was so high a church that the bishop refused to consecrate it as Holy Cross; it had to become St Saviour.

The thirteenth century was a popular model for Victorians who wanted large elegance: the cathedral-like bulk of St Bartholomew, Armley, is rendered perfectly; the soaring spire of All Saints, Bradford, stands on the already grand base of a Southeast tower with polygonal apsed chancel; the disturbing proportions of St John Evangelist's massive tower, big bold pinnacles and grotesquely stretched lucarnes on the spire still make one gulp. The more simple lancet church as favoured by the Commissioners is everywhere. Pretty, below a mountainous tree-clad hillside as at Hebden Bridge, dominating at St George's, Great George Street, Leeds, and arresting in spikey unity with tall spire and flying buttresses at Oulton. The latter by Thomas Rickman, 1827, was described as 'one of the most chaste and elegant churches' shortly after it was completed. The Unitarian cotton magnate, John Fielden, gave a thirteenth-century style church at Todmorden. It stands in a romantic position at the foot of a hill behind the town. Also thirteenth century was Crossley's Congregational church and Akroyd's All Saints by Scott in Halifax. Sir Titus Salt's Congregational Church is more chapel-like with arched windows and peri-style drum of Corinthian columns, making the entrance a base for its dome and cupola.

The turn of the twentieth century is marked by conspicuous and lavish neo-baroque buildings mainly for commerce, but also industry, for example at Armley. One of the glories of Leeds is the extent of complete neo-Baroque streets off Briggate with matching turrets of fantastic composition. Edwardian arcades by the theatre architect Frank Matcham link Queen Victoria Street to County Arcade by a Cross Arcade to create a flamboyant trading village of wonderful theatrical effect. In Batley the civic area also dates from the turn of the century and has a marked flavour of Art Nouveau in decorative glass and staircases.

Modern buildings are principally of technical or engineering interest but one may still appreciate the spatial or sculptural qualities of new build. In Leeds the controversial Quarry Hill House has a strategic function to occupy a prominent site, the eastern focus of Sir

Overleaf, left: St Bartholomew, 1872, Leeds;
right: All Souls, Blackman Lane, George Gilbert Scott, Leeds.

Reginald Blomfield's 1930s avenue, The Head-row. The architect's huge atrium marked by shoulders of ashlar is engagingly monumental; the wings of large windows divided with squared lights remind one of a 1930s power station – very appropriate for a northern industrial city. It has firmness, independence and resolution; it occupies its prominent site with assurance. The modern steel sculpture on the roof, however, is neither northern nor of the essence of the building but should be regarded lightly. Another new building of note is the Metropolitan University tower known locally as the 'Rusty Pin'. It is tall, brown and has facets removed from the corners asymmetrically. It defies the received wisdom for towers and engages the visual sense without resolution. It could genuinely be termed sculpture. Another new building known as the Sail in Beeston is prominent from every part of Leeds, a sail-shaped extension to a tower which, ironically, is uncomfortably shaken by wind. Also at Beeston within the historic terminal basin of the Leeds and Liverpool Canal Basin a tall round tower has been inappropriately sited. It is not possible to see any justification for this imposition. It does not add to, facilitate or complement its listed neighbours. But in Leeds modern sculptural thinking lies behind the irregular façades of buildings on East Street where the use of asymmetry, out of vertical and multi-coloured facing relieves otherwise daunting cliffs of large modern blocks. Leeds is a truly cosmopolitan city with a developed commercial centre, mature arts and entertainment facilities, and park-like country estates within its boundary. Although Bradford, Leeds and Sheffield all have their Windy City of tower blocks they are largely without aesthetic merit. Leeds, however, has pioneered palatable new architecture with some consideration for the foot passenger.

Gazetteer

ABERFORD   Attractive village strung out along the former A1 road. The eighteenth-century Swan Inn with canted bay windows overlooks Aberford Bridge carrying Main Street high over Cock Beck. On the north bank of the Beck at a little distance are Iron Age earthworks known as Becca Banks. Nearby is Becca Hall, a two-storeyed Georgian house with canted bays and a pediment over the five bays, built for Warren Hastings' secretary in 1785. Opposite the Swan Inn is Aberford House, like a pair of distinguished townhouses in lime-stone with twin pedimented doorways and balustraded parapet. St Ricarius' Church, a unique dedication, was almost entirely rebuilt by Anthony Salvin in 1861; his is the nave with clerestory and plate tracery, but the early Norman tower with short Perp spire is old. Salvin rebuilt because he claimed such 'barbarous' cutting of the dog-tooth and zigzag mouldings of the chancel arch 50 years before prevented restoration. 'Massive herring-bone masonry' and arches were also taken down. We think differently today. By the church gate is an ancient

GASCOIGNE ALMSHOUSES, ABERFORD.

market cross with chamfered square shaft and four-gabled coping; removed in 1644 during the plague and restored in 1911 to commemorate the Coronation of George V.

Out of the village to the south is an early RC chapel, 1793; then an isolated, tall, early Georgian house of two and a half storeys and hipped roof. But on the west are the amazing Gascoigne almshouses, 1844, a multitude of gables with round pinnacles and crosses surrounding a Tudor tower with empty niches similarly embellished; converted to offices. Just beyond the almshouses is a pair of handsome lodges – blank arches (horseshoe shape) enclose sash windows below a little pediment. The lodges are linked to quadruple-shafted gate piers capped with ball finials. They heralded a Georgian mansion called Parlington Park which stood to the west. It was occupied by the Gascoignes (see *Lotherton*). On the death of Sir Thomas in 1810 it was left to a relation, Richard Oliver, on condition he became a Gascoigne, and it remained in Gascoigne hands until the twentieth century. After use by the army in the First and Second World Wars it lay abandoned until demolished in the 1950s. Along the former North Drive at the other end of the village (opposite the estate office, two storeys despite appearances) is an avenue leading to a Triumphal Arch

ARCH TO US REBELS, PALLINGTON PARK, ABERFORD.

with Doric pilasters and flanking pedestrian gateways. It was designed by Thomas Leverton in 1783, as the inscription says, to commemorate 'Liberty in North America Triumphant'. The explanation is that Sir Thomas Gascoigne was, like the Marquis of Rockingham, strongly on the side of the colonists in the American War of Independence. The village lodge faces the avenue and has a pyramid-shaped roof. A remnant of the former park is the deer shelter, a now ruined circular Gothic building designed by William Lindley. The Gascoignes moved to *Lotherton* in 1905. [11]

ADDINGHAM Wharfedale village in most attractive country to the west of the county where it adjoins Yorkshire Dales National Park. Many stone cottages and Georgian houses are in Main Street, including a shop with classical pediment and pilasters which was built in 1826 as the Piece Hall, and an old farmstead with outside steps. Some mullion-windowed cottages date from the seventeenth century. A stone mill with big square chimney is now apartments. Away from the village to the east is St Peter's Church in rural seclusion. From the lane one sees the church lying in a meadow near the Wharfe with a faerie path to it across a hump-backed bridge over a brook. Mostly Perp, in spite of appearances, it was built for Rector Leonard Vavasour by his father Sir Henry in 1475. The North arcade and aisle windows demonstrate that period with arched lights under straight heads. The dilapidated South arcade, however, which collapsed, was replaced by a plain wall with classical arched windows in 1756: the date also of the tower and West gallery – a sort of naval-timbered construction painted like the poop of a warship. The splendid roof with tie beams and king posts was exposed in 1952. Riverside walks lead to Ilkley and to higher Wharfedale. Bolton Abbey is three miles northwest. Explore Low Mill Lane towards the riverside meadows to see the pedimented former rectory and, by the river, Italianate Hallcroft Hall – Regency, with broad soffits and hipped roof.

Down the lane, west towards Bolton Abbey is Farfield Hall, a Georgian mansion built by the Quaker George Myers in 1728. Giant Baroque fluted Corinthian pilasters support the projecting three-bay front with a high-relief pediment enclosing carved arms; in the frieze are carved seahorses and serpents' tails. The doorways are framed by segmental pediments on brackets. A new wing was added by Keith Douglas, the conductor, in Edwardian times to accommodate a music room. There are limited views from the road. The Myers were Quakers and gave the site for the preserved Friends Meeting House, 1689, which has mullioned windows and Myers's tombs in the graveyard. [1]

ADEL Charming, leafy suburb to the north of Leeds fronting open country. By the cricket field is a jewel of a church, St John the Baptist, a beautiful and complete Norman chapel of 1150 with twin belcotes (rebuilt by Robert Chantrell in the nineteenth century) and outstanding South door, now protected from the elements by a wood-and-copper gable. The large projecting doorway is decorated with arched zigzag and beak-head on shafts. Above is a gable carved with a lamb and symbols of the Evangelists. The original Norman bronze door ring was stolen in modern times by thoughtless robbers, the current piece is a reproduction. The nave and chancel have carved corbel heads of primitive faces under the eaves – many are renewed. The North and West of the nave and all the chancel are lit by tiny Norman windows, splayed to the interior, with exterior stone renewed in 1839. The chancel arch is another magnificent Norman affair, the outer order grotesque heads, and inner zigzag. Capitals are carved with Christian symbols. Pulpit and chancel screen are by Temple Moore, 1890. Paintings of the Crucifixion and Ascension are by Vanderbank,

Left: CENTAUR BITTEN BY DRAGON, ST JOHN BAPTIST, ADEL; *below*: NORMAN CHANCEL ARCH, ST JOHN BAPTIST, ADEL.

1748. The old rectory to the east dates from medieval times – its timber frame encased by stone in 1652. This is to the rear of the present pedimented Georgian building whose stables form the parish rooms. [9]
Open Sunday a.m.; Wednesday a.m.; Thursday p.m.

ALLERTON St Peter's Parish Church is a tall high-roofed lancet building with a strange tower reducing by angled stages, a fancy parapet of crenellation and a little tiled pyramid spire. It is curious in that it appears all of a piece with Allerton Mill – a four-storey textile mill with cast iron gates and cast iron water tank on its tower. Further up the hill and left down Allerton Lane is the Jacobean Old Hall. Up the rising village street to Dean Head are views of the Pennines and, sadly, of the Holling Hill wind farm on Ovenden Moor. To the south is a cluster of hamlets curiously known as Jerusalem, Egypt, and on Egypt Lane the former Walls of Jericho – high retaining walls of millstone grit to keep the road open through friable shale but which proved unequal to the task. Similar walls may be seen between Shelf and Northowram where a cutting is lined with great black stones. The biblical names doubtless originate from the same fierce, upland chapel devotion as caused Welsh villages also to be named Jerusalem etc. [8]

ALMONDBURY Pretty hillside village above Huddersfield with distinguished Perp church of All Hallows. Its sturdy tower, buttressed diagonally, has four gargoyles flying out. Although the chancel chapels were extended in the nineteenth century, original EE lancets still look through to the chancel from within. The Perp nave, aisles and nave roof, 1522, are finely carved with instruments of the Passion picked out in gold; the corbels carved with local arms (North aisle) and grotesque heads (South aisle). In the North aisle an Elizabethan altar table. Under the tower is a seventeenth-century font with pagoda-like Perp cover – tiers of arches and crocketed pinnacles. Outside are the old village stocks. Opposite the church gate is Wormald's Hall, a seventeenth-century timbered building over a stone lower storey of mullioned windows and doorway, 1631. The timberwork oversails the ground floor.

West of the village on the exposed Castle Hill is an isolated and high tower in Cardiff Castle Gothic with belvedere, 1897, for Queen Victoria's Jubilee. The hill was earlier occupied by the Brigantes as a fort in the Iron Age, and then by a Norman motte and bailey. The hill is very steep and breezy but affords tremendous rural views south towards Black Hill and Emley Moor, and north to industrial Huddersfield whose chimneys, towered mills and oblique rows of cottages stand in the landscape like a Lowry print. You can drive up a lane called 'Hillside' to the tower car park, but there is nothing between the road and a spectacular fall. In this place you readily acquire the feel of West Yorkshire and the Pennines. Forever windy, the harebells are not even still in August, but at weekends boys fly their kites; and on bank holidays the tower is open to the public. [20]

ALVERTHORPE Pretty well part of Wakefield these days. The perfectly Perp-style church, St Paul's, 1823, stands broadside on a hill; large tower, six big symmetrical transomed windows but, unusually, no pinnacles. In the village is renowned Silcoates School, of routine architectural importance apart from the former headmaster's house, a nice Georgian residence in brick with canted bays rising two storeys and capped by ogee domes on the half storey. To the left is a hall with a big Venetian window under a pediment on twin pilasters; another block copies features of the headmaster's house and was rebuilt in 1904. A new hall and chapel are in 1930s neo-Georgian. [16]

ARMITAGE BRIDGE Still a garden mill village built by the Brooke family, and lying deep in a wooded valley with narrow lanes and the rushing River Holme. The Brookes built the handsome stone-slated Dec church in 1848 (Robert Chantrell), its pinnacled West tower is thickly buttressed with gabled niches, short chancel and low South chapel with sundial. A fire caused substantial rebuilding some 20 years ago. Brooke Mill has ceased operations but family house, Armitage Bridge House, black ashlar with sash windows and big porch on fluted Ionic columns, looks across meadows down the valley. [20]

ARTHINGTON Set in silvern pastures by the side of the River Wharfe, with no village to speak of is St Peter's, 1864. Elaborately bold, with mini transepts, the tracery is diagrammatic Dec The tower is tall and carries angst with a disproportionately short broached spire – all in stone. The adjacent Gothic vicarage is as big as the church. Approaching the village from the east, on a difficult road, you can see the Nunnery, a sixteenth-century house in isolated splendour – manifold mullions with two-storey oriel above the door, 1585. Reportedly contemporary plasterwork is in the parlour, vine trails on the beams and panelled diamonds with foliage. There is no convenient parking so prepare for a glimpse only of this interesting old house which stands east of the church. The name derives from the priory of Cluniac nuns which was founded in the twelfth century, but of which there are no remnants. Arthington Hall is a survivor of many rebuildings, lastly by John Carr in the eighteenth century who reused windows and balustrades from an earlier Baroque building. Alfred Waterhouse

THE NUNNERY, 1585, ARTHINGTON.

made some additions, but the present appearance can only be described as strange. [3]

BADSWORTH Limestone village in the east of the county, its roofs are slate and red pantile. On high ground the almost entirely Perp church of St Mary dominates. The South aisle, high clerestory and chancel windows are wide four-centred. The fourteenth-century tower, rebuilt in 1935, opens into the nave and aisles through lofty arches. The Perp font, octagonal with eight styles of window tracery carved on the panels, is originally from Barnsley church. On the South sanctuary wall is an inscribed tablet to Sir John Bright, the Parliamentary campaigner who lived here and died in 1688. His monument is capped with extravagantly carved scrolls, foliage, urn, shield, etc. Of Sir John's hall only the gatehouse remains, the arch walled up to form a house now called Badsworth Hall. The old hall ruins, a Gothic feature for almost 150 years, were finally demolished in 1976 for new houses in Badsworth Court. Badsworth gave its name to the miner's hunt. Now combined with the Bramham Moor (founded by Fox-Lane), the kennels are at Thorpe Audlin. At Rogerthorpe half a mile east over a dip in the fields is a Jacobean manor, now a hotel. [23]

BAILDON In a cleft of the escarpment from Rombald's Moor high above the River Aire clings this old village. The sloping square has a memorial drinking fountain replacing the village cross, its polished granite column and cap somewhat bizarre. St John's nineteenth-century church on a step of the hill has simple lancets and bell turret – its width was doubled by a second stone-roofed chapel in 1848. The tower was added in 1928. The level churchyard provides a belvedere overlooking stone-roofed cottages down into the Aire Valley. The old village has many vernacular styles: Tudor at the Malt Shovel, an ancient inn with improbably tiny mullions, sixteenth-century doorway and a little Yorkshire wheel window. Up Northgate stands *Baildon Hall*, a seventeenth-century house with mullions in the gables and stone sash windows with one large mullioned and transomed window. Drip moulds have Catherine wheel stops; gables have finials of a Saxon character with concentric circles and Saltaire cross. Batley House has Georgian sashes and a hipped roof. Down the hill on Hallfield Drive is *The Hall*: transitional seventeenth/eighteenth-century – stone sash windows, but with a grand seven-light mullioned and transomed hall window under a drip mould. Below the gables are square cross-mullioned windows. The rear of the house, not seen, is a substantial timbered structure of the fourteenth century.

Along the cliff-top west is Baildon Moor, a windy place of public resort up above the erstwhile smoky regions of Shipley, Manningham and Bradford. Shipley Glen, to the west, is a steep and picturesquely wooded valley. A little, twin-track, cable railway winds the adventurous uphill through the glen. [8]

BARDSEY Sandstone agricultural village in undulating wooded country close to the market town of Wetherby. The church of All Hallows has a Saxon tower, twin Saxon arched openings divided by a round column can be seen high up the south side of the tower. The corbelled-out top stage is Perp. The Norman South doorway has zigzag and beak-head in the arch. Also Norman is the nave whose arcades of circular piers have scalloped capitals. Roof lines of the Saxon church can be distinguished, also blocked Saxon openings, which mean that much of the nave fabric is Saxon. The roofs were raised in the nineteenth century; this church is a history of architecture in stone over a thousand years. Note in particular how the early tower (and porch) was embraced by twelfth-century aisles (lancet windows); then two hundred years later more widening with fuller Perp windows.

In the churchyard is a Georgian sundial of 1751 on a pillar. To the west of the church is an Elizabethan

BARKISLAND HALL, 1638.

6

timber-framed cottage mostly encased in stone but exposed on the first floor. [4]

BARKISLAND High Pennine village whose main street descends an eastern spur of bleak Norland Moor. Below the village Barkisland Hall, a tall gritstone manor house ('I.G.S.G. Gledhill, 1638', over the door), looks over Black Brook's pleasant valley; it is a strong and bold Jacobean mansion of three storeys, three gables of mullioned and transomed windows; a projecting porch also of three storeys with columned frontispiece to the first two. Doric below, Ionic above and then a rose window. Next door is Lower Hall, another seventeenth-century house, old transomed windows at the back and at the front eighteenth-century square mullions with sash windows. The village stocks are opposite.

Above the village is the plain parish church which is Victorian Dec – steeply pitched aisle roofs, no tower but west belcote. From the crossroads, in the direction of mysterious Krumlin are gateposts to another sixteenth/seventeenth-century house, Howroyd Hall. Many gabled, big chimney stacks, good drip moulds and carved stops. The mullions were removed by Lady Mary Horton who replaced them with sash windows in the eighteenth century as at her Ledston Hall. The original house was timber framed of which a wall and door survive. The hall is Jacobean with gallery of turned balusters, 18-light window, nice ceiling rose of acorns, fruit and heraldic devices, and big fireplace of Ionic columns with Royal Arms of Charles I over. The latter was concealed behind boards in the Civil War. There is panelling of the sixteenth and eighteenth centuries, and a Georgian stone fireplace in the dining room installed by Lady Mary. Horatio Nelson visited and Ivor Novello wrote *Perchance to Dream* here – the original stage set was a copy of the sitting room. [13]

BARWICK-IN-ELMET Rural village east of Leeds well separated from the dreary eastern suburbs and municipal housing by farmland – quite pretty. In the centre of the village is a very tall maypole. There are many stone cottages and within the village centre old farm houses. The church of All Saints has an embattled Perp tower and is built both of limestone and gritstone. The aisles, arcades and clerestory are Perp but the origin of the church is Norman witnessed by some herringbone masonry and the window in the north of the chancel. The chancel and ogee-headed door to the vestry are probably Dec. A fifteenth-century statue on the tower is Sir Henry Vavasour, patron, who lived at Hazlewood Castle five miles to the east; stained glass is to the Gascoignes of Lotherton. The former rectory is seventeenth-century, rendered brick, with a hipped roof.

A mile or so north is Potterton Hall in Potterton Park, a tall eighteenth-century house of two and a half storeys, five bays. Also an additional wing of seven bays with Tuscan porch – south-facing as part of an L-shape, well proportioned and very pretty; the west facing elevation is slightly austere. [10]

BATLEY Broken wool mills and stone terraces stagger about the hillsides. Station Road, still cobbled, is lined with individual Italianate warehouses: three storeys with carved leaf and fruit capitals, polychromatic stone arches, shafting and heavily corbelled cornices. The toothy gaps from the ruins will be hard to fill sympathetically. Opposite the station at the junction of Upper Station Road and Warehouse Street is a finely carved and decorated Italianate warehouse, keystones of carved birds of prey and a circular oriel rising from a stem carved with a large bat. The view over the cobbles from this corner, through the broken, gapped warehouses into a valley punctuated with chimneys, water tower and steeple rising through woods, is an unremediated industrial landscape. At the foot of Soot Hill Lane is another fine warehouse with shafting, foliated capitals and polychromatic stone arches – it has the addition of a French mansarded roof. Batley is a town gutted by the collapse of the cloth trade.

The town centre is up Hick Lane from the crossroads past yet more Italianate buildings and a pedimented chapel with swags of foliage above double Tuscan doorways. Opposite is the former West Riding Union Bank, 1877, Italian Gothic – heavily carved porch and shafts with fruit and foliage capitals. Turning right into Cambridge Street is an estate of municipal buildings in plainer rock-faced neo-Baroque. First the Technical School, then the baths with decorative stone water tank, then the First World War Memorial and Garden. On the left is the Carnegie Library, grand neo-Baroque, 1906 – again rock-faced with ashlar dressings and a pediment carved with gryphons and a clock tower with ogee leaded dome. The upper storeys of the wings have windows divided by Doric pilasters and choice Art Nouveau stained glass. En suite with the municipal buildings is the Post Office with its name carved in stone like a town hall department. The road widens into Market Square, cobbled and sloping. Here is a classical Town Hall – pedimented on fine Ionic pilasters draped with swags of carved flowers, but actually the same date as the other municipal buildings, early twentieth century. It is fitted out with Arts and Crafts glass and a vigorous plaster coving of vegetation. Upstairs is a hall where tea dances take place – pilasters divide walls decorated with Ionic horns and garlands. A spiralling Art Nouveau balustrade completes the staircase. The inner porch entrance

ALL SAINTS, PERPENDICULAR GOTHIC, BATLEY.

has a fine door screen with a pediment of carved oak and Art Nouveau glass panels of tulips. The interior is well preserved and nicely decorated in white, blue and gold.

On the far side of the square is Batley Central Methodist Church, 1869, a crowded classical composition beneath a pediment. Southwest of the town centre is the ancient Parish Church of All Saints, discreet and countrified. A medieval pixie church in a wood in the middle of town. It is slightly overlooked only by the sadly abandoned Taylor's Mill whose Edwardian profile includes a serried roof line and water tower – each gable is crowned with an elliptical stone pediment. The Parish Church of All Saints is conspicuously antique, even rustic, amid so much Italianate and Edwardian glory. The tower is robustly Yorkshire, like a castle turret with well corbelled-out parapet and stubby obelisk-like pin-

nacles. Essentially Perp, the East window has panel tracery under a low arch and the East chapel windows have square heads, round arches for the lights. The South aisle appears in a somewhat battered condition but has all its original Perp windows. Sundial. The clerestory has mullioned windows. Within, the South arcade has Dec quatrefoil piers; the church is airy and bright with figures from old glass inserted in new clear windows. An alabaster monument to Sir William and Lady Mirfield is in the North chapel. The South chapel screen is richly

Opposite, above: GAPPED ITALIANATE WAREHOUSES, STATION ROAD, BATLEY.
below: WAREHOUSE ON WAREHOUSE STREET, BATLEY.

carved. The pulpit is Jacobean. At the foot of the tower is a copper tablet enscribed:

Requiem of the Late Three Bells of Batley Church

[We] were taken from that turret grey, Where we for long have hung

Like worn out lumber thrown away, Forever mute each tongue . . .

And now our changes all are rung, Here ends our dying song

Our last and final peal is done, Farewell, farewell, ding dong!

(1851)   [15]

BINGLEY Within a green and wooded valley the Harden Beck joins the River Aire at Beckfoot; the Leeds and Liverpool Canal begins its climb up Five Rise Locks through the Pennines towards the west coast. The mills are on the east side of the River Aire and from above them is an interesting industrial prospect looking down towards the bridge. Beckfoot Lane and the old packhorse bridge give a more rural view of Bingley from the south side of the River Aire. Park Road looks across the railway and canal through mills to the outrageous Modern former Bradford and Bingley Building Society. North is the old village centre. Here in a close around the churchyard is a cobbled street of cottages, many with mullions, and some lurching through age in a slightly alarming fashion. By the main road the Old Whitehorse Inn is reputedly thirteenth century with a gable certainly of the seventeenth. Across the main road is Damart Mill, its name on the chimney.

All Saints Church on Old Main Street is Perp – a previous building was destroyed by Scots who invaded England after the Battle of Bannockburn in 1314. The aisles have octagonal piers; much of the East end has been rebuilt as has the South aisle and stone-slated roof. There is a huge counterweighted Gothic cover to the font of 1881, and a carved runic stone on a pedestal which bears the name of King Eadberht. The Perp tower was raised to its present height in 1739; it has a large gold-figured clock and sundial. In the North aisle is a stained glass window by Burne-Jones, but this can no longer be seen from within – the space is taken up by the organ. This is a shame because the novel window tracery and strong colours would look well if back-lit. It is also apparent from the East end that whatever recent rebuilding has taken place the huge masonry of the East chancel and its chapel walls is old. [8]

BIRSTALL Joseph Priestley, discoverer of oxygen, was born here at Fieldhead in 1733. His bronze statue stands in the little cobbled marketplace off Low Lane. It is a former agricultural village retaining some old buildings around the marketplace; most are early nineteenth century converted to shops. The Parish Church of St Peter is across the Bradford road in a wooded situation opposite a mill pond – given over to angling. You see at once a Yorkshire tower with aggressively corbelled-out parapet; the Perp top with transomed openings stands on a Norman tower. The rest of the church, embattled throughout, is in a distinctive flaking cream limestone and dates only from 1863. From the higher churchyard west of the tower the width of the large doubled aisles is very evident. Grand and equal porches enter both the North and South aisles – gargoyles at the corners. The East window is a full-scale Victorian essay in Dec, but is artificial and uninspiring. The Black Bull Inn immediately west of the churchyard is ramshackle seventeenth century with square mullions but an older window to the rear.

Northwest of Birstall is the hamlet of *Oakwell* with a country park and Tudor/Jacobean mansion. It was 'Fieldhead' in *Shirley*, one of Charlotte Brontë's novels, and the home of Shirley Keeldar. At that time it was a boarding school for young ladies. Charlotte visited with Ellen Nussey who lived at nearby Moor Lane House. On approaching the house you see two truly massive chimneys and small mullioned windows between. To the south are two cross-gables and a gabled entrance porch to the hall. The hall window is spectacular consisting of 30 lights glazed with tiny diamond panes. Behind this big transomed window is a grand fireplace and a gallery with seventeenth-century balusters.

The house was built by Captain John Batt of Halifax in 1583, his mother's family were then owners of Shibden Hall. The date over the porch with his initials was replicated above while still legible. Although principally of stone, much of the house has a medieval timber frame. Masonry joins indicate the western portion was built later; in 1611 the parlour was 'new' and there was recorded a hall chamber, that is, a bedroom over the hall. The hall now is open to the roof – the Jacobean gallery shows when the enlargement took place. The massive hall windows may also date from this time, but the small diamond lights look wrong and may be a more recent 'antiquarian' alteration. It is open to the public as a furnished house. Teas or good for picnics. [15]

BOOTH WOOD Exhilarating location below the Pennine watershed where a long thin reservoir gathers plentiful water – in the frequent westerly squalls waves cascade over the dam wall whisking jets of spume into the air. From here look upward and east to an original M62 bridge of some splendour – the converse of a suspension bridge – a wide parabolic arch supporting a carriageway linking the B6114 between ridges. [19]

BOSTON SPA Owes its Georgian foundation to the discovery of warm mineral springs in 1744; it is a choice creamy-white limestone village by the River Wharfe. There was no church until 1814, but prosperity quickly dictated a replacement for the first humble structure. The present St Mary's, by W. Parkinson, was built in 1884 in big EE with clustered lancets. A forceful building, its massive tower is a focus of attention. Within, the proportions are grand but successful: circular piers sustain the arcades, angel corbels the massive roof. In the Lady Chapel is the original late Georgian altar table rescued from the boiler house. The baths, grandly called the Pump Room, were down by the River Wharfe but have become a private house. The long and narrow bridge, 1770, with cutwaters has not been enlarged since horse carriage days and presents attractive views up and down the Wharfe. The bridge links it with *Thorp Arch*, its neighbouring village over the river. The lengthy main street has many good houses from this period, including Georgian limestone terraces, some with bow windows, some at right angles to the main street in a large block called The Terrace. Boston Hall also is on the main street – Georgian with Doric porch. [5]

BOTTOM BOAT North of Wakefield on the River Calder where the sinuating river used to freeze on 'The Oxbow Pastures' – fields of solid ice used for skating. There used to be two ferry boats operating from Altofts, the Top Boat and the Bottom Boat, known to work from 1605. The ferrymen lived in the Ferry Boat Inn. In 1672 ten passengers were drowned. [16]

BRADFORD Set in a bowl of the Pennine hills and connected to the River Aire and its valley by a north-flowing beck, Bradford has for long been a market town. Like the other wool towns, it grew from multitudes of spinners and weavers whose cottages lodged in the hills and who sold at Bradford's market. In the sixteenth century it was described as 'a praty quik market toun . . . it standithe much by clothing'. Cloth was made and sold by the 'piece' in the Piece Hall built in Kirkgate in 1773. In the nineteenth century domestic production was overtaken by industrial-scale mills. Bradford soared on the power of steam engines with factory scales of production; from the middle of the nineteenth century it became the principal exporter to the world giving rise to fantastic new wealth. Worsteds were a speciality of Bradford made from long staple wool; 'cloth' is made from short staple wool. The centre of Bradford, which runs north along the beck to Shipley and up adjacent hillsides, was lined with stone-built mills each with its chimney: the hilly centre of Bradford was crowded with merchants' warehouses stacking up on the valley sides, many of which remain today. In the present retail part of town some have become shops, but the quarter called 'Little Germany' of grand warehouses in their dignified original state remain. Huge trade rendered the Piece Hall inadequate. It was demolished in 1873 and superseded by the Wool Exchange, a magnificent Italian Gothic design by Lockwood and Mawson which would not disgrace Venice. The skill and erudition of Lockwood and Mawson, especially in the application of Italian Renaissance Gothic, made them very popular. It was they who designed St George's Hall for concerts in 1851, the Town Hall in 1873, Bradford Markets in 1877 and many of the warehouses in Little Germany.

The quality of the stone and ambitious interpretive Renaissance designs with expensive carved detail made Bradford a city of architectural wonders. Unfortunately, rather like Exeter after the Second World War, the Council destroyed many historic buildings in pursuit of modernization with concrete redevelopment. The fine Grecian Court House, 1834, the Gothic Mechanics Institute, 1839, Exchange Station, 1886, and Kirkgate Markets, 1877, with warehouses along the Leeds Road have all been demolished in recent times. At the behest of the City Engineer and Chief Planner, who were one and the same, S. G. Wardley, the integrity of a blackened feast of Victorian splendour was destroyed. Not content with that the Council has recently demolished the 1960s shopping centre without replacing it. The result is a hole in the centre of Bradford and a massive boarded-up site paralysing half the commercial and retail centre. The parts of the city where the politicians and developers have not played God remain of great interest and a useful exploration can best be made on foot. [8]

Opposite, above: SALVAGED STATUARY FROM OLD KIRKGATE MARKET, BRADFORD; *below*: MONUMENT TO ABRAHAM BALME, 1796, BRADFORD CATHEDRAL.

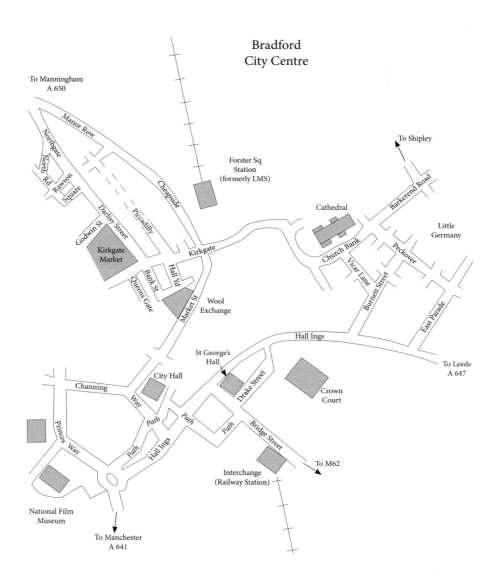

Bradford
City Centre

To Manningham
A 650

Manor Row

Northgate

North Rd

Rawson
Square

Godwin St

Darlsy Street

Cheapside

Piccadilly

Kirkgate Market

Bank St

Queens Gate

Hall Yd

Market St

Kirkgate

Wool
Exchange

Forster Sq
Station
(formerly LMS)

To Shipley

Cathedral

Church Bank

Vicar Lane

Burnett Street

Barkerend Road

Peckover

Little
Germany

East Parade

Hall Ings

To Leeds
A 647

St George's
Hall

Drake Street

City Hall

Channing

Way

Path

Path

Path

Path

Hall Ings

Crown
Court

Bridge Street

To M62

Princes Way

Interchange
(Railway Station)

National Film
Museum

To Manchester
A 641

Bradford – walk through the City Centre Arriving at Bradford Interchange, a modern steel-and-glass bus station combined with railway station, you see the Italianate nature of the town. Opposite is the Great Victoria Hotel – pavilion roofs, shafted arches and Venetian windows of cheerful buff sandstone from nearby Bolton Woods Quarry. Next to it is St George's Hall, 1853, built like an Italian temple with arched windows between attached Corinthian columns and with a strong modillioned cornice. It stands on a rusticated basement storey. The architects, Lockwood and Mawson, had books of careful Italian Renaissance precedents and a gifted sense of proportion. They dominated the nineteenth century in designing the building of Bradford's institutions and also the nearby mill and town of Saltaire. St George's Hall demonstrates their chapel-building experience with a large flat ceiling supported on cast iron columns which also support double galleries round three sides for 3,000 people. Rich ornamentation of foli-

age, flowers, fruit, musical instruments and figures is displayed 'in most harmonious colours and happy taste'. The stage is steeply raked with a grand organ casing – Bradford wanted cultivated architecture for its arts performances – it had come up in the world. Then turning into Drake Street are the Law Courts by Napper Collerton Partnership, 1992. A good low building which shows obeisance to local tradition. In local buff sandstone to match the Great Victoria Hotel across the square, the Courts are a natty combination of modernized Renaissance elements: pillars, drum bays, square bays with glazing lines of mullions and transoms, and a vestigial cornice moulding. The lead-sheathed roof storey is quiet. It is a good modern occupant of the demolished Exchange Station whose tracks came in under Bridge Street. Descending to Hall Ings the stone ramparts built for the station give the Law Courts the air of a modern castle. Now go east to Leeds Road and East Parade.

Here is a solid piece of old Bradford: the Cathedral on

St George's Hall, Bradford.

LITTLE GERMANY, BRADFORD.

its hill, and a cascade of nineteenth-century warehouses known as *Little Germany* on the same hill. The area is so-called since many of the traders were German. Caspian House at 61 East Parade was built by D. Delius & Co., whose senior partner was Frederick's father. Opposite, 46 Peckover Street is by the prolific Gothic architect George Corson. As elsewhere he combines Renaissance elements with Baroque and baronial Gothic – oriels, turrets, shafts and novelty cornicing. On Peckover Street is Festival Square where tea may be taken. On the corner with Burnett Street is Atomik House, 1859, and next door is Biscot House on whose site the Independent Labour Party had its inaugural conference in 1893. Descending Burnett Street to Vicar Lane is No. 66, 1867, by Eli Milnes which has a two-storey cart entrance and massive iron doors with a spoked-wheel design. Huge battered plinths support the columns. No.

62 Vicar Lane, 1871, by Lockwood and Mawson has a triumphal corner entrance – a segmental pediment on garlanded brackets enclosing a carved eagle astride a globe. Opposite, Law Russell's premises at No. 63 has archetypal wedding cake tiers of Corinthian porticos diminishing as they rise to a penultimate set of finely carved Venetian windows. On the corner of Well Street and Church Bank is Pennine House by Eli Milnes, 1864. No. 39 by Milnes and France, 1867, has a grand entrance set obliquely on the corner with garlanded Ionic capitals on polished granite columns.

Then east up Church Bank is the **Cathedral of St Peter**, the medieval parish church, raised to cathedral status in 1919. Standing on a step of the hill it still shows its stubby Perp West tower of 1500 to the town. The tower was strung with woolpacks in the Civil War to protect it against Royalist cannon fire, seen in a memorable print; the entrance to the Cathedral is under the tower through a tremendous arch which itself is the western part of the nave. It looks over the town showing a huge six-light Perp window and large blue clock. The arcades have Dec quatrefoil piers, the Perp aisles are embattled. The piers are deeply moulded creating the impression of clustered shafts. The North aisle carries memorials of the wool town from medieval days to the twentieth century, which once included a controversial memorial to the surgeon William Sharp of a half naked Grecian girl, removed because the authorities thought it salacious. Remaining memorials of pictorial interest include Joseph Priestley building canals and carved figures by Flaxman of a young couple being instructed by wise Abraham Balme, 1796. Looking east there are three extensions designed to elevate the Cathedral by Sir Edward Maufe; first the Choir east of the chancel arch which, with the raised organ loft, is in a square tower under a low pyramid roof. Here is the bishop's throne in a seventeenth-century Renaissance style with obelisks; then the Sanctuary rises by five steps to the High Altar flanked by high Gothic arches; the Lady Chapel is beyond and then the reset East windows with Morris glass. New buildings were placed either side of the West tower, 1954, by Edward Maufe to make offices and a Song School. North of the Cathedral is a small traditional close of neo-Georgian houses for the dean and canons. On the hill above the Cathedral is the only other old building in the centre, Paper Hall, 1643, with 18-light mullioned and transomed hall window, Tudor door arch and stepped lights in the gable. The right-hand wing has later pedimented cross-mullioned windows.

Opposite: LITTLE GERMANY, BRADFORD.

Built by Williams Rooks as a house, James Garnett installed Bradford's first commercial spinning machine here in the eighteenth century.

From the West steps of the Cathedral cross into town via Cheapside to the Midland Hotel by Forster Square (was Midland) Station. French mansards and an octagonal tower are over the main entrance displaying mournful dragons within the spandrels; the many balconies stand on cornices and have cast iron railings. The former station entrance down a wooden ramp reeks of nineteenth-century steam. From this point go west along lower *Kirkgate* to the junction with Market Street to the former Bradford District Bank (now NatWest), 1873, by local architects Milnes and France with giant attached columns and turret in golden local sandstone. Continuing west to the next road north, Piccadilly, are the Grecian Public Rooms which once had a bowed façade decorated with pilasters. Its rebuilding now gives a Roman façade; but on the Piccadilly side remains the former robust Grecian entrance with Doric columns. Early eighteenth-century Bradford met here. Looking up Piccadilly are more buildings of this period, early wool warehouses with expensive Grecian portals and façades. This is the best late Georgian material in town. Opposite Piccadilly and across Kirkgate, Piece Hall Yard was the site of the Piece Hall until 1873. It was part of Georgian Bradford and fronted the Public Rooms.

The Grandly Gothic Bradford Club, 1877, by Lockwood and Mawson has a lantern projecting over its entrance. Although not easily accessible, the interior contains a fine library. Emerging south into Hustler Gate on your left is Lloyds Bank, 1920, representing Art Deco with ranks of giant pilasters whose capitals show a winged lion's head and Greek key emblems. Glazed lantern lights in the banking hall. Walking west, on the corner of Hustler Gate and Bank Street is the former Bradford Commercial Bank, 1867, by Andrews and Pepper showing the bank's original colourful Arms. In Italian Gothic like the Wool Exchange, its neighbour, it has big lancets, marble shafts, angled towers and sharp gabled dormers. In the banking hall is a coved ceiling. More Gothic on Bank Street at Bank House which was originally the Liberal Club, 1876, by Lockwood and Mawson. Returning to Kirkgate, go west once more to Queensgate – the Exchange Chambers was built in 1850 like a series of villas with couple-arched windows descending the hill like domestic houses. Opposite is a show of Baroque pedimented windows at random levels.

Facing Queensgate is the Kirkgate Centre, 1975, by John Brunton & Partners – when concrete was king. This modern monstrosity replaced the Kirkgate Market of 1877 (Lockwood and Mawson) which was demolished. The interior had colonnades of iron and a glass roof with a carved stone frontage and a very fine frieze. The friezes were retained and at first shown in Lister Park, then relegated to the Industrial Museum. Now to hide its guilt the council has placed these carvings in storage. Looking west from here is a further excess in concrete by John Brunton & Partners, Highpoint House on Godwin Street originally for the Yorkshire Building Society. It is a deliberately out of scale concrete tower whose dominating upper four storeys above the roofline of its neighbours looks like a solid water tank with slits of pink glass windows. It can have done the building society's reputation no good. The tendency of building societies, such as Halifax, the Bradford and Bingley and the Yorkshire, to spend investors' money on ephemeral concrete has proved irresistible in Yorkshire.

To regain a sense of civilization look over the crossroads from Kirkgate to the Santander Bank (originally Bradford Bank), 1858, with large Venetian windows within a rusticated ground floor. The showy architecture above with attached Corinthian columns rises to a cornice and balustrade – it looks particularly grand from an oblique angle. From here go north up Darley Street, the main shopping street, to the junction with Godwin Street where is a remnant of Rawson Market, the provisions department of the Kirkgate Market, again by Lockwood and Mawson, 1871.

Now a loop to the north which may be omitted – if time is short go directly to the Wool Exchange. Going north up Darley Street after Godwin Street is *Rawson Square* where on the west corner stands the Masonic Hall, 1876, grand independent Italianate Gothic. A statue of Richard Oastler used to stand here but has been moved to North Parade, a little to the north. He was a factory owner who became a prime mover in legislation for the protection of children in industry with his 10 Hour Act. The statue, erected in 1869, shows him with a mill girl and boy when he was:

> . . . *the King of the factory children.*
> [But] infant's labour was assailed,
> And petty tyrants writhed and wailed,
> But gratitude the chain has broke
> Which bound them to the tyrant's yoke,
> The prison house no more's the walls
> Of the King of the factory children.
>   (Pamphlet, 1844)

Opposite, above: MANNINGHAM MILL, BRADFORD; *below*: JAMIYAT TABLIGH-UL-ISLAM MOSQUE, BRADFORD.

North Parade leads off Rawson Square opposite Darley Street and on the right may be seen Church House, originally the Church Institute, 1871, by Andrews and Pepper in a strong continental Dec style, with gables in the roof. Close by is Devonshire House, 1898, an Art Nouveau version of a medieval chateau-style with serpentine balcony. The most dramatic building, however, is the **Yorkshire Penny Bank**, 1893, on the prominent corner between North Parade and Manor Row. It is a serious neo-Baroque composition with a corner entrance rising through stages of twisted shafting and balustraded arched balconies to a proud Baroque octagonal clock tower. Although no longer a bank, its interior retains period plasterwork, mahogany woodwork and marble mouldings. The crowded Renaissance detail is startling and not easy to assimilate. From here are open views across the valley of the Bradford Beck and former canal as far as the new mosque on the hill opposite and, a little north, to Peel Park and Bolton Woods. Manor Row leads back into town from the Yorkshire Penny Bank past Regency houses, warehouses and the former County Court – identified by its rustic stone arches and Royal Arms. York House on the right, 1866, by Lockwood and Mawson is more Venetian Gothic and was built as a club. The Register Office, which also bears the Royal Arms, was built as the Poor Law Guardians' Office in classical Italianate style, 1877. Next to it is the former office of the Bradford Canal Company.

Descending the road which changes from Manor Row to Cheapside is Market Street and, at the junction with Hustler Gate, the sharp triangular site of the **Wool Exchange**, a glorious Italian Gothic creation by Lockwood and Mawson, 1864. The Venetian Gothic has tiers of arched windows, corner pinnacles and a parapet of pierced and pointed merlons. The tiers of arched windows have plate tracery on the ground floor, reducing to double lancets on the first, triple lancets on the second, and are ideally proportioned. As you arrive at the site from Cheapside and Market Street the thin part of the triangle bears an Italianate clock tower with octagonal pinnacles and short round spire. On the tower is a statue of Bishop Blaize, Patron Saint of Woolcombers. It declares serious business, although sadly the business of wool has been eclipsed and the premises are in multiple occupation. Between the arches on the ground floor are carved heads of the heroes of manufacture and trade in the eighteenth and nineteenth centuries: James Watt, Titus Salt, Sir Richard Arkwright and Lord Palmerston.

Before building the Wool Exchange the Woolmasters invited John Ruskin to advise them on the correct style. His advice was reported, 'There are a great many odd styles of architecture about; you don't want to do anything ridiculous; you hear of me as a respectable architectural man milliner, and send for me, that I may tell you the leading fashion . . . [but] I do not care for this exchange of yours . . . [and] you cannot have good architecture merely by asking people's advice.' They did quite well without his endorsement; his sourness may be attributable to his enthusiasm for Venetian Gothic whose popularity in Victorian pubs he regretted.

Then on Market Street is the magnificent **Town Hall**, again by Lockwood and Mawson, 1873. On a high day the view from Market Street of the Town Hall with its large flags blowing in the breeze makes an inspiring sight. It is early French Gothic spiced up with a flavour of northern Italy. There are similarities with G. E. Street's Royal Courts in London: big Dec shafted windows on the first floor; breathtakingly long arcades on the second enclosing statues of the monarchs of England. Elizabeth I and Victoria are in pride of place either side of the Gothic arched entrance with its octagonal turrets and oriel. It is bold and simple, the opposite of the Yorkshire Penny Bank, the long repetitive elevation is a good foundation for the audaciously tall Tuscan tower (220ft) based on that of the Palazzo Vecchio, Florence. Contrasting extensions by Norman Shaw and F. E. P. Edwards in 1905 highlight the successful boldness of the original design. Shaw is caught up with fussy neo-Baroque oriels, dormers and intricate circular stair window of many mullions. The original Court Room by Lockwood and Mawson has Gothic arcading; but the dining hall is by Shaw where Arts and Crafts domestic is writ large with a big inglenook.

Beyond the City Hall and across Prince's Way is the **Alhambra Theatre**, 1914, on Morley Street. Not the usual neo-Baroque: the architects Chadwick and Watson described it as 'the English Renaissance of the Georgian period' which, within the constraints of theatre architecture, appears to have been carried out. It was going to be demolished and replaced by a new theatre off Little Horton Lane but luckily escaped and the latter site became the National Museum for Media, Film and Television with an IMAX cinema. The museum is a nationally funded institution with three auditoriums and galleries devoted to media. It is easily possible to spend the whole day here. Note the statue to J. B. Priestley, a son of

Overleaf, left: TOWN HALL, BRADFORD;
right: THE WOOL EXCHANGE, BRADFORD.

Outer Bradford

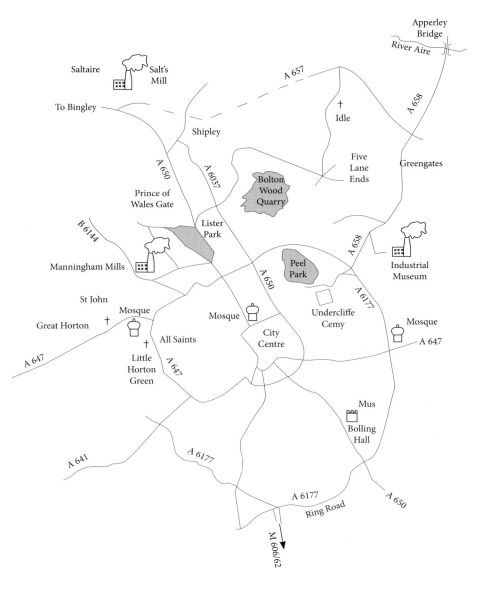

Apperley Bridge

River Aire

A 658

Saltaire   Salt's Mill

To Bingley

A 657

Idle

Shipley

Five Lane Ends

Greengates

A 650

A 6037

Bolton Wood Quarry

Prince of Wales Gate

B 6144

Lister Park

A 658

Manningham Mills

Peel Park

Industrial Museum

A 650

Undercliffe Cemy

A 6177

St John

Mosque

Great Horton

Mosque

Mosque

A 647

A 647

All Saints

City Centre

Little Horton Green

A 647

Mus

Bolling Hall

A 641

A 6177

A 6177

Ring Road

A 650

M 606/62

Bradford, before negotiating the underpass beneath the Jacob's Well roundabout towards Hall Ings. Here is a curious building, the Bradford Telegraph and Argus, partly built in 1980 with a glass front to the printing works but coupled to a former wool warehouse built to sell *stuff*. It is grand Italian Renaissance with pedimented windows and a heavy cornice, and was built for the merchants Milligan and Forbes in 1853.

Outer Bradford – car or cycle

Take the A650 north from the City Centre. Notice the Jamiyat Tabligh Mosque to the right built in traditional local stone. Towards **Manningham** the stone terraces are of roomy Italianate houses. Shortly on the left is Cartwright Hall in Lister Park. The wooded park was the home of Samuel Cunliffe Lister, proprietor of Manningham Mills, the greatest silk and velvet mill in Yorkshire, which towers over the park from the west. Its scale is colossal; style Italianate with a massive chimney over 250ft high which was topped out personally by Cunliffe Lister. The east side has a battered basement storey, arched windows and entrance incorporating the Cunliffe Lister Arms. The elevation to Patent Street rises by six storeys of windows with continuous sills, strong arched profiles to the fifth storey, then a big cornice and attic storey. The most dramatic viewpoint is from Patent Street towards the campanile chimney. Still manufacturing until the 1980s, it has now been converted into apartments. This mighty building has been demeaned by the placing of curvaceous prefabs on the roof.

Samuel Cunliffe Lister made a fortune, went into politics and became a peer. He presides in marble over the south entrance to Lister Park. The park also gives room to a statue of Sir Titus Salt under a Gothic canopy at the north entrance. The thirteenth-century style gatehouse with crenellated towers commemorates the visit of the Prince of Wales in 1882. It carries the Prince of Wales' feathers on its machiolated parapet with carved Yorkshire roses. Inside the park is the **Cartwright Art Galley and Museum**, 1903, a self-regarding Baroque monument to the academic machinery inventor. The utility of its function is subordinate to the flamboyant design. It is the opposite of the Hepworth in Wakefield. From the pleasant terraces of the park with its boating lake may be seen the Grammar School, 1937, a large Art Deco scheme. The district has many strong Gothic terraces of houses, some with cottage Arts and Crafts roofs over bays and porches.

Take the byroad opposite the Prince of Wales Gate east to the lower valley. Ahead is Bolton Wood Quarry, the source of many golden stone Victorian buildings in Yorkshire and beyond. Go right then left up the hill gaining a view of Bradford's valley situation. Although originally built in the country, Titus Salt's Saltaire can be seen to the north as part of the Bradford conurbation. It may be visited in the same expedition as Manningham Mills. On the hilltop make east for Five Lane Ends and turn north for **Idle**, a hillside village above the valley of the River Aire, retaining its old streets. Around the church some pretty stone mullioned houses and cottages survive: one has an ogee-shaped door lintel of the seventeenth century and in Town Lane are two others with moulded mullions. At the foot of Town Lane a seventeenth-century chapel has symmetrically arranged doors, one dated 1630 and the other 1883; the mullions have round-headed lights, those at the rear have transom bars. The chapel and other buildings are now studios for the performing arts. North of the church is the Grange, 1734, gabled and mullioned in seventeenth-century style. Holy Trinity Church is not so old: broad, aisled, late Georgian and distinctive with West tower pinnacles inelegantly capped with 'gate pier' gables. Then descend to the Aire Valley and follow the A657 east to *Greengates* and a rural corner at Apperley Bridge.

Greengates is a riverside suburb of Bradford which, surprisingly, has never been completely built up. Its uninspiring Parish Church of St John, 1893, with lancets, octagonal turret and spirelet, looks north into a wooded section of the Aire Valley. By the river is the ancient Apperley Bridge surviving alongside the new, together with a picturesque inn, the George & Dragon; of the three gables two with mullions are Elizabethan, the third, taller, was added in 1704. The Dog & Gun in Harrogate Road also has mullions.

From the junction of the A657 and A658 go south towards **Undercliffe**, turning left after the first roundabout for a museum of textile machinery which may be seen operating (signed). At Undercliffe workers' housing has engulfed earlier agricultural cottages. Once a worsted spinning mill, Moorside Mills (1875) is now Bradford's industrial museum, displaying processes of woolmaking both domestic and industrial. Spinning and weaving machinery operates on the first floor. Motive power down the years is exhibited, particularly the horizontal steam engines which used to power local mills. There is a transport section which includes a tank engine, Nellie, in service at Bradford sewage works until 1970. It would be kinder to lend her to the Worth Valley Railway than keep her here. There are remnants of former Bradford trades including printing and motor manufacturing – for example the Jowett car. One tram and one trolley bus are immured in a shed. The mill owner's house is also open to view and is furnished with Victorian and Edwardian furniture. Once displayed here were the salvaged vestiges of Kirkgate Market: the pierced ironwork canopy, the neo-Baroque archway, iron galleries, carved stonework and fancy gate piers, but these guilty remnants have been removed to store. The museum itself is a wasted opportunity which might have shown the history and glory of the Bradford worsted trade to a new generation; it should be in a museum for unimaginative museums. Evidently starved of cash, it could be a selling point for the town. From the museum return to the A658, cross the Ring Road and in a quarter of a mile is the gothic cemetery at Undercliffe displaying the symbolic hopes and fears of the Victorian settlers to this town, both mill owners and mill workers. Where the 'A' road turns due south there is an entry to Peel Park, an excellent inner city Victorian Park with cast iron gates and glasshouses. Returning to the ringroad, on the left in Thornbury Road is seen the distinctive outline of the *Madni Jamia Masjid Mosque* with dome and minarets built in local ashlar sandstone. In an architectural competition run by a Muslim youth charity and the Council of Europe these minarets won a prize for the most beautiful mosque structures from a field of 50 in Europe.

Reverting to the Ring Road and travelling south to the junction with the A650, turn into the City once again for *Bowling*. Bowling is a suburb of Bradford, but ***Bolling Hall*** is an accessible part-medieval house looking down to Bradford from the south. (Bolling: OE *bolla*, a hollow – on the hill.) The hall's south elevation shows windows of many ages caught between two broad square towers. The west part is thirteenth century and was the semi-fortified home of the Bollings, Lords of the Manor. Ogee-headed windows in this wing are further evidence of medieval building; the ashlar wall behind the hall was part of a medieval timbered range. It passed from Bollings to Tempests in 1497 as a dowry for Rosamund – the Bollings' only child, and it was the Tempests who gave the hall its present shape. They built the kitchen range behind the medieval tower, the Elizabethan embattled bays and magnificent hall with 30-light window of little panes. The Lindley Wood family (later Lords Halifax) acquired the estate in 1668 and Captain Charles Wood employed John Carr of York in

Undercliffe Cemetery, Bradford.

UNDERCLIFFE CEMETERY, BRADFORD.
Opposite, above and below: BOLLING HALL, JACOBEAN PLASTER CEILING, BRADFORD.

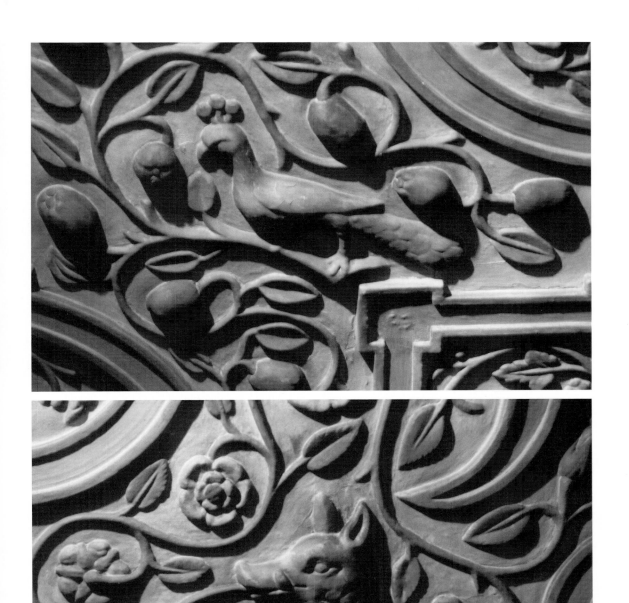

the eighteenth century to update the house. Carr made the Adamesque drawing room and designed the plaster ceiling with its acanthus leaf centre and spokes of cornear panels filled with arabesques and urns. The big mullioned and transomed hall window has heraldic glass for the Bollings, Tempests and Stanleys – it was brought from Copt Hewick Hall. The hall was owned by the Bowling Iron Co. and surrounded by pits and iron workings in the nineteenth century. The house was given to Bradford Corporation by G. A. Paley in 1912 and is now sensitively furnished again as though a home. The Ghost Room has an Elizabethan plaster ceiling of strapwork and acorns, but the lurid frieze is Victorian. The oak mantel and overmantel provide arched portrait frames; the oak four-poster was occupied by the Earl of Newcastle in 1643 prior to his assault on Bradford in the Civil War. In a dream a ghost implored him to 'Pity poor Bradford'. It is believed he did. An enduring image

SUFFA-TUL-ISLAM MOSQUE, BRADFORD.

of Bradford in the Civil War is the tower of the parish church strung with woolpacks for protection.

From Bolling Hall revert to the Ring Road and travel clockwise, crossing the M606 junction with the A641 to the tall spire of All Saints at **Little Horton Green**, a very large and distinguished EE-style church of 1864. Its proportions are more elegant than St John at Great Horton although there are common Dec elements. The tall Southeast tower has conical pinnacles and elegant parapets of foliated tracery. There is a richly decorated apse to the east, crocketed gables over shafted windows and blank trefoils carved on the balustrade. It was considered as a possible cathedral for Bradford. Little Horton Green retains seventeenth- and eighteenth-century cottages like a village, but the very fine seventeenth-century Horton Hall and Horton Old Hall have been demolished in recent times to be replaced by new housing – they were opposite the church. Here only a mile from the City Centre remains a cluster of distinguished old houses and cottages.

West of the church opposite Kennion Street is a low stone farmhouse with many mullioned windows. Walking up the road west you find a tiny (unusually) brick seventeenth-century cottage with stone roof and mullions – only one bay wide. After the nineteenth-century cottages is a picturesque sixteenth-century house with a spreading low gable and no room for a bedroom. More nineteenth-century cottages then a grander seventeenth-century house with broad twin gables, finials, five-light mullioned and transomed windows, and an ancient leaning chimney breast. There follow more cottages and some formal eighteenth-century houses with quoins, sashes and tripartite windows. Over the road junction and still on All Saints Road is a new mosque. Considerably larger than Bradford Cathedral it is faced in pink and red stone, the fenestration is within tall blank arches of grey stone. Its four minarets have corbelled-out stages which reduce to octagons and green caps. Two large green domes echo the minarets. It is an attractive and ambitious building – will there be cricket between the mosque and All Saints?

Continue west to another old village engulfed by Bradford at **Great Horton** where opposite a cluster of seventeenth-century cottages in Walshaw Street (with mullioned windows, stringcourse and round-arched doorway dated 1697) is the terrifyingly bold tower and spire of St John's, 1871–4, by T. H. and F. Healey. The tower has sharp obelisk finials rising straight from the tower table and ghastly exaggerated lucarnes (long dormers) on the spire. A house of horror in the air, it is prominent on the hillside and can be seen for miles. The Methodist Church, 1862, is distinctive with a delicate pediment and colonnade like a cotton estate mansion; it looks over a gardened forecourt. Also in Great Horton Road opposite the Crossley Mending Co. (Burlers, Menders, Picking and Tinting) by Bartle Fold is a transitional house of 1746. Although it has a stone-hipped roof the windows are still mullioned with a high transom bar, the doorway also is Jacobean – but has a Georgian eighteenth-century door. And so return to the City Centre by the A647.

To carry on through western suburbs which rise to 1,000ft go via *Clayton Heights* to *Queensbury*.

BRADSHAW In the blackened heights west of Bradford, a modest village swept by inhospitable cloud and wind. From the War Memorial are good open views east towards Scout Edge. Here also is the lychgate for St John's Church, 1837, whose big lancets contain a transom and twin lancets. It is neat and better proportioned than the description may appear, the small nave is well lit. [7]

BRAMHAM Agreeable stone village gathering in the shelter of a tributary valley of the Wharfe, with a distinguished old church. The tower is Norman but the embattled upper storey and spire were added in the sixteenth century. There is a North arcade of tall round piers with unmoulded round arches, also 1100s; the EE South doorway has colonnettes and a dog-tooth carved arch. A little later is the South aisle with octagonal piers. The re-formed EE chancel has lancet windows and Art Nouveau screens. Memorials are to Foxes, Lane Foxes and Lord Bingley. The former Great North Road is the main street with old limestone buildings from 1600s to 1800s.

The A1 bypass sweeps close to the village but a bridge to the south allows you to cross the tide. Here is Bowcliffe Hall, a handsome classical mansion with broad Tuscan porch, tripartite window over – all under a pediment. The A1 has ruined the privacy of the house but fortunately it is now a company headquarters. From this point (and with signs from the A1) a drive leads to Bramham Park, for long the home of the Lane Fox family. The park and interesting gardens are open in the summer. The drive crosses undulating parkland of pasture and woodland. You pass Bramham Biggin, a seventeenth-century house with gables of mullioned and transomed windows and 1756 addition of bowed and Venetian windows. *Bramham House* itself comes into view across a rising brow of parkland: it is elevated on a half-storey to maximize its prospect of the park. It was built in 1710 by Lord Bingley, Lord Mayor and Member of Parliament for York – he was a favourite of Queen Anne. The house is plain classical of 11 bays over a low rusticated basement and has a balustraded flat roof. It is

very horizontal – this emphasized by flanking pavilions stepped forward, also flat roofed – and joined to further pavilions by Tuscan colonnades. The house looks bigger because the Italianate classical stables, at right angles to the main house, accompany it to form a courtyard. The stables are later and richer than their house, with a pediment on Tuscan columns, clock tower and lantern (John Wood Snr). Well forward of the house and overlooking the park are massive isolated rusticated piers, very Baroque. Also Baroque is the interior. The Stone Room entrance hall – a 30ft cube – has stone walls, great stone Corinthian columns and florid coved cornice. After a fire the garden front was remodelled by Detmar Blow in 1907 to form a gallery looking into the garden.

To reach the formal gardens and grounds, which are laid out in the manner of André Le Nôtre, go through the rear of the stables. The West elevation of the house has a double staircase down to the garden, part of Blow's Edwardian rebuilding. The West Front looks out over rising woods with beech avenues radiating from a round and domed temple (half a mile south of the house) with six avenues to other eye-catchers: for example north is the Summer House with Ionic portico by James

MEMORIAL TO RAILWAY WORKERS, BRAMHOPE MONUMENT.

Bramham House, baroque piers.

Bramham House, garden.

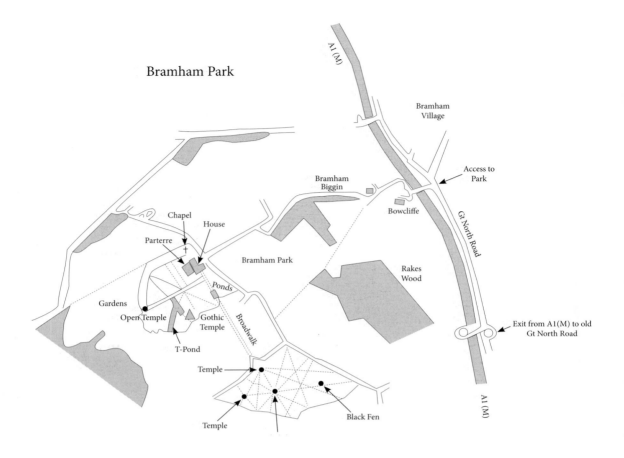

Bramham Park

A1 (M)

Bramham
Village

Access to
Park

Bramham
Biggin

Bowcliffe

Gt North Road

Chapel

House

Parterre

Bramham Park

Rakes
Wood

Ponds

Gardens

Open Temple

Gothic
Temple

T-Pond

Broadwalk

Exit from A1(M) to old
Gt North Road

Temple

Black Fen

A1 (M)

Temple

Paine – now made into a chapel; a mile to the south is an obelisk with urn finial, a memorial to the second Lord Bingley's son. From here radiate ten forest rides interconnecting like stars. The park suffered severely in 1962 when a gale felled 400 mature trees but now, through replanting, is well recovered. The formal gardens are also laid on straight paths and parterre principles. Best formal garden in the county.

House: Open only to groups by appointment.
Garden: Open daily in summer. [5]

BRAMHOPE Bramhope Cross is at the village centre with a number of old stone-roofed cottages. The Methodist church is Gothic with a little spire, 1895. The hall is no more but across the A660, along Hall Drive expensive commuter homes tumble over the escarpment of Wharfedale trespassing on the landscape. By the junction, however, is Bramhope Puritan Chapel, 1649, that is, during the Commonwealth. It is a simple box with belcote, stone roof, and arched lights in straight-headed windows. The East window has five lights. The clear space within is roofed with thick oak beams, purlins and king posts. There are oak-boxed pews with bobbin heads. The pulpit has a reader's desk in front and carries a sounding board above. Very charming, open to visitors on Sundays. Not now in use for worship, it was the Anglican church from the late eighteenth century to 1881 when St Giles (lancet style) was built in the village. Glorious views are to the north looking into Wharfedale as you travel towards Otley. [3]

BRAMHAM HOUSE, GARDEN.

PURITAN CHAPEL, 1649, BRAMHOPE.

BRIGHOUSE A busy small wool town in the Calder Valley at the nexus of seven principal roads. A link road effectively divides the town from its wooded suburban hill to the north with stone-built mansions and stone terraces – many with unadopted streets of complete nineteenth-century terraced courts. One of the best merchant's houses is The Rydings, early nineteenth century, Grecian with ashlar and Ionic-columned porch (still in a garden it is now the public library). Also on this hillside is the Parish Church of St Martin, 1831 – ashlar with big lancets divided by Y tracery; lumpish battlements and a tower which is not robust; gloomy churchyard; later chancel, 1905 – Arts and Crafts Gothic. Below the church is the slender red-tiled spire of Central Methodist Church in a Gothic, again influenced by Art Nouveau. In the centre of the town is Thornton Square where the stone-roofed Black Bull with Doric porch is late Georgian. To its left is Briggate leading over the Calder and

Hebble Navigation by a humped back bridge. Attractive waterside walks. Two massive flour hoppers are now redundant. Also in Thornton Square is the former town hall whose public office is a pastiche of Renaissance styles. Some elevated three-storey buildings in stone demonstrate Victorian prosperity. On Bethal Street is the nineteenth-century chapel where the founder of the Salvation Army, Colonel Booth, was minister: plain eaves but a cornice to each storey of stone sashed windows. Proudest and saddest is Bethel Chapel of 1878. Two towers with mansard roofs are linked by arched windows under a carved foliage band; under each tower are symmetrical thirteenth-century style doorways: it has become a pub. The Old Ship Inn in Bethal Street has a 1920s timber façade made of wood from HMS *Donegal*, a Man o'War, built in 1858.

South across the tumbling River Calder and canal are pleasant stone-built leafy suburbs up to Toothill. A little to the west is **Rastrick**, part of the Brighouse township and partner in the famous Brighouse and Rastrick Brass Band. Rastrick is up the A643, towards the skyline where the M62 appears to fly above you. A mile out of Brighouse stands the singular Church of St Matthew: joint Methodist and Anglican, built in 1768. The squat tower is reminiscent of a stable yard adornment, shallow pediments to the tower parapet support a stone dome carrying a Doric cupola and fancy weathervane. The nave is symmetrical with corniced entrances at each end like a Sunday school, blank arches between but pierced with Georgian fanlights. A curvaceous apse has a Venetian window. Inside are galleries on Tuscan columns. St James on Bradford Road has excellent Morris glass. [14]

BUCKSTONES EDGE One of the loneliest heights in England at the very west of West Yorkshire on the summit of the Pennines. Here are gigantic waves of moorland, its rough grass bent east by the ever blowing wind. Buckstones Edge belongs to the National Trust and is part of the 2,300 hectare Marsden Moor estate. Only cotton grass, bilberry and heather decorate these desolate moors. Gryphs of washed-out peat channels show the greasy blackness beneath. The Pennine Way follows the Pennine spine and traverses the horizon southwest along the watershed of the Irish and North Seas. Holme Moss with its aerial beacon signals Derbyshire on the southern horizon. [West of 19]

BURLEY-IN-WHARFEDALE Bordering the River Wharfe just above the flood line. The river meanders attractively through meadows, and from the elevated gazebo in the park are views north to Askwith Moor. St Mary's Church is picturesquely situated near the wooded river bank, model Dec, 1843, with sharp features and attractive tower – octagonal pinnacles support the spire with flying buttresses. Large lancets are filled with crisp diamond lights. The hall, between the church and the river, is late Georgian: bow windows, shallow-pitched roof and wide soffits supported on large 'S' brackets. Near the roundabout on the Otley Road is Burley House: smart classical with a three-bay pediment, doorway with Tuscan columns, Venetian window and balustraded first-floor windows. [2]

CALVERLEY On the A657 overlooking the rural Aire Valley and Leeds and Liverpool Canal. The church is on a bend in the road and may easily be missed; it has a Dec tower with Perp upper storey and corbelled-out parapet. The nave is made of large hewn stones and has a clerestory of straight-headed Dec windows. The stonework is much renewed. The West window in a kind of plate tracery may be a renewal; also the East window with its flowing tracery. Some good memorials are in the churchyard, which opens to farmland under lime and beech trees. Next door to the church is a handsome eighteenth-century house – straight-headed twin porches, two and a half storeys with moulded stone sashes and a big cornice. Calverley Old Hall on Woodhall Road is medieval, Elizabethan and Jacobean – a happy jumble of gables, mullions and Perp windows. [9]

CAPHOUSE A village consisting of the Reindeer Inn – formerly The Cap House – and a colliery. The colliery, now owned by a trust, is a listed building and operates for visitors to observe the conditions for winning coal. Although small it is typical of many pits which operated in West Yorkshire until recently. Most have disappeared without trace. Caphouse began operations in 1791 when the present winding shaft was sunk as 'shaft no. 17'. In those days there were many shafts because operations below ground could not stray far. The mine was bought by Sir John Lister Kaye in 1827 and, as its date stone declares, the present winding house was built by his daughter Emma Lister Kaye in 1876. Remarkably the pit headgear is wooden and dates from that time, although now strengthened with steel. Inside, the steam winding engine was second-hand even in 1876 and has an antique appearance with its pistons cased in wood like the Titfield Thunderbolt. The tall square chimney is for the boiler furnace to provide the necessary steam and you should find the steam engine working. You can descend to see the coalface and underground equipment, although the last coal was brought up in 1985. Visitors descend in a cage wound at slow speed by a modern electric motor. All the domestic features of the colliery are preserved including the lamp room and baths where you hear ghostly miners sing. In its latter days coal was brought up from a drift entrance down the hill by a conveyor system which still runs. The coal then passed through the washery and screens, all of which remain. A small railway connects Caphouse with another shaft, Hope Pit. There is an exhibition of mining techniques and history. [21]

CASTLEFORD Once a ford held by the Romans it has a fine elliptical three-arch bridge over the Calder built in 1807. Its cutwaters and arches are rusticated, blind arches mark the buttresses either end, and the parapet is decorated with cornice moulding. To the west is a spectacular weir with the remains of a large steel barge crashed over the fall and well embedded over many decades. A better view may be had from the Millennium footbridge which (confidently) staggers over this broad reach of river. By the weir is an old flour mill originally

CAPHOUSE COLLIERY.

worked by water power. It retains overhanging gantries from which corn and flour were collected and delivered by barge. Allinson's used to grind corn between stones. Today the air is sweet from a chemical works, and the down-at-heel sense of the town is explained by its past dependence on mining and glass manufacture. To the north where a cut of the Aire and Calder Navigation bypasses the centre of Castleford coal barges are moored up with their tugs. These are operated in trains called 'Tom Pudding Boats'. Local coal is too sulphurous to burn and unless the power stations can find a new abstraction process they may never put out again.

A path downstream to Bulholme Lock at the end of the pound leads past pretty narrow boats and cruisers. On the far bank dangerous chemicals were reprocessed until recently. Nevertheless, looking towards Castleford from the lock is a pleasing prospect of water, grass and trees. From here a footpath leads to Fairburn Ings, an area of open water and a nationally important wetland for breeding waders and wildfowl – the wetlands developed from subsidence caused by coal workings some

half a mile beneath. A walk leads via Hicksons Flash, Lin Dyke and Spoonbill Flash to the visitor centre. Current barge traffic on the Navigation includes sand from the Trent and fuel oil from Hull docks. Coal is suspended. A scheme to ferry multitudes of butty boats from the Continent for further penetration into Yorkshire was abandoned owing to adverse reaction at Hull Docks. All Saints Church, 1866, stands on a small eminence over the town, model cruciform with a central tower, stair turret and Yorkshire-style corbelled-out tower parapet. A little 'Disney' but a clean might work wonders. Much of the housing is by the Earls of Mexborough for their mines. See also *Whitwood* in this conurbation. [17]

CHEVET PARK The house and park of the Pilkington baronets. The park includes the large lake at Newmillerdam and the woods around the lake have public access. The house has been demolished. (See *Newmillerdam.*) [22]

ALLINSON'S MILL, CASTLEFORD.

CLAYTON HEIGHTS Here the suburbs of Bradford climb laboriously west uphill into the Pennines towards Queensbury – a conventional mill settlement of blackened stone in a moorland setting at 1000ft. On the Bradford side are many curious single storey, stone-roofed cottages of the eighteenth and nineteenth centuries. Up on the heights, and contrary to commonsense, new houses are being built on the skyline along main roads. There appears to be a strong irrational element in Bradford's planning mind. [8]

CLAYTON WEST In lovely undulating country in the East Pennines. Terminus of the Kirklees Light Railway which follows an old BR branch line and which can be found at the former BR station. The steam locomotives were especially built for this railway. [21]

CLECKHEATON Opposite Coach Lane is the former Congregational Church of 1857–9 with its elaborate and expensive portico of six Corinthian columns, handsome now that it has been cleaned. St John's Church is

down towards the River Spen and although the tower is of 1830, it is the only remnant of the Commissioner's Church; the conventional steep roof and lancet windows, aisles and clerestory are later Victorian, Lockwood and Mawson. On Whitechapel Road is the last rebuilding of the Old Chapel, 1831, with large lancets, intersecting tracery and a polygonal bell turret. Here is a good Norman font with rudely carved figures in its arcading. The Town Hall is neo-Baroque, 1890; the library shows the influence of Art Deco and has its original oak interior. [14]

CLIFFORD Village of honey-coloured limestone, delightfully roofed with red pantiles. At the top of the village is St Luke's Church, 1841, rather toy-like with large lancets. The tower is a step too far and spoils the composition with big double lancets within tower arches. From the top of the village descend past Georgian houses gathered around the green, and past the War Memorial and baptismal well in its little stone pavilion. Clifford Moor is north of here – it is where combatants

gathered for the Pilgrimage of Grace and also the Rising of the North. It does not look dangerous ground.

The High Street winds satisfactorily down, lined by cottages of a consistent limestone hue to frame the Romanesque style RC Church of St Edward. Its tall tower in the same stone might have jumped from the middle of France. Patrons were the Grimstones of Clifford Flax Mill (in the village) and the design was derived from continental sketches, seen by chance in Scotland and used by the architect J. A. Hansom. Other contributors present a snapshot in history: the Pope, the Queen of France, the King of Sardinia and the Duke of Palma. The large tower has five storeys and was originally accessible to carriages within the base; its pyramid roof stands over an open loggia storey. Within, the Romanesque theme is overdone with chubby piers and arcades; the sanctuary is screened by an arcade through which a Madonna appears in an apse to the east. There is a rose window in the East nave; an organ in a West gallery on arches; twin-light clerestory windows; and a pitched roof with barrel-shaped braces. One of the circular aisle piers is spiralled and stands on a carved turtle whose eyes show some pain. The statue of the Madonna was carved by Hoffmann, an Italian Jew who converted to Catholicism through working on it. There is some glass by A. W. Pugin. The door is fastened by the most massive lock but do not hesitate to swing the handle (which must weigh about 20lbs) it works with ease. Opposite the church is a little castellated lookout tower by the entrance to the now demolished mill. Clifford's Mill spun flax for patent yarn and bootlaces; flax grew in the fields here and the workers were supervised from the tower. [5]

CLIFTON   After the M62 junction towards Brighouse a lane on the right ascends the side of the Calder Valley to Clifton, a small rural village perched on the edge of the escarpment looking over fields to the north and east. Old cottages and an inn of the seventeenth century are accompanied by the Dec style St John Evangelist chapel of 1859. The graveyard looks out over acres of warehouses in the Calder Valley below. Just east of here is ancient Kirklees off a lane ostensibly leading to a garden centre. It was a priory for Cistercian nuns but not very large; there are no remains but its name has been given to the unitary council for Huddersfield and surrounding area. The Priory's Elizabethan gatehouse is post-Reformation, partly in stone with mullioned windows and partly timber framed, now in a parlous state. One of the

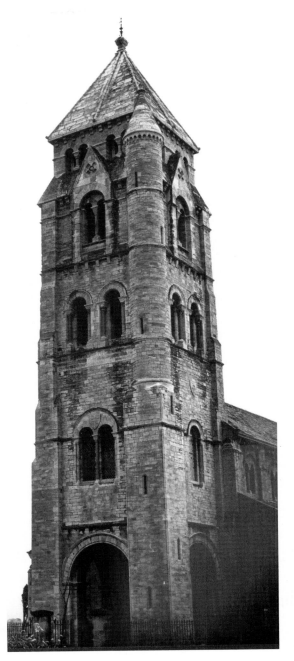

St Edward, Clifford.

Opposite, above: Tom Pudding Tugs laid up, Castleford;
below: Sea-going boats on the Calder, Castleford.

39

KIRKLEES HALL, CLIFTON.

many graves of Robin Hood is nearby but is not worth seeking out. Kirklees Hall is a mighty jumble of Elizabethan and Jacobean building with massed chimneys and runs of mullioned and transomed windows. A little difficult to understand, its plan is E-shaped with the spokes hitting you as you approach. Therefore the main front faces north. Although built in the seventeenth century it was converted to stone sashes in 1780. The parapets over the wings are decorated with semi-circular merlons like embattling. Earlier sixteenth-century building shows large raw mullioned windows of an earlier age; the massive chimneys to service big rooms are seen before the formal front – it is as though the mansion's petticoat is on display. The pretty stable block with mullioned and transomed windows would make a handsome house in its own right. The main house is divided into a number of units and permission should be obtained to visit. The estate reaches down to the foot of the wooded Calder Valley, and occupies an oasis entirely out of view of industry and commerce. [14]

COLLINGHAM 'A pleasant village in a calm and tranquil situation on the Wharfe', according to Dr Whitaker the antiquarian. St Oswald's Church stands in a rural location east of the village with a path through the churchyard into a meadow by the river. The North aisle and tower are Perp; the South aisle EE, delicate and slightly leaning; the North arcade has good circular piers of 1200. A small Norman arch was saved at the nineteenth-century restoration by insertion into the sextant's hut in the churchyard. The North aisle contains stumps of two Anglo-Saxon crosses: one carved with figures of the Apostles on each face and the other displaying interlaced beasts and foliage, dated to the eighth and ninth centuries. Below the pulpit is a stone with eight hollows thought to be for grease and wick to light the medieval church. The Royal Arms on the South nave wall 'AR 1706' are those of Queen Anne. The village extends west along the river's meadows and a road doubles back to the north behind – it leads to a grandly arched bridge over the Wharfe which lands on a tree-clad bluff above the river and goes on to Linton. [9]

COOKRIDGE Beyond Headingley on the outskirts of Leeds towards Otley. A large burial ground was made in the nineteenth century at Lawnswood, designed by George Corson, 1875. Without the rigidity of Undercliffe the paths wind attractively through woods with rhododendron, azaleas, etc. Arthur Briggs, owner of the largest colliery in Europe (see *Whitwood*), is buried here. There are some unusual memorials; a house porch

TOLL HOUSE AT COPLEY BRIDGE, COPLEY.
Right: ST LUKE AND ALL SAINTS, NORMAN AND 14TH CENTURY, DARRINGTON.

Page 44: TOWN HALL, DEWSBURY.

for departure and a chimney memorial to a steeplejack. To the west, but gained by the Old Otley Road and Hospital Lane, are the sad remains of Cookridge Hospital, sad because its architect in the main parts was Norman Shaw with trade mark big timbered gables – but its sale for development appears to jeopardize what remains. The lodge is a superb example of Arts and Crafts, a timber-clad gabled chalet with a tall steep roof, the first floor is cantilevered forwards on braces; bay window on more braces, and the gable projects yet again. Cookridge is the highest point for miles and has a huge underground water reservoir for northwest Leeds. The telecom mast is to signal, inter alia, through to Lancashire via Windy Hill in the Pennines. [3]

COPLEY An early paternalistic industrial estate by Colonel Edward Akroyd established south of the River Calder below the steep declivity from Halifax. It predates Akroydon and Saltaire. The very grand classical mill (1847) sadly is demolished but the grid of cottages remains and the large gloomy and austere church by W. H. Crossland, St Stephen (1865). It is in the hands of the Churches Conservation Trust, through which a visit should be arranged. [13]

CRAGG Village in the outstandingly pretty Cragg Vale. Cragg Brook tumbles down to the Calder from wild lunar landscapes on Great Manshead Hill and Turley Holes Moor where the peat is driven into furrows, craters and islands: and where in June a white sea of cotton grass bobs over all. Halfway down this wooded vale old cottages and an empty-windowed chapel cling to the hillside; below them the Church of St John-in-the-Wilderness, 1839, lancet style with Perp tower, is much enhanced by the location. Over the little hump bridge to the west a lone chimney fingers the sky, silent and now unsmoking – Cragg Vale Mill has been demolished. It will remain a monument to the Hinchcliffes, woolmasters who inhabited an Italian Renaissance style mansion in the wooded and rhododendroned east side of the vale. The mansion, built at the turn of the nineteenth century, burned down and the grounds are filled with modern houses. [13]

CROFTON Former hilltop pit village. Colliery houses in New Crofton retain old seventeenth-century farmhouses of some character – one dated 1665 has mullions and a stout chimney, is now the Manor Public House. Another rather less grand is dated 1677. In the High Street there remains a group of old cottages with pantile and stone roofs. A curiosity in Hare Park Lane is a house whose end gable has a theatrically large Doric doorway. The Parish Church of All Saints dominates from its hill – cruciform with Perp crossing tower, embattling and transepts. It is said to have been built about 1430 by Bishop Fleming of Lincoln but may originally date from the early twelfth century. There is a handsome stone-ribbed porch and in the North transept parts of Saxon crosses, one with creatures in interlacing and one with a horned head. The spire has been taken down. The bell frame of 1663 was replaced by steel in 1922 and its wood made into a lychgate to commemorate the Great War. To the east of the church is an arched mausoleum guarded by an arresting and frightening winged angel for the Wilson family who used to live below Church Hill. [22]

CULLINGWORTH Urbanized village uphill and south of Bingley. St John's Church is in the Victorian lancet style but is an unusually nice composition in the arrangement of the windows; transept and nave face the street and embrace a tower with stair turret. From a plain table the square tower sweeps into a short octagonal spire. In the village are old cottages and farmhouses, many with moulded mullions and continuous dripmould, as well as the more usual square mullions. Small mills are now converted to flats. [7]

DARRINGTON Beige limestone village just off the Great North Road. The medieval church of St Luke and All Saints stands on a little hill in the middle of the village. The Norman tower (with Perp battlements) is embraced by the west third of the nave; evidence of its steep-roofed predecessor is on the tower – it must have been short and stubby. It was rebuilt very early to judge by the EE lancets in the arcades of tall, round piers. The South doorway is also EE and has three orders of shafts – slightly decayed though sheltered by a later stone-roofed porch on stone arches. The porch roof has pinnacles on columns over the gable and corbels. A glory of the church is the Dec aisle windows with interweaving reticulated tracery; proportionately smaller windows in the chancel give it a very satisfying appearance; its East window also has reticulated tracery. The North chancel chapel is Dec and impressively crooked (it has long been held in place by a substantial buttress) it appears rebuilt about 1300 from the nail head decoration on the arch capitals. A turret projects out of its roof – also a little crooked – it accommodates the rood stairs which were not destroyed and from which a choirboy sang at the Christmas service until recently. The contribution of the fifteenth century appears to be limited to a big East chancel window with panelled tracery, and the chancel wall – the exterior most unusually has a panel of carved quatrefoil. Very dignified interior: there is a stone effigy of Sir Warin de Scargill who died in 1326 within an arch

Opposite: SHODDY MILL, DEWSBURY;
above: DEWSBURY WAREHOUSES.

stone terraced houses. It was built in 1897 to commemorate Queen Victoria's Jubilee. Holy Trinity lies up its own drive, built in 1939, with unusual thick chevron window tracery impaled on straight, square mullions. Within, reinforced concrete arches open progressively towards the chancel above which is a low tower. The chandeliers display symbolic medallions, for example of the Creation and Ascension. Denby Dale is famous for the massive pies it bakes periodically. The first was in 1788 to celebrate King George III's recovery from insanity. The pies are made on an 'as required' basis but may be expected to be baked on a great occasion, such as the Battle of Waterloo, Queen Victoria's Jubilee in 1887 (when the pie went bad), and for the Millennium in 2000. The profits from a pie made in 1964 were sufficient to build a community centre known as The Pie Hall. It is likely that in today's world the massive pie dish will no longer be used and it has accordingly been put on display outside. The town is still in business making woollen cloth although Kenyan's Mill has closed; Hinchcliffe's has a modern mill and has been in business since 1766, today spinning cashmere. [26]

DENHOLME Bleak one-mill town high on Thornton Moor – entirely in black stone with the moors rising behind the houses. The little Mechanics Institute, 1880, has round-arched windows with Gothic drip moulds. Even in the hills the houses cluster in terraces. The lancet-style, aisled church, St Paul (1843 by J. B. Chantrell), has double lancets in the clerestory, a prominent tower and spire. Lavish memorials are to Fosters, mill owners who paid for it – but why on a hill a mile out of town? It has paid the price and is now abandoned. The great mill chimney marking Denholme on this moorland road has long been demolished. [7]

DEWSBURY Newly cleaned with many excitements in architectural terms. Stone throughout it displays a variety of nineteenth-century buildings on its hillsides. Wool mills and warehouses display the richest Italian carving and ornamentation on local honey-coloured sandstone which gleams in the sun. The Town Hall, 1889, is an exuberant Renaissance chateau where either side of a central tower stagger others with French mansards; the ornate tower has an awesome clock stage, then a turret. Situated on the hill to the north it is a joyful swaggering piece. Barclays Bank is like an Italian palace with shafted arched windows, keystone heads and windows on the first floor with elliptical hoods. By the railway station are three- and four-storey classical wool warehouses. The Co-op 'Dewsbury Pioneers Industrial Society' is outrageous neo-Baroque but in keeping with the town's fizzy architectural mood. It was famous for 'shoddy':

of the North chancel wall but his lady is relegated to the South aisle. Note the scalloped capitals in the Norman tower arch; also the Perp tracery carved on bench ends.

Close to the churchyard is the former nineteenth-century school with white diamond iron tracery in the Gothic windows; it is now a house. Within the churchyard is *Church House*, with a pyramid roof and Gothicized wooden lights; part of the building has a bricked-up Gothic arch, red pantiles. Sadly the original village building material, beige or honey-coloured limestone with pantiles, has not been much respected in new building. [23]

DENBY DALE In a deep valley under the shadow of a huge stone railway viaduct carrying the Sheffield to Huddersfield line through the Pennines. The gaunt outlines of the Methodist Memorial Hall are up the hill to the north, its gable rearing above the slate roofs of the

cloth made from wool and silk ends. Not found today, it was referred to by W. S. Gilbert in the lines, 'When you have nothing else to wear, but cloth of gold and satins, for cloth of gold you cease to care – up goes the price of shoddy' (*The Gondoliers*). A five-storey shoddy mill still stands in the centre, its painted name a sign of times gone by.

The churches and chapels are also exuberant. On Long Causeway is the United Reformed Church in well-ornamented Dec style with plate tracery and shafting. On Daisy Hill the Methodist Church has a restrained façade of arched windows. At the foot of the town is *Dewsbury Minster* – otherwise All Saints – a large cruciform church from the thirteenth century. Its North arcade is a curiosity, the piers consisting of groups of independent shafts. Some Saxon masonry is claimed in the spandrels but is doubtful. The nave and aisles were substantially rebuilt in the eighteenth century by John Carr. The North doorway has an ogee head and almost ogee pediment. The windows of Carr's North aisle are modern in spirit: large arches divided by mullions, the lights also with round heads. In the North transept is

ALL SAINTS NAVE, DEWSBURY.

medieval stained glass rearranged and showing medieval life, for example harvesting and pig killing. The fabric of the transepts and chancel, however, is late nineteenth century. This big church has suffered some radical surgery recently, switching worship from East to West in the nave so as to free the chancel for support facilities. That in turn has been divided into two storeys with prayer rooms, offices and refreshments. The church's possessions, an Anglian cross and other ninth-century carved fragments, including a very early Madonna and child, are on display. The large carved reredos by Temple Moore has been retired and is placed on a side wall to be viewed near the entrance. Open daily, parking south of the churchyard, leaflets for tours and tea. [15]

DRIGHLINGTON Pronounced Drig-aling-ton. A green oasis between Bradford and Leeds. St Paul's Church, 1878, is in a somewhat lugubrious Perp style built of small stones. The seven-light East window has glass by Charles Kemp, and the chancel arch spandrels a mosaic of St Paul. An attractive chancel roof has hammer beams and gilded angels. In the churchyard many urn-finialled memorials and obelisks are more gothic than the contrived church. Seventeenth-century Lumb Hall was occupied by Parliamentarians in the Civil War. The three gables all have mullions; the ground floor windows are grander with transom bar. The projecting porch bay has a little Yorkshire rose window over, and carved in the doorway keystone is a fanciful likeness of Charles I. Chimneys are in stout banks. Nearby at *Adwalton* is the site of a famous Royalist victory in the Civil War on 30 June 1643. After Marston Moor the Battle of Adwalton was the most important. The site is now surrounded by housing but there is public access to the battle terrain where much imagination is required. [15]

EAST ARDSLEY The centre of the village is north of the A650. Turn off by the petrol station for the hall whose west flank is on Thorpe Lane showing a stout chimney breast. It is a clothier's house with a gabled porch and gables of mullioned windows either side. The porch is dated 1632; there are ten lights in the left and eight in the right-hand gable. Crocketed finials to the gables. The church of 1881 replaces a much earlier building but the Norman doorway with zigzag and beak-head decoration was preserved. Stone terraces of houses for mill workers are laid about the hilly terrain higgledy piggledy with allotments and pigeon lofts interspersed. [16]

EAST RIDDLESDEN HALL SOUTHSIDE.

EAST HARDWICK Brick village. The church is a steeply gabled EE exercise of 1875; its diminutive tower oddly placed in the crook of the South transept and nave. Curious triangular dormer lights are set in the steep tiled nave, chancel and transept roofs. [16]

EAST KESWICK A farming hamlet northeast of Leeds which in spite of some new housing retains a rural atmosphere. Outcrops of sandstone are indicated in the building material. St Mary Magdalene, 1856, has a conical bell turret and stone-roofed lychgate memorial for

the First World War. It is an essay in EE with tall chancel arch; crossbeams support purlins in the open roof. [4]

EAST RIDDLESDEN Yorkshire Jacobean Hall pleasantly situated in Airedale – just above the flood plain. It is the site of a medieval hall of which fragments remain but the Jacobean mansion of today was the creation of James Murgatroyd, 1640. The porch has a large Yorkshire wheel window of eight cusped lights above an arched entrance with Doric columns; it is embattled and with pinnacles like the main gable to its left. That gable

49

is replete with mullions, twelve lights made of four windows joined together; then high in the gable stepped lights. Chimney stacks present a diamond aspect. The medieval hall was right of the entrance where now stands the ruin of Edmund Starkie's wing, built in the 1690s. Its cross-mullioned windows are out of line with the pinnacled gables. It became derelict and the roof was taken off in 1905; its shell forms part of the formal gardens behind.

The best room inside is the hall with a big elliptically-arched fireplace flanked by Doric pillars. Facing the fireplace part of the medieval hall projects from the 1690 wing. The fine Jacobean staircase came from Northamptonshire. Much panelling and seventeenth-century plasterwork, the latter from sixteenth-century moulds, was made by Francis Lee of Wakefield, so it is in a sense Tudor. The beams are encrusted with plaster foliage and creatures; the ceiling with little pendants and crests. The tall fireplace in the drawing room is carved with semi-circular devices like the lintels at Oakworth Hall. Good contemporary furniture includes the vast oak dresser described in *Wuthering Heights*. At the rear of the house

is another similar porch, wheel window and mullioned gables replicating the north elevation, and a formal garden. In the grounds is the Bothy, accommodation built for farm workers and now a tearoom. There are two large seventeenth-century barns – the Great Barn is 120ft long with a cobbled floor and king post roof. The Airedale Barn was taken over during the Second World War by the Ministry of Food who removed the aisle posts, but they have been restored by the National Trust. The house was more than once on the brink of demolition but twins William and John Brigg of Keighley bought it in 1934 to make it one of the earliest gifts to the National Trust. [1]

ELLAND   An intriguing little wool town rising on the south side of the Calder Valley. It has an ancient heart centred on the Perp Church of St Mary with an embattled tower. Though parts of the South aisle are renewed with straight-headed windows, that which embraces the tower is certainly medieval. The West door and outer South door have pretty wooden intersecting blank tracery – the latter with spikes on top like a court house or

EAST RIDDLESDEN HALL, 17TH CENTURY PLASTERWORK.

Great barn, 1980, East Riddlesden.

prison. The East windows of the chapel are also Perp, the buttresses at the East end step in with crocketed gables and quite alarming gargoyles. The finial over the porch is like a square vase and surely not original. The church key can be obtained from Dobson's Sweet Factory. Opposite the church tower is a small stone-roofed sixteenth-century house of three gables – mullioned and transomed windows, two have stepped lights. This is next door to the sweet factory, the home of Elland Historical Society. On Church Street is a bank in modest EE style with stone-shafted entrance, also a late Georgian pub the Savile Arms with Doric porch. All is stone in the town centre save for the outrageous Elland House, an eight-storey concrete formula building. Concrete tene-

TRANSMITTING TOWER, EMLEY MOOR.

ments are used to infill the town centre around stone Victorian shops, three-storey terraces and classical chapels. Thoughtful development has been absent. A short walk up Northgate brings you to the late Tudor Fleece Inn, an excellent stone-roofed sixteenth-century house of two low gables – each with mullioned and transomed windows – flanking irregular gables in the centre. On Victoria Road is Bethesda Methodist Church with large plate-traceried West window – punchy, like a revolver magazine. Twin towers are on either flank with pyramid roofs and EE-style entrance doors, each within a shafted Norman arch. On Southgate is another Methodist church, this time in Arts and Crafts Gothic. From here the former mills stand independently a little east of the town as though musing; they retain great dignity.

A new road between Huddersfield and Halifax swoops over the valley here in a patronizing fashion causing those by the old waterways terminal on the canal at Elland Bridge to look up. The old road by the river is to be preferred, past abandoned mills and stumpy grass-topped chimney stacks. On Saddleworth Road the Pennine Yarn Dying Mill is finished. A walk over Elland Bridge gives views of the fast-running Calder and a little further the Calder and Hebble Navigation with eighteenth-century stone-built warehousing to the west. By Elland Bridge, and wholly out of place, is a grandiose former bank with twin polished granite columns and vigorously carved pediment on which sits the figure of Neptune. From the bridge also is a good view of Valley Mill, Italianate with two towers – one Baroque. Behind it rise the woods of Elland Park, an uninterrupted bank of greenery. Here by the river stood Elland Old Hall, sadly demolished in 1976, which revealed a medieval timber frame when it was split open. [14]

EMLEY   On a spur of the Pennines already 800ft high the slender needle of Emley Moor Television mast dominates this part of Yorkshire. Like an enormous missile poised to spring at the stars, a further 1,084ft of elegant concrete penetrates the clouds from a surprisingly broad base. Inside is a three-man lift to the broadcasting antennae. Its predecessor was a guyed steel structure that fell to the ground in a storm in 1969. It was similar to Holme Moss. One of the steel guys cut through the roof and walls of a chapel. Fortunately there was no loss of life. The new structure dares the heavens and can be seen from most parts of the county.

The lower village of Emley has some good recent housing, and a robust Norman church, St Michael's, overlooks the Calder Valley, its stout Perp tower visible for many miles. Some Norman masonry and a tympanum carved with a dragon, lamb and cross is in the South wall. The tie-beam roof may be not unconnected

Mills on the River Calder, Elland.

with the windy location. In the chancel is an excellent, large brass candelabra, still with candles, and an East window with fifteenth-century glass depicting the crucifixion, the Virgin and St John. A medieval market cross is in the centre of the village. [21]

ESHOLT That rare thing, an agricultural village between Bradford and Leeds in the Aire Valley. Away from the main road, the picturesque village grouping of Old Hall Farm, church and vicarage look through trees to the river and canal, and over to Buck Wood on the hill opposite. It will be familiar as the original fictional village of Emmerdale from the TV series. The chapel-like Church of St Paul is small with a belcote and flagpole in lieu of tower. The twinned windows along the nave are almost lancets; in the nave is a new gallery for the organ. A Dec-style chancel arch and three lancets form the East window. The Elizabethan Old Hall has one particularly huge gable containing a high mullioned window and embraces two bays of mullioned windows at ground level; it is very pretty. Home Farm displays excellent seventeenth-century Yorkshire features: shaped lintels, mullions and big drip-mould stops. About a mile away east, within a water treatment plant, is the early classical hall of the Calverleys. Pedimented, of seven bays, it was built in 1706 by Joseph Pope. Its 100-acre park is now Bradford's modern sewage works, and the mansion has become offices, but it remains leafy and tranquil. It incorporates part of a twelfth-century nunnery whose last prioress, Elizabeth Pudsey, died in 1540. Until 1970 a steam tank engine hauled sewage to and fro, it is now retired to the *Underhill* industrial museum. [2]

FARNLEY (LEEDS) Now part of Leeds and occupying the west valley side of Farnley Beck. The old village is high up on the hill and fronting open country. Victorian ambition destroyed Carr's little classical church in 1885 and now the fraying Dec/Perp St Michael and All Angels which replaced it is too big; but the cupola from Carr's church still stands in the churchyard. Across the road is Lawns House, Georgian, with central three-bay pediment. A little to the north is Farnley Hall, also Georgian, down a wooded half-mile drive: somewhat broader than Lawns it has a nice Tuscan porch and frontispiece in the projecting central bay. The hall is offices and its large garden a public park. New Farnley to the southwest was built to house employees of the Farnley Iron Co. Terraces remain but now there is no smelting or forging of iron. [9]

FARNLEY TYAS High on a plateau south of Huddersfield with the mills hidden in the deeply riven valleys of the Holme and Fenay Beck, this old farming village

presides over many hectares of pasture clear of the busy industrial lives in the valleys below. Grand views to the west. Much nearer is Castle Hill at Almondbury where in the foreground a spectacular too-high tower commemorating Queen Victoria's Jubilee-crowns the already high mound of an ancient British hill fort. On its own little eminence in the village is the church of St Lucius, 1840, of darkening gritstone. Plain tower with diagonal buttresses and a thin corbel table from which a stumpy octagonal spire rises out of a low-pitched roof. The broad nave has Perp-style straight-headed windows; it is plastered within but the beamed roof shows the trusses. [20]

FEATHERSTONE The mining town continues to dribble its parallel rows of terraced houses over a wide area. The collieries have gone, leaving behind shuttered shops and boarded-up houses. All Saints Parish Church is in the old village. Essentially a stone-roofed Perp church with tower, it looks south from its little hill over fields and woods. Until recently mountainous slag heaps occupied this ground, its restoration is unbelievable to those who knew it. This entry made in 1975 was, 'All Saints Church remains today, looking out over the winking lights and gantries of the colliery and its vast heaps of waste dragged up from the bowels of the earth.' Older parts of the church are in evidence in the porch, tower staircase and in some of the masonry, especially in the Perp East window. The ribbed stone-roofed porch and South doorway are fourteenth century. The South chapel, South aisle arcades and octagonal font are fifteenth century. [17/23]

FELKIRK A traditional West Yorkshire view of fields and trees but with a prospect of industry. There is still open cast mining in Royston behind the churchyard in this suburb of Barnsley. The Norman, EE and Perp church of St Peter is approached through a lychgate (commemorating the Great War) and displays an unusual big Perp East window, all lights arched including those below the transom. The tower arch is Norman and has cushion capitals. The octagonal piers of the arcades are fourteenth century and the chancel chapels fifteenth century. Also fifteenth century is the Perp clerestory with a sundial to the south side. In the aisles is much original large masonry. Some good table tombs in the churchyard which swoops down to a stream before rising up with more memorials beyond. The churchyard contains a pretty Jacobean schoolroom with renewed mullions, a big buttress by the central doorway, and a steeply pitched stone roof. Now the church rooms. [22]

FENAY BRIDGE Where the A629 into Huddersfield crosses the Fenay Beck. It now gives its name to develop-

Opposite: WOODSOME HALL, 1600, FENAY BRIDGE.

POWER STATION, TURBINE HALL, FERRYBRIDGE.

ment between the A629 and the A642 which meet at Waterloo. It is a dormitory area and suburb of Huddersfield, but east of the Penistone Road and over the Fenay Beck is some good unspoilt country: Woodsome Road, for example, rises through wooded hills to Farnley Tyas. Fenay Lane rises to Almondbury and passes some palatial residences of the nineteenth and twentieth centuries, especially in Burkes Lane area and going west towards Almondbury Common. Off Fenay Lane is Fenay Hall of the seventeenth century, with carved timbered gables.

Also up Woodsome Road is Woodsome Hall, an Elizabethan mansion once owned by the Earls of Dartmouth who had considerable land hereabouts. The gabled Elizabethan house of 1600 was built for Arthur Kaye. It has a broad front of gables with mullioned and transomed windows. The porch storey is outflanked by a large gable to the left and the hall has a long transomed window of ten lights with cross-mullioned windows either side. In the former stable yard some Elizabethan timbered buildings are in need of repair. Inside the old hall has a spectacular fireplace over 20ft wide, still in use; the crook beam construction is exposed; it has oak panelling and a gallery with turned newel posts; a Jaco-

bean clock dated 1652 is fixed to the chimney breast. To the right of the hall is a good Elizabethan chamber with recessed ceiling and mouldings of fruit and foliage. Nice staircase with good turned balusters. The inner courtyard has a loggia and displays mullioned windows under triple gables. Stewardship by a golf club has given spare and proper conservation to a delightful Elizabethan mansion. Members and guests must wear a jacket and tie every evening. [20]

FERRYBRIDGE   At this old crossing of the River Aire by the Great North Road are remnants of a Georgian Posting village. Now bypassed, Carr's handsome classical three-arched bridge over the gloomy and dangerous river still stands; to the west is an old Toll House with canted bays of sashes. Little remains of the Georgian village although in coaching days the Angel, the Golden Lion and the Greyhound were busy with staging coaches and there was a customs house for river traffic. Sir Walter Scott is said to have written part of *Heart of Midlothian* while staying at the Ferrybridge Inn. But it is now part of the most unreformed industrial area of West Yorkshire. The village is dramatically in the shadow of

Ferrybridge A and C Power Stations – coal fired generation, C with a grand listed 1930s Turbine House. Six massive cooling towers for Power Station A stand behind, dominating the view. Shadows from their cloud wisps cross the scene. St Andrew's Church is situated just south of Pontefract Road. Some good Norman features: the North doorway has waterleaf capitals, and tower arch is Norman. Some EE windows. South aisle and arcade are Perp as is the tower summit. This church stood with the now demolished Fryston Hall at Water Fryston just east of the A1(M) crossing of the River Aire. As the name implies it was regularly flooded and often unusable. During the Second World War it was temporarily closed and a new site bought. The Revd C. H. Branch loved his old church and fought the bishops of Wakefield and Pontefract to remove it stone by stone to the new site. The plan was eventually agreed by all concerned but the builder omitted to number the stones and not all the building was correctly reassembled. The South porch was deliberately moved to the North side for access reasons. [17]

JOHN CARR'S BRIDGE FOR GREAT NORTH ROAD, FERRYBRIDGE.

FLOCKTON Hillside stone village on the A637 running up to the Pennines. Despite its ersatz timbering, the George and Dragon is a genuinely old house which used to be known as the 'Chained Poker' owing to pokers kept fixed to the fireplace. Henry VIII is said to have visited, no doubt on a peregrination from his home at Pontefract Castle. It was renamed the George and Dragon in Victorian times when the stone mullions appear to have been renewed and pretty iron tracery inserted. The principal timbers and structure, however, are old. In the village are some redbrick terraces and the stone-built St James the Great, a chapel with West belcote in Victorian Dec style. Tremendous views to the huge Emley Moor TV transmission tower to the south. [21]

FULNECK South of Pudsey is a historic Moravian settlement. Its mainly eighteenth-century buildings overlook the green oasis of Tong between Bradford and Leeds. A school for boys opened in 1748 being moved from Wyke and a little later for girls who were moved from Chelsea. Moravians did not believe in promoting the family, but rather the community, so that boarding schools were best. The movement caught on with West Yorkshire weavers and hence the establishment of this settlement on Lambs Hill. The buildings are all in a line overlooking the valley and consist of the Georgian church showing a gable to the north with stone cupola and clock; to the south it has an ashlar façade with tall round-headed windows, decorative keystones, prominent cornice and parapet. Segmental and elliptical gabled dormers in the roof, and good eighteenth-century plasterwork within. The terrace overlooks open country and either side of the chapel are the brick boarding houses for boys and girls, three-storeys high and each with pediments. Access to the terrace is from the car park by the burial ground. The Moravian Museum is open Wednesday afternoons. The famous American architect Benjamin H. Latrobe was the son of the schoolmaster here, born in 1764. He became the leading late Georgian architect in the United States, designing the White House in Washington DC. [9]

GARFORTH Formerly part of the mining empire of the Gascoigne family of nearby Parlington Park and Lotherton Hall. The Victorian main street, unusually for West Yorkshire, is in red brick. St Mary's Church is in an ornate lancet style, 1844; the tower and stair turret derived from EE; small stone spire with broaches; excellent modern church rooms in stone linked to the church. [11]

Overleaf: MORAVIAN SCHOOL, FULNECK.

Moravian Church, Fulneck.

CLAY HOUSE, 1650, GREETLAND.

GOMERSAL Nicely wooded stone village south of Bradford. A charming seventeenth-century manor house stands at the junction of Moor Lane and Knowles Lane, just off the A651. Of three broad stone gables, the mullioned windows are protected by drip moulds and stand asymmetrically within the gables. The hall window is eight lights from two window sections; the parlour window has six continuous lights with transom bars. Continuous drip mould follows both and rises high in the left gable to accommodate a Victorian window. Carved finials are on the gables.

Countryside borders the village which incorporates a number of old farms. Going south through the village and opposite open farmland is Red House, a low red-brick Georgian house ('Red' because brick is unusual here), protruding Victorian stone bays and a good fanlight to the main entrance. Georgian staircase hall within. It is now a museum showing the home circumstances of the Taylor family, cloth manufacturers who owned a mill at Hunsworth. Charlotte Brontë visited Mary Taylor here and the Red House plays a part in her novel *Shirley* as 'Briamains', home to Hiram Yorke. John Wesley was also a visitor who scratched his name on a window in 1768. The village was a strong non-conformist centre in the nineteenth century with chapels and a Moravian settlement established in 1751. The Sisters House, 1798, was built for the school. South in the village is Pollard Hall, another excellent many-gabled Jacobean house. The house has been divided into three but the oldest portion includes its former hall, rising through two storeys and lit by a massive transomed hall window. St Mary's Church overlooks the steep road to Cleckheaton, with a Dec-style tower, 1850. [15]

GRANGE MOOR The ruined tower is called Black Dick's Tower. It was the summerhouse of Sir Richard Beaumont, alias Black Dick of the North, alias Baron Whitley Beaumont. He died in 1631 and was interred at Kirkheaton Church in the family chapel, but is reputed still to walk in the grounds carrying his head under his arm every 5 July. Whitley Hall has disappeared through mining subsidence. Black Dick's Tower is a ruin but was used by the Observer Corps in the Second World War. (See *Kirkheaton*.) [21]

GREETLAND The B6113 main street descends from Norland Moor on a col to the valley of the River Calder. Near the top is St Thomas's Church, 1860, of impossibly awkward architecture. Fat lancets with plate tracery

Overleaf, left: BARRY'S TOWN HALL, HALIFAX; *right*: DEAN CLOUGH AND AKROYD'S CHURCH, HALIFAX.

are squashed together in a nave of blackened stone with white pointing. The South transept has a tripartite shafted window with inelegant high plate tracery. The square West tower has lancets and thick pyramid pinnacles. The West window is ill-digested lancets, shafting and plate tracery. To be frank, it is irremediably ugly but nonetheless appears much loved. Descending the main street gives views down the Calder Valley over mills to hillside pasture beyond. The green mass of Elland Park Wood is to the northeast. At the foot of the main street is Jacobean Clay House, 1650, in a little park; its entrance is by some seventeenth-century cottages with diamond-shaped mullioned windows. Set on a terrace of the hill, Clay House has four symmetrical gables each with distinct fenestration. All are mullioned and transomed but that left of centre has 12 lights on the ground floor – a demonstration of some wealth. No porch, but the entrance has an elliptical hood moulding with beehive-shaped stops. The arched doorway's over lintel has a pattern of semi-circles – compare fireplaces at *East Riddlesden Hall* and *Oakworth Old Hall*. The house is used by Calderdale Council for social functions and can be hired. Next to it is a large medieval aisled barn recently restored and converted to a residence; the little arched ventilation openings of the barn are retained. In the crowded valley bottom by the brook and next to Victoria Mill a cricket field is miraculously preserved. Victoria Mill is a handsome stone building with a glazed-tile string course rhythmically following the arches of the windows. Some textile manufacture remains in the village but not at Victoria Mill, now a multi-floored sales emporium. [13]

GUISELEY   Slightly dour mill town where weaving and garment manufacturing continues. Not the most architectural mills. Not far from the town cross (which replicates a Saxon cross in the church) and old stocks is St Oswald's Church built on a rock eminence. East of the church is the old rectory, a Pennine-type manor house built by the Revd Robert Moore in 1601. In medieval times it had been a hall of the Ward family and an original timber-framed wall lies within the building. The south front has pleasing symmetrical gables, round-headed mullioned windows and a projecting porch gable. It can be seen partially from the churchyard. More accessible is St Oswald's Church. Save for the Perp tower with its Yorkshire corbelled-out parapet it does not seem old because of heavy new work by Archdeacon Howson in 1910. The original Norman nave became the South aisle and was recased. The new nave was designed by Sir Charles Nicholson who made the awful South aisle 'Norman' windows set in little gables and the heavy foliated lancets in the clerestory. The rood

beam statuary is by *Guglielimo Tosi*. The new building exhausted the Archdeacon's wealth; he is commemorated by a window in the North aisle. Some better news: the Norman South arcade has original Romanesque arches, quatrefoil piers and scalloped capitals; the South doorway has chevron decoration, and the chancel arch has shafts. The South transept is thirteenth century with big lancets to the east and plate tracery to the south; it is one of the best examples of thirteenth-century architecture in the county. The oak box pew belonged to the Calverley family of Esholt Hall. The hatchments are of two other Esholt Hall families, the Cromptons and Stanfields. [2]

HALIFAX   A prosperous cloth town since the Middle Ages, it is spectacularly set amid hills. The medieval church with its tower – the largest for many miles – vied with Wakefield to be Cathedral of the Diocese when formed out of Ripon. Roads helter-skelter round the hillsides so that twin headlights in the night signify traffic not aeroplanes. The town occupies a mound between the River Calder and the Hebble Brook and was a famous centre for sheep farmers and cloth weavers down the centuries. Cloth was sold by individuals in the Piece Hall – a magnificent eighteenth-century market for wool. The early transport connection was by branch canal, and today the railway ducks in and out of tunnels to reach the town. Nineteenth-century prosperity led to the building of massive mills – bigger than palaces – and to the prosperity of merchant princes who made long-lasting contributions to the fabric of the town. The determination of the Victorian town to be noticed led to the commissioning of Charles Barry to design a monument of a town hall with a huge pyramidal spire embellished with neo-Renaissance detail. [13]

Halifax – walk 1   Beginning a tour at the *railway station*, on the right of the bridge to town is the parish church; left is the Eureka exhibition for children which embraces the old station building. That is a grand Italianate composition with projecting Doric porch and upper storey of rusticated arches; the chimneys and broad parapet are supported by consoles. The actual railway station is now restricted to an island platform, but this has fine cast iron columns with red-painted wagon wheels in the arch spandrels. Looking south from the platform the tracks interweave as they descend into the valley. In town to the west the valley is filled out with mills and chimneys – and above these cars and lorries enter by bridge from Beacon Hill, with its latter-day signal station of radio masts.

From the station going west is the *Square Chapel* (brick in a stone town), 1772, by Thomas Bradley – a

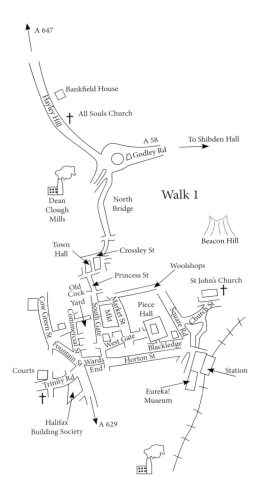

Bankfield House

All Souls Church

A 58   To Shibden Hall

Godley Rd

Walk 1

Dean Clough Mills

North Bridge

Beacon Hill

Town Hall

Crossley St

Woolshops

Princess St

St John's Church

Old Cock Yard

Market St

Mkt

Piece Hall

Square Rd

Church St

Cow Green St

Commercial St

South Gate

West Gate

Blackledge

Fountain St

Wards End

Horton St

Station

Courts

Trinity Rd

Eureka! Museum

Halifax Building Society

A 629

ened hulk of Halifax Minster is best observed from the north side below the Perp West tower; the buttressed aisle displays Y-traceried lancets and a tiny embattled porch. A North chapel with Perp West window and crocketed gable was added, above which the chancel clerestory shows elliptical arched windows, embattling and heavily crocketed pinnacles. In spring against the green of Beacon Hill it is less austere but in the grey days of winter it is gaunt indeed. The chancel chapel (North) is like a mausoleum: crocketed gables and ogee cresting surmounted by fern merlons, built in 1521 by Archbishop Rokeby. The East end of the church maintains its height against the descending hill. Although much Perp regalia, the North aisle is essentially twelfth century containing reused zigzag carved stone. The tower and remainder of the church were built about 1450. Inside is a nice Jacobean communion rail with intricately carved leafy balusters. The old box pews have knobs and an unusual poor box is the seventeenth-century figure of Old Tristram, bearded, life sized and newly repainted. The *Commonwealth Windows* in the South aisle are plain glass but leaded in star and lozenge patterns. The glorious East window by Hedgeland in luminous colours reads as though there were no mullions. The seventeenth-century wooden ceilings are handsome; the Gothic-spired font cover has openwork arches and is fifteenth century. The church has a gloomy but warm ambience.

Next turn west uphill to the Square for *Piece Hall*, 1779, by Bradley, a perfectly preserved Georgian cloth market built as loggias or colonnades on two and three storeys round a yard. On the lower storey are rusticated pillars, Tuscan columns on the first floor; it is a remarkable survival containing dozens of trading rooms and although cloth is no longer sold it is still used for exhibitions and fairs. The council is entertaining a scheme to turn it into shops. The Westgate exit is through a pedimented arch with little white cupola above. But avoiding Westgate with its *lèse majesté* glazed roof, turn right into Market Street where on the corner of Albion Street is *Borough Market*, a fine neo-Baroque ashlar composition with pyramid towerlets, mansards, dormers and tall sharp spires – reminiscent of Leeds Market. At its junction with *Wool Shops* is a view over the rooftops to the wooded lower slopes of *Beacon Hill*. Here is a much-restored remnant from the seventeenth-century days of timber construction – with an oversailing second storey, herringbone gables, wooden mullions with square-leaded windows and a stone roof. There were many timber-framed houses in Halifax in the sixteenth century. Turn west up Russell Street to the high arched entrance into an arcade leading back into the Market Hall whose arcades are glazed on tall cast iron columns and arches like a cathedral. This is a terrific Victorian survival.

stone Doric porch and stone Venetian window contrast with red brick. The upper lights of the round-arched windows have intersecting tracery – an elegant façade. Next to it is the ruin of Square Congregational Church of which the spectacular EE spire remains. The angled buttresses and spire itself carry pinnacles in ascending series, each with dormers copying the spire. Like the chapel next door it is a finely balanced architectural composition. A former transept window shows a tremendous whorl of lunettes and quatrefoil in the most intricate Dec style. Built in 1855 by the Crossleys it replaced the eighteenth-century brick chapel which became the Sunday school, and is now an arts centre. It was rescued in 1989 from a ruin; its intricate eighteenth-century plaster mouldings have been well restored.

Opposite and below is the ancient parish church; nestling in its shadow is a seventeenth-century inn, the Ring O'Bells, with a gable of mullioned windows. The black-

PIECE HALL, HALIFAX.

There are clusters of columns; horned Ionic capitals, leafy with acanthus; in the spandrels are stars of fleur-de-lis; the clerestory of arched windows is crowned with a dome at the junction of the transepts. Below it a gilded classical column with branches of ornate lanterns carries an iron clock.

Turning left on Southgate is the Theatre Royal, 1904 – classical pastiche with a pediment on attached Ionic columns. Underemployed. The balconies are garlanded with fruit and dragons. Then turning right is Wardsend, and a primitive eighteenth-century three-storey house with a Doric entrance; next are the twin projecting gables of a grander house with Venetian windows in the gables; it is of brick with stone sashes, quoins and a stone string course. At the top of Wardsend a pair of three-storey stone Regency houses contrast with the

Second floor loggia, Piece Hall, Halifax.

BOROUGH MARKET, HALIFAX.

overbearing HQ of the Halifax Building Society which stands on massive stone-cased pillars, each as big as a house; the entrance vestibule is a large space below the office block which is cantilevered towards the roofs of its neighbours. Its effect is rather unpleasant. To the right is a stone-built former cinema with 1930s vertical panelling.

Opposite on Fountain Street is the Victoria Theatre, neo-Baroque, with a wide circular entrance and attached columns – a small Baroque cupola above. On Blackwall Road just behind the Halifax Building Society is a now redundant but rather stately classical eighteenth-century church, Holy Trinity, a little reminiscent of Horbury. Built in 1795 it was designed by G. Bradley and has a giant Palladian south elevation, a large Venetian window standing on a pediment on Ionic columns. The Venetian window also has Ionic columns and below this a rusticated basement. Either side are balustraded windows and doors with blocked architraves. The tower is octagonal with a Doric storey and pediment then a low dome with ball and cross. Although now offices, it is one of the more splendid classical Yorkshire churches. The Magistrates' Court opposite is 1898, a neo-Baroque pastiche of Italianate features in a nice domestic rendition; the door to the Warrant Office is prettily carved with swags on the overdoor; an Italianate belvedere tower has arches and an octagonal lantern over. Now west up Commercial Street the Arcade Royale is again neo-Baroque, white faience tiling. The Post Office is a contrast of distinctive EE Gothic, arched and shafted windows, corner shafts rising into finials above the roof. The TSB then appears on the left, independent, very florid with twin polished granite columns upholding its big garlanded pediment. It is like a country house stranded in the middle of town.

In **Old Cock Yard** opposite, a seventeenth-century inn with stone roof survives – mullioned on four storeys, a later Doric porch (straight cornice) and Regency wing with arched sash windows. It is quite big. Silver Street further west is furnished with more Victorian Gothic where arched and shafted windows rise to steep roofs with mansards. Crown Street is principally Victorian of the late nineteenth century, tall elevated buildings, put up in the same wave of prosperity as the Town Hall again in Gothic and with classical decoration. At the corner of Princess Street and Old Market is a former Burtons decorated with stone-coloured tiles – Art Deco but an unusual theme of the East with elephant heads and zigzag moulding. The White Swan Hotel has four storeys of pedimented windows with massive cornices, garlanded cartouches and beautifully carved swans in the spandrel of the porch, 1860. On the right, frenetically carved oriel windows project below a garlanded

pediment. Next door the big first-floor windows have elliptical pediments.

The big pyramid tower of the **Town Hall**, by Barry 1862, has three storeys of reducing Renaissance proportions below the pedimented clock – thence rising by three further storeys of spire to a crow's nest decorated with wrought iron; then the fourth spire stage ends in a gilded crown and woolpack weathervane – the source of Halifax's glory. The Town Hall building to the right of the tower has two storeys of loggias or arcaded recesses, the roof a cast iron ridge piece. The ceremonial entrance is a porte-cochère to the south which proclaims 'Love Mercy', 'Act Wisely' and 'Justice'. The best elevation faces south – into the sun – tall storeys of arched windows sandwiched between Doric columns; with three storeys of balustrading and a steep roof crowned with cast iron cresting.

In Rawson Street is a town house like a continental palace – **Somerset House**, built c.1766 by John Carr for the wool merchant John Royd. Somerset House has been restored. The first-floor grand salon with its spectacular carved plasterwork by Guiseppe Cortese depicts allegorical scenes of Neptune, Britannia, etc., alongside vignettes from Aesop's Fables. The building is very grand with gabled wings projecting into Rawson Street and a central gable crowned with classical urns; on the ground floor is a Doric porch and loggia of Doric columns and arches. Unfortunately the South wing has a bookshop built into it. In Clare Road, a few minutes from the town centre, is Hope Hall, now the Albany Club – a Georgian mansion with pediment spreading over five bays and stone sashed windows. The porch projects on four Tuscan columns with a Venetian window above.

North Bridge spans the deep valley of the Hebble Brook – good cast iron parapet – and Dean Clough Mills below, the most massive assembly of wool mills in West Yorkshire. All in stone and up to ten storeys high. The restored mills are handsome indeed. Now occupied by leisure and commerce, these mills recently produced acre on acre of Crossley carpet. The approach to the Town Hall was not named Crossley Street for nothing. A short distance up the Queensbury Road is **Akroydon**, a suburb where the Akroyd wool dynasty held sway. Here, opposite the church of All Souls, was Haley Hill Mills (now demolished), but much remains of Colonel Akroyd's work and high sense of social responsibility. He paid for the church designed by Sir George Gilbert Scott who, without modesty, called it his best church. It is thirteenth century in style with French influence and richly decorated with shafting and carved capitals. The spire was calculated to be slightly higher than the Square Congregational Church of the Crossleys. It overlooks

MARBLE PULPIT IN ALL SOULS, HALIFAX.

CAST IRON GATE TO PIECE HALL, HALIFAX.

the valley, proudly tall, balanced, but now too grand for its little congregation; on the road in front is a statue of Colonel Akroyd, a little verdigrized. Scott chose the Permian limestone from Nottinghamshire badly, it conflicted chemically with the sandstone and has eroded. Although 'closed' it still opens for high days through the Churches Conservation Trust. Its polished granite, elegant traceried windows and the tall steeple demonstrate the priorities in life in a deliberate way to the rows of workers' terraced homes opposite. The Vicarage, also by Scott, remains next door. Up the hill is Colonel Akroyd's former home, now a museum, *Bankfield House*. Grandly Italianate with triple arched windows and wide soffits on brackets, the main entrance is under a Venetian window and rises up a flight of stairs to the main hall. The hall has classical depictions of the gods and the elliptical ceiling has lozenge-shaped medallions. A fine Italianate fireplace has caryatid figures and encaustic

tiles. The stair hall has spiral balusters and brass lions on the newel posts. The magnificent library, with cast iron columns 20ft high and a gallery, is actually the public library. Colonel Akroyd built houses for workers in terraces of gabled Gothic or Tudor windowed luxury – the best of them are assembled round a large grassed square where a Gothic Dec monument has ascending gabled stages surmounted by a cross. It is inscribed 'A Monument of Christian Reverence ... and of Loyalty to Our Sovereign Lady Queen Victoria by Edward Akroyd, the Founder of Akroydon'.

Halifax – walk 2 From Swine Market in the centre of Halifax go left up Gibbet Street which crosses Burdock Way by a bridge, and on the right at the junction of Bedford Street is the site of the old gibbet where sheep stealers were beheaded – such was the value of wool to the local community. Then turning south down Clarence Street is St Mary's Catholic Church, Arts and Crafts flavoured EE with presbytery en suite. At the junction of Bond Street is Hopwood Hall – a three-storey Georgian mansion with an elliptical pediment over the door and bold rustication to the ground floor. Turn up Hopwood Lane, right, and after some late Georgian terraces with Tuscan porches are the Sir Francis Crossley almshouses, tall Gothic terraces built in 1855, best seen from Margaret Street with their myriad towers, chimneys and gables; big cross-transomed windows, labelled 'FC'. Next door is Sir Francis Crossley's mansion, *Belle Vue*, in its own grounds and further west the Crossley Housing Scheme for Workers in elegant, if slightly heavy, Gothic terraces. The mansion itself is very continental and looks over Hopwood Lane through iron railings. It used to be the public library and accessible, but is now closed off. A French tone is set by the mansard roof behind a pediment ornately carved with Crossley Arms. Round-arched windows, doorway and oval dormers supported by consoles complete the continental effect. On the east elevation are wrought iron balconies and a very fine architectural orangery with a satisfying apse.

SQUARE CONGREGATIONAL CHURCH, HALIFAX.

Opposite is the *People's Park* where on the terrace is an arched Renaissance-style pavilion. In the architrave is written 'Blessed be the Lord who daily loadeth us with benefits'. At the back of the shelter is a statue of Frank Crossley Esquire MP in a niche. Either side are grotesque heads mouthing water into shells. Just down the grassy slope to the south is a coy bandstand – green-

71

SHIBDEN HALL, HALIFAX.

painted cast iron, elegant pillars and ogee-domed roof. The large sundial was given by Alderman Matthew Smith in 1873 to remind us 'First the hour then the day steals away'. A round lake displays shells and dolphins while cast iron bridges on inlets pretend to bridge more extensive water. It is a clever park giving a big impression of space in about three acres.

South from the People's Park on Arden Road are Joseph Crossley's almshouses, a large quadrangle of Gothic terraces exhibiting Romantic features, for example mansarded turrets, a castellated tower with crenellated oriel and octagonal staircase turret. The windows are transomed and some have inventive EE-type tracery.

The Arms of Crossley and a carved stone gives the date 'AD 1863'. From the south corner of Joseph Crossley's almshouses go west up Haugh Shaw Road, a district of pleasant stone terraces and trees, to Haugh Shaw Hall on a bank. The wing to the right has stone sashes and quoins, the ridged and stone slated portion to the left has modern windows, but in the centre is a two-storey seventeenth-century porch with arched doorway and three-light transomed window above.

Then turn south along Moorfield Street past neat stone terraces with cobbled streets to Savile Park, a high open green space with playing fields and fronting the Crossley Park School, another ambitious Crossley

Medieval painted glass, Shibden Hall, Halifax.

enterprise which was originally an orphanage. Shaped gables, big transomed windows, mansarded roofs crested in wrought iron and a Baroque clock tower. From here industry in the valley of the Hebble is elided with views rising beyond to the green of Signal Hill or away east along the Calder Valley and up to the moors of Emley Mast. This expansiveness heralds no barrier to ambition at Crossley Heath School. Up Free School Lane can be seen the proud corona of the **Wainhouse Tower/Chimney** for the Wainhouse Dye Works. At Skircoat Moor take the vertiginous Delph Hill Road, cobbled (and possibly dangerous by car) to the base of the tower. There are 404 steps to the top which spiral round the flue; it is 253ft high, octagonal and of stone – the corona has two viewing platforms, the first corbelled and balustraded out, then an octagonal colonnade with balcony giving magnificent views over the Calder Valley. It is usually open on bank holidays. The Dye Works are demolished.

Down Delph Hill on Woodhouse Lane is Elizabethan Wood Hall, 1589 – two three-storey symmetrical gables with the porch and its five-light transomed window under a projecting gable. Sadly the ground- and first-floor windows have been abased and the interior ruined. From the junction with Wakefield Road the first turning right up Washer Lane leads to the more comely Old Hall, 1690. Big transomed hall window, eccentric left-hand gable with stepped lights, high gabled porch also with stepped lights. Nice carved mould stops, Tudor doorway – 1930s door. Return via Sowerby Bridge or Elland to Halifax centre. About three hours.

Halifax environs – by car or bike   Take the A58 across Beacon Hill to Shibden Dale where the tumbling brook is dammed into a lake for Shibden Hall's park. Boats are available. **Shibden Hall** is concealed behind trees from this point and stands up the hill to the west. It is the best timbered building hereabouts, quite substantial with gables either side of a double-storey hall (called a housebody). The gables each have diagonal timber strutting – herringbone style – with more strutting around oriel windows. Very handsome effect. Between the gables the ten-light transomed hall window has armorial glass to the earlier possessors: Oates, Saviles and Waterhouses. The hall fireplace and gallery, however, were inserted by Anne Lister in 1830. The staircase newels have heavy carved finials like Kempe's Temple Newsam staircase. Anne Lister 'improved' the hall with flat vertical timber strips to simulate timber construction and built the tower in 1839 with its French mansard. She created the southwest elevated garden whose parapets have over-large funerary urns. Anne Lister has become a social and literary figure of national importance, blazing an early trail with female lovers and recording her exploits in a diary. The last Lister bequeathed the house to Halifax and died in 1933. The house is well kept by Calderdale Council and furnished with excellent oak, laid out as though still a home. There is an exhibition – which includes the Lister's coaches – in a seventeenth-century aisled barn with kingpost roof. Trees and rhododendron stand above the hall.

From Stump Cross at the foot of Shibden Dale is an attractive unclassified road to the north. Weavers' cottages look west across the dale to tree-clad hillsides. If ready for *very* steep hills, take the turning down Blake Hill for **Shibden Mill**, of the eighteenth century, and now an inn. As you descend Blake Hill look for Scout Hall on the far side of the valley, and also Lee House to its left – a former pub – four square with pediment, ashlar, five bays, commanding tremendous views. It is attached to an old stone-roofed and mullioned farmstead of the seventeenth century. Rising towards Lee House where the climb is steepest, the lane reverts to cobbles. From Lee House a track skirts the west flank of the valley through undergrowth and foxgloves to the impressive ruin of **Scout Hall**. The windows of this three-storey seventeenth-century mansion (cross-mullioned) have remained unglazed for decades and weeds sprout from the chimneys. Nine bays of windows and in the centre a tall corniced door with a carving of sheep. Bays of corniced ovals mark the second and sixth bays. Stone roof. The house is arresting and dominating: strangely it has one gabled roof end and one hipped roof.

The head of Shibden Dale to the northwest looks unspoiled with wild tree-clad steep valley sides, but a careless planner has allowed new housing on the summit. Travelling to the very top of Lee Lane you come to a small artificial ski slope. Then turning south towards Halifax along the side of the ridge, where the blustery wind makes ceaseless ripples in the rye grass, are true 'Last of the Summer Wine' views down to Halifax: terraced houses, mills and their chimneys with dappled green hills and moors beyond. On the horizon are the twin masts of Pole Moor radio broadcasting station. The wind seems always to be singing in the wires up here and on a sunny day the view will make your heart sing. At the diagonal crossroads go straight ahead and turn right at Lower Range by Amblers Terrace, down the steep hill towards Colonel Akroyd's Church. The spire and a very fine chimney with elegant corona seem to burst upwards out of the trees. The church on the right is the RC Church of the Sacred Heart, 1895, with nominal Dec fenestration. The chimney with the fine corona, 1857, is best viewed from a gennel off Woodside

Opposite: Scout hall, Halifax.

Road. It belongs to Lea Bank Mill in Dean Clough below. Here the A629 on concrete stilts and cradles flies over the roofs of mills and factories in Dean Clough towards the blackened stone heights of Queensbury. Higher up this valley on Ovenden Road is a handsome abandoned mill with sightless windows and pedimented gable on its east façade, giving it a quizzical look. To restore it would be good. To go on from here see *Holmfield*, *Illingworth* and *Bradshaw*.

HALTON (LEEDS)   St Wilfrid's Halton is a remarkable and exciting 1930s concrete church by Randall Wells. The stone-faced gables of the church brood castle-like over a landscape of housing from their well-elevated terrace. Within, the effect of the concrete arched nave is amplified by aisles through transverse arches formed within angular arcades. There are short transept chapels and a full-length gable window in the South transept where a big transom at one-third height tenses the atmosphere. It is a concrete sculpture of poise. The interior is adorned only by the 1930s woodwork of the architect's original scheme, for example wooden screens of tiny shuttles and bobbins to reflect the cloth trade. Statuary is by the workshop of Eric Gill; there is an effigy of St Wilfrid, the founder of Ripon Minster. Very properly the beneficiary of an EH grant to repair its leaking concrete to preserve this sculpture of the 1930s. [10]

HANGING HEATON   From here are tremendous views over industrial Dewsbury and Batley. The newly cleaned church of St Paul with its tall clear lancet windows and West tower is a model of elegance. [15]

HAREWOOD   A Georgian palace set above the edge of Wharfedale with long and attractive views of woods, hills and water below. The entrance from the A61 is through an arched Grecian gatehouse. The drive meanders through undulating parkland to the house set at the very lip of a hill looking south. It was built by Carr of York in 1759 for Edwin Lascelles out of trade in the East and West Indies where the family had sugar plantations. It is an exquisite Georgian mansion with original Robert Adam colour schemes and matching furniture by Chippendale.

On approach the house appears a little squashed at

South front, Orpheus and Leopard, Harewood House.
Overleaf, left: State bedroom, Adam and Chippendale, Harewood House.
right: Long gallery, Adam ceiling, Harewood House.

78

79

LONG GALLERY, RESTORED FIREPLACE, HAREWOOD HOUSE.

one and a half storeys under a pediment on six attached Corinthian columns. The reasons lie partly in the failure to show the rusticated basement storey on which it stands – the ground was never scraped away as originally intended; also the convenience of arriving by carriage just outside the piano nobile mattered; and also because of the addition of Charles Barry's heavy roof. Barry's brief was to engineer more accommodation and Italianize the South façade looking over Lancelot Brown's park completed over nine years.

Visitors come to the North door under a pediment with exquisitely carved Lascelles Arms, which includes vigorous trailing foliage. Georgian lanterns on wrought iron stands are the only external furniture. The entrance is into a grand *Grecian Hall of Heroes*, walls festooned with plaques and roundels showing symbols of martial arts and architectural devices. A frieze of white Greek

key and rams' heads is supported on fluted Doric pilasters. The Wedding of Neptune with the Chariot of Phaeton is shown on medallions. Chippendale's Grecian chairs exaggerate the sense of space but a large statue of *Adam* by Jacob Epstein is out of scale. Is it a bad joke? The more grotesque parts were hidden for a royal visit. Turning left is the Old Library – a grand coved ceiling above rich cornice, and Bath guiloche on green and tiny acanthus corbels to the coving. The colours are original. Over the white marble fireplace is a grisaille by Biagio Rebecca, that is, imitation antique bas-relief in shades of grey, and over it a semi-circular painting of antique scenes by Angelica Kauffman. Chippendale chairs here were made for the room; in the corner is a bust of the former Princess Royal, the late Earl's mother. Then in the East Bedroom Adam is less flamboyant but the curl of the frieze is matched by Chippendale's state bed

80

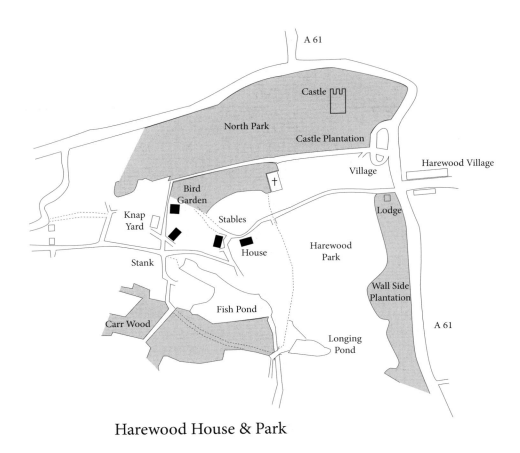

Harewood House & Park

picked out in gold. Lord Harewood's Sitting Room follows with dark blue walls, white fireplace and a restrained frieze of anthemion and palmette. Next the State Bedroom was converted from the Princess Royal's Sitting Room with its magnificent Chippendale bed. Reassembled from store, its gilded dome on fluted columns is furnished with green silk curtains matching green silk walls in which a white Ionic screen is set.

The Spanish Library, leather wall covering, was made by Barry from the former State Dressing Room. His are the wooden bookcases, but the coved ceiling with delicate bands of antique colour is Adam. Then the Saloon, another library with brass-inlaid mahogany bookcases; the Adam ceiling is coved over a simple cornice; apses flank the North door – also lined by bookcases. This was the family's main living room until they removed to the second floor. Next is the Yellow Drawing Room – for which straw-yellow silk was bought by Edwin Lascelles for Adam; with two large mirrors carved by Chippendale. In the Cinnamon Drawing Room Chippendale console tables with inlaid tops have corbels of gilded rams' heads standing on serpentine rams' legs. Nineteenth-century coving contrasts sharply with Adam's style. *The Long Gallery* runs along the entire West elevation; it has Venetian windows at either end. Chippendale carved the 'taffeta' pelmets and mirrors sub-divided by strings of urns and acanthus leaf; also the elegant torchères and giltwood chairs. The 16 ceiling paintings are by Biagio Rebecca. Lord Harewood reversed Barry's brutal alteration of the Venetian windows and restored the original chimney piece with female caryatids. Turning back towards the entrance hall is the Dining Room, furnished by Chippendale's sideboards and dining chairs; here Barry raised the ceiling with a modelled acanthus leaf cove. The last room, the Music Room, shows circular reliefs by Angelica Kauffman. The Adam ceiling design is reflected in the carpet design, and the room has Chippendale giltwood chairs.

The **South Terrace** was made in 1840 by Barry; here dwarf-box parterres are filled with colourful masses of flowers in sinuating shapes as though a carpet. The central statue of *Orpheus with a Leopard* is modern, by Astrid Zydower. The distinctly Italianate South elevation and terrace overlook a private valley of landscaped woods and lakes. Downhill to the southwest the stables and yard are almost out of sight; the Doric loggias are used for tea and exhibitions; exhibitions are also in the Terrace Gallery.

The Park and Castle   From the A61 and in Wharfedale the remains of the **Norman Castle** are visible, rebuilt by Sir William de Aldeburgh in the fourteenth century as an oblong castle with 100ft-high angle towers. Turner's watercolour in the house shows the state of the ruin even in the eighteenth century. It is not always accessible but the picture shows medieval remains of a crocketed ogee gable and cusped arched recess from the Great Hall. After William de Aldeburgh, the castle passed to Redmaynes until Elizabethan times when it was sold to the Gascoignes of Gawthorpe Hall, almost the present site of Harewood House. Sir William Gascoigne was an assertive Chief Justice to Henry IV – he refused to try Archbishop Scrope for high treason. The estate later devolved to the Earls of Strafford, and Alexander Pope criticized the second Earl's meanness:

For very want he could not build a wall . . .
Banished the doctor and expelled the friend;
What but want – which you perhaps think mad,
Yet [all will] thus feel – the want of what he had!

If Gawthorpe Hall fell down that may have been what Henry Lascelles bought in 1738. The park is in a tributary valley of the Wharfe in which Capability Brown composed lakes and wood-clothed hills like a little kingdom. The views are at their best in spring when the rhododendrons are out – the Lascelles' collection of rhododendron is renowned. Behind the stables is a bird garden with aviaries where endangered species from overseas are bred. A flock of flamingos from Chile lives on the lake.

The Village and Church   The village used to be in the area of **All Saints Church** halfway down the drive on the right going from the present village. It had six pubs. Edwin Lascelles rebuilt it as a model village outside the park gates. The architect was the same John Carr, but maybe to maintain contrasts the new village was built in terraces of working people's houses, two and a half storeys like a model industrial village. The houses line the road approaching the estate gates and bring an unwelcome urban sense to the scene. An attempt was made to establish a mill here but that was not a success. A consequence of leaving the church behind is that it has become redundant although now in the hands of the Churches Conservation Trust. Built contemporaneously with the castle it is Perp with an embattled West tower; its glory is the collection of medieval tombs and monuments. Sir Henry and Lady Redmayne, 1426, are north of the chancel, and other incumbents are Sir William and Lady Ryther, 1425; the daughters of Sir William de Aldeburgh; and Sir William Gascoigne, former Chief Justice of the King's Bench. The church is usually open and entrance free. [4]

HARTSHEAD   In rural isolation overlooking the Calder Valley is St Peter's Church and a hamlet of farm, vicarage and cottages. The squat tower is Norman with much-worn random sandstone between gritstone quoins. The body of the church is neo-Norman of 1883, with stylized triple Norman windows to the South aisle, and a stone roof with an odd Norman/Venetian dormer. The East window is a triple Norman affair with crafted zig-zag and columnettes – rather vulgar. But the chancel arch is actually Norman as is the South doorway which has double columns, scalloped capitals and original zig-zag in the arch. The parish was an early appointment for the Reverend Patrick Brontë. [14]

HAWORTH   Famous home of the Brontë family. The picturesque village tumbling down the hill beside the cobbled High Street would be an attraction in itself. Reminiscent of a Cornish or Yorkshire fishing village – you look down onto higgledy-piggledly roof tops of houses below. But this is high moorland and can be wintry for nine months of the year when snow and mist cling to these desolate hills; the summer contrast of sunshine and heather is truly illuminating. Most of the cottages had their origins as weavers' houses as shown by the breadth of the mullioned windows. Piecework was still undertaken in homes in the early twentieth century. Gaunt mills stand on the valley floor and there is an intact nineteenth-century railway with gas-lit stations which runs to Keighley.

EDWARD, YORKIST COMMANDER, AND ELIZABETH, 1510, HAREWOOD.

St Michael's Church and churchyard obliquely abuts the High Street. The church of the Brontës' time was demolished and rebuilt in 1880; their church was Georgian with some Gothic revival: arched windows and Perp transoms. These survive in the present tower, which is eighteenth century. The 1880 church is by Healey in more schooled Victorian Perp and is warmly ambient with a richly painted West window by Capronnier. It has octagonal piers to the aisles, a Dec-style clerestory and a steep Dec-style roof supported on hammer beams. The pulpit and font are finely carved marble. The reredos is a vigorously carved depiction of the Last Supper. The South chancel chapel is the Brontë Memorial Chapel and a plate marks the family vault

below the chapel arch. Ends of pews from the old church are preserved in the Brontë Museum. The list of incumbents interestingly designates some as 'Puritans' and some 'Expelled'. The bleak open churchyard of the nineteenth century is now wooded; cottages gather close to the north side of the church as though sheltering from the cold, and stone-paved gennels lead to the main street.

The Brontë Museum is in the former parsonage, now divided from the churchyard by a wall. Years ago the parsonage was across fields at Sowdens Farm where the zealous Reverend William Grimshaw lived in the eighteenth century – he partially rebuilt the church, and was known as 'The Prophet of the Moors'. The Brontës' father, Patrick, obtained the living in 1820 only because

STONE ROOFS, HAWORTH.

his predecessor was hounded out after a year's incumbency. The house has five bays, pedimented doorway and sash windows, built in 1779. Well cared for by the Brontë Society, it has original or authentic furnishings and demonstrates chaste living – but to a good middle-class standard especially in comparison with, for example, Patrick Brontë's childhood home.

Many buildings are of the seventeenth to nineteenth centuries in the village, including inns, Baptist and Methodist chapels, the old Manor House and, at the foot of Main Street, the seventeenth-century Old Hall with gabled porch and eight-light hall window. On a fine day there is a good view of the village from Browside, east of the valley, off the A6033. Over the last 20 years there has been a degree of development which is not sustainable and threatens to ruin the village charac-

ter. The establishment of a modern windmill in the face of the village on Brow Moor is regrettable. At the foot of the village near the station is Bridgehouse Mill, four storeys, continuing in a niche trade making traditional frogging, aiguillettes, sashes, epaulettes, olivettes and gorgettes for the Duke of Plazatoro and others.

Brontë excursions can be made to *Hartshead*, a Norman church where Patrick Brontë was curate. Here he met and married Maria Bramwell in 1812. Three years later he became vicar at *Thornton* where Charlotte, Bramwell, Emily and Anne were born. The family moved to Haworth in 1820 but Maria Brontë died in 1821. After that Patrick struggled: Emily and Anne boarded at

Opposite: HAWORTH VILLAGE.

HAWORTH PARSONAGE.

the Clergy Daughters' School in Lancashire. Unsanitary conditions, cold and hunger caused their withdrawal. On their return the three sisters and their red-headed brother Bramwell were able to explore the high moors above Haworth: Emily wrote *Wuthering Heights* in 1847 for which the tumbled-down farm at Top Withens was the model.

Anne wrote *The Tenant of Wildfell Hall* in 1848, a didactic novel showing empathy for women and the heroine: 'My heart sank within me to behold that stately mansion in the midst of its expansive grounds. The park as beautiful now, in its wintry garb, as it could be in its summer glory: the majestic sweep, the undulating swell and fall, displayed to full advantage in that robe of dazzling purity, stainless and printless – save one long, winding track left by the trooping deer – the stately timber-trees with their heavy-laden branches gleaming white against the dull, grey sky; the deep, encircling woods; the broad expanse of water sleeping in frozen quiet . . .', and memorable description on approaching Staningley: 'The very fact of sitting exalted aloft, [on the coach] surveying the snowy landscape and sweet sunny

sky, inhaling the pure, bracing air, and crunching away over the crisp frozen snow, was exhilarating enough in itself; but add to this the idea of to what goal I was hastening, and whom I expected to meet . . .'

Charlotte's *Jane Eyre* depicts North Lees Hall and Hathersage in Derbyshire but *Shirley* was based on a Luddite attack at Rawfold's Mill, Liversedge, in 1812. The plotters met at the nearby 'Shears Inn'. Also, in the novel was the 'Red House at Gomersal', home of her friend Mary Taylor, which became the millowner's home. The heroine, Shirley Keeldar, lived at 'Fieldhead' based on *Oakwell Hall, Birstall*. Another of Charlotte's friends, Ellen Nussey, was the daughter of a millowner in Birstall – her grave may be found at St Peter's, Birstall.

The walk from Haworth to 'Wuthering Heights'
From the Parsonage take the path west, stone-paved to West Lane, then via Cemetery Road to a road junction. Straight ahead is a track over Haworth Moor. In one and a half miles it drops to Sladen Beck, an attraction for the Brontë children. Upstream north is the waterfall – small cascades of water flow over stones in a steep

descent. Close to the path is the Brontë Chair standing in the stream and shaped like a mounting block – here too at the confluence of paths is the small stone Brontë Bridge. Climbing west out of the little valley follow South Dean Brook path until it joins the Pennine Way. Top Withens is a little to the southwest along the Pennine Way, and a most desolate place. From here return along the Pennine Way passing Middle Withens and Lower Withens, now ruined farmsteads – deserted sheep crofts. Keep northeast for Stanbury via Back Lane and Ponden Hall (believed Thrushcross Grange). The distance is seven miles of hill walking, say half a day. (See also *Pennine Way* for *Ponden*.) [7]

HEATH A village remarkable for its grand historic houses just east of Wakefield, uphill and indeed on a heath – bright in spring with yellow gorse and fields of oilseed. The village is set around a large green and consists almost entirely of distinguished Georgian houses. The *Old Hall* was a spectacular Smythson Elizabethan mansion with canted bays, embattled and overlooking the River Calder in the valley below. Professor Pevsner noted its ruined condition in the 1960s which is now complete, although two modern houses have grown from it. Its tall Georgian gates with big acorn finials remain. A huge chimneypiece was, however, removed and installed in the rear hall of Hazlewood Castle. Immediately east of the green is Heath House, hipped roof with pediment on Ionic pilasters – double pilasters at each end of the façade. The ground floor has a notionally rusticated base; swept volute mouldings to the first-floor window pediments; James Paine, 1744.

Then clockwise round the heath (or green) is *Heath Hall* by John Carr, 1754. Splendid enough to be an independent stately home in a park, it has 11 bays with canted bay windows at either end. In the centre is a pediment on giant Ionic columns. The roof is lined with big balusters. Its grandeur is enhanced by flanking pavilions with pediments and cupolas. Continuing southeast is the *Dower House*, again by John Carr, 1740, plainer but with a simple pediment over the South façade facing the heath. Carved stone sashes and carved consols support corniced windows. From here is a good view of the village. Next, south, is a group of cottages which include the *King's Arms* pub – parts dating from the seventeenth century – it displays a huge Royal Arms. It is still lit by gas and is a summer venue for citizens of Wakefield. There are a number of old cottages, including one with particularly small mullioned windows, before Beach Lawn, an early nineteenth-century classical house with canted bays, hipped roof of stone and pedimented entrance. From here the beauties of Wakefield are just visible through trees. There is no church. [22]

HAWORTH STATION.

HEBDEN BRIDGE In the high wooded valleys of the Upper Calder where Colden Water and Hebden Water flow into the River Calder once were grimy mills. Now it has the quality of an alpine retreat with stone weavers' cottages and farmsteads lodged on the hillsides below gritstone crags towering out of the tree-clad slopes. Tucked into the hillside at the foot of Colden Water is the Church of St James; big chamfered lancets to the tower, self-conscious but charming. The little town is overlooked by three-storeyed terraces of eighteenth- and nineteenth-century weavers' houses. Narrow stone streets of cottages built for those performing hard and distasteful labour are now cleaned, pedestrianized and made fit for tourists. The 'bridge', incidentally, is over Hebden Water before it emerges into the River Calder and is part of a centuries-old Cross-Pennine track. Hope Baptist Church is a tall classical affair with Doric pilasters, arched windows and pedimented doorway. Even the picture house is classical and built in stone. The

White Lion Hotel, mullioned, 1657, has a big decorative cornice. Hebden Bridge Mill with a conspicuous round chimney at the roadside is used for exhibitions. Other mills have been converted to retail use, a good transformation from the smoky days of industry.

Taking the 'A' road to Keighley and Haworth north up the valley observe terraces swell round the hillside in toy-town parades, rising and falling with the contours. The parapet of Heptonstall Church tower appears over the treetops to the west. A turning down Mitchell Road takes you along Hebden Water to Hardcastle Crags where the silvern valley is crammed with birch, oak and sycamore. Leaving the car at the National Trust car park, a path follows the stream into the high hills. Glades of pasture lie in the valley bottom and the crags – protruding cliffs of gritstone – open up through the trees. A track leads to Gibson Mill, an exemplar of conservation using alternative technology, which is open to the public (NT). [12]

HECKMONDWIKE   Mill town conurbation with Batley and Dewsbury. The Parish Church of St James, 1830, is distinctive with large lancets separated by crowding gable-capped buttresses. The tower has big lancets at the bell stage and a stone octagonal spire with broaches rises directly from a corbel table. The Congregational Chapel, 1890, in contrast is a traitor to simplicity. What would John Wesley have said of this Baroque palace? An ornate portico of mixed Ionic and Corinthian capitals is flanked by towers, one with arched belvedere, the other with a leaded dome and each crowned with urns – florid and lacking tastefulness. Next door is the Independent School of 1856, plain and proper, five bays of round-arched windows, now used as church rooms. The town centre is defined by a marketplace with eclectic unambitious buildings. Cottages of the seventeenth century mingle with a glaze-tiled pub, Italianate bank, 1950s brick, and a Georgian hotel with hipped roof. By the edge of the market square is a fountain, 1863, on the marriage of the Prince of Wales to Princess Alexandra of Denmark. It is, bizarrely, a drinking fountain with consoles supporting ancient carved heads and little gables, a clock then a lantern! [15]

HEMSWORTH   Former agricultural village in the east of the county once overwhelmed by mining but now miraculously cleared. A few old cottages remain in the centre where the church of St Helen stands prominently

HEATH HALL.

on a little knoll at the crossroads. Originally Dec of which remains a pretty five-light window demonstrating flowing tracery with lunettes clustered either side of a quatrefoil; in the South chancel chapel is a window with reticulated tracery and on the north side an ogee-headed door. These items appear to have been saved in J. L. Pearson's rebuilding of 1867 which otherwise relies on unsatisfactory emblem-like plate tracery windows. The West tower has a plain parapet. The North aisle stands parallel to the nave and is also stone roofed. The elevated churchyard overlooks old pantiled cottages; it misses its great yew which perished in a gale in January 1884. The stump remains 120 years later and must be 500 years old. [23]

HEPTONSTALL High on the shoulder of the hill between the valleys of Hebden Water and Colden Water. Quaint narrow streets of angular weavers' cottages tumble down the hill in terraces linked by little cobbled ways. It is one of the spectacular villages of West Yorkshire for dark-stone charm and elevated views over tree-clad valleys where isolated mills stand with their chimneys. The cottages and steep cobbled paths remind one of Robin Hood's Bay. Weavers' Square is the centre where fairs are held with the 'Pace Egg Play' on Good Friday which tells of the heroic deeds of St George. The Parish Church of St Thomas à Becket and St Thomas the Apostle finds a flat shelf: a solid amalgam of early Victorian Dec and Perp; tall Perp clerestory; strong, embat-

HEPTONSTALL.

tled tower with ogee-flared bell openings; pinnacles and pierced merlons – it is the fruit of Victorian wealth. Inside big quatrefoil arcades and the truly lofty roof are divided by a large 1960s-style screen with a loft and modern organ. The West part is for socializing and the East for worship. Around the churchyard are stone-roofed weavers' cottages. Within the churchyard flat gravestones tip and heave in waves as though hit by an earthquake. 'King' David Hartley is buried here – he was leader of a gang of eighteenth-century coiners who clipped money to make their own sovereigns.

The ruined old church also stands in the churchyard, intact apart from its roofs. It burnt out following a lightning strike in 1830. The tower has an aggressive corbelled-out Yorkshire parapet with protruding stair turret. The empty fifteenth-century windows have a mid-height transom bar; the East window looks through to crowded stone-roofed weavers' cottages behind. The North aisle has domestic-type mullioned windows; the North chancel gable has stepped lights as though a house. The porch is roofed with gravestones. Well enough on a summer afternoon for a little family to picnic but in the grey mist of winter it is a daunting location. Below the churchyard cobbled pathways run horizontal with the hill, for example West Laithe. At the crossroads of Northgate and Church Lane Georgian windows mix with square mullions from the previous century. Church Lane leads past three-storeyed weavers' cottages to a short eighteenth-century terrace with Venetian windows. The octagonal Wesleyan Chapel is

ACKWORTH SCHOOL, HIGH ACKWORTH.

said to be the longest chapel in continuous use in the country. [12]

HIGH ACKWORTH Distinguished stone village centred on a triangular green. It has a ball-topped medieval cross and spreading trees. South of the green are the former almshouses, Mary Lowther's hospital, 1741, long and low with stone sash windows and, beneath a central pediment, a doorway and windows with Gibbs surrounds. The Georgian mansion, Ackworth Park, stood north of the green but is demolished. Immediately north in its churchyard of yews is St Cuthbert's which burned down in 1852. The Perp tower and stone-vaulted porch are old, but the nave and chancel are nineteenth century. Over the porch entrance is a niche

Opposite: HEPTONSTALL OLD CHURCH.

enclosing an effigy of St Cuthbert. Inside against the North wall is an incised tombstone with floriated cross. There are two interesting fonts: that under the tower is Norman, rescued from a garden; that by the South door commemorates the restoration of Thomas Bradley, chaplain to Charles I, to St Cuthbert's and of 'This font thrown down in the war of the Fanatics . . . and set up again in the year 1663'. West of the green on the Castleford road is the Old Hall (a farm), three storeyed, gabled with many mullions and said to possess a priest's hole.

Going south from the green on the left is Ackworth House, a Georgian mansion with canted bays and a Venetian window. There are many other smart Georgian properties, some with Tuscan porches. Then on the right is the Quaker School in premises built in 1758 by Thomas Coram as his Foundling Hospital in the north. Disease affected the foundlings badly, the project was

HOLME, MOORLAND.

abandoned and the premises bought by Dr John Fother-gill when on a journey to Wensleydale in 1778 for the Society of Friends. The hospital became their school in 1779 and so remains to this day. From the road the appearance of the buildings is confusing. However, down a passage, by steps to the south is the great court-yard and an austere classical range of 13 bays with a pediment. A courtyard is formed by a pair of opposing buildings also with pediments, and crowned by white lanterns. Connection to the main range is achieved by quarter-circle Tuscan arcades. Between here and the road is a tall archway leading to an arcaded court like its counterpart in Coram's Fields, London WC1. [23]

HOLME   Head of the valley of the River Holme above Huddersfield abutting high moorland to the south. A village of quaint weavers' cottages and mullioned farm-steads. It had its own hydroelectric supply from Rake Dyke until 1934. [25]

HOLMEBRIDGE   In the shadow of Holme Moss and its radio mast, stone weavers' cottages and mills straggle along the valley side. If you wander down Old Road, a narrow lane, you will find three-storeyed weavers' cot-tages, look over stone roofs and see former wool mills. St David's Church, 1840, is a neat and balanced lancet style framed by sycamores. Here there is just room for a cricket ground and nearby is the Bridge Tavern, typi-cally of three storeys with three-light mullioned win-

HOLDSWORTH HALL, 1633.

dows and a date stone of 1809. Above the village are good views of moors and Brownhill Reservoir. [25]

HOLME MOSS High wild moorland within the Peak District National Park. At 524 metres stands the dramatic architecture of a big radio transmitter with a further 228 metres of steel and cable. It is the highest in the UK and was erected in 1984. A predecessor was an original BBC TV transmitter in 1951. Its compound has a GPO-style office. A special warning sign announces that the mast sheds lumps of ice in winter. From here are distant views south over the Derbyshire border to Bleaklow and Kinder Scout. The rough terrain is heather, reed and bilberry overlaying a peat morass whose interior bleeds like black treacle. To the south the A6024, surely over-classified, clings to the hillside on a vertiginous descent. To warn of unprotected cliffs below the road the Highways Department has erected wooden poles with reflectors to permit navigation in fog. Below Twizzle Head Moss to the east are the enclosed headwater valleys of the River Holme with picturesque reservoirs banked

with trees. Only tracks intrude, a path winds through Ramsden Clough to *Holmebridge* and may be walked from Dunford Bridge (South Yorks). Fine landscape. [25]

HOLMFIELD On the road north from Halifax Beck by abandoned mills and tin-roofed industry, austere and mountainous Pule Hill keeps you company. At Holmfield is a gem of a 'Halifax' house in a hamlet of seventeenth-century buildings. The farm to the north has long runs of mullions, but Holdsworth House demonstrates the wealth of a seventeenth-century gentleman. Into a discreet front garden with grand finial-topped piers and toy-like garden cottage is the rich façade of Abraham Briggs' 1633 clothier's house: the left gable has a run of nine mullions, and right of the two-storey porch a transomed window of 11 lights. Its wide spreading gables give an unusually comfortable sensation even with snow on the ground. It is now a hotel. [13]

HOLMFIRTH Hugging the sides of the river the old wool town perches on a hillside; mill chimneys protrude

through foliage below. From Holmfirth Town Gate stone cottages and warehouses ascend the hillside in higgledy-piggledy fashion linked by steep cobbled paths and stone steps. Like a warehouse also is Holy Trinity Church which blends into the townscape. It is the second building (first 1632), rebuilt in 1777 after damage from floods. The Perp tower was rebuilt in 1788. It is a charming Georgian church with side galleries and pillars decorated in white, blue and gold; the ceilings decorated with geometric corn ear mouldings; original box pews may be seen in the North and South galleries. The West gallery has been turned into a meeting room with views down the church. Opposite here is the former Valley Theatre, 1912, neo-Baroque. By the riverside is a ball-capped column, 'Erected in 1801' to commemorate the *Peace of Amiens*, which also indicates the height of the flood in 1852 when Bilberry Reservoir breached its wall with the loss of 81 lives. In 1944 another flood drowned three people and swept away a bridge of shops built over the river. From the bridge is an unmodernized view of eighteenth- and nineteenth-century buildings. A plaque on the parapet shows the layout of headstreams and hills of the River Holme. Many visitors and ramblers congregate here in summer as this was the setting for *Last of the Summer Wine*, the TV series. [25]

HONLEY Weaving village of old and new cottages with mullioned windows climbing the west slopes of the Holme Valley south of Huddersfield. The parish church, St Mary's (R. D. Chantrell), stands well but has disagreeable proportions with its lancets, tall thin tower and elongated pinnacles. Within, however, it is quite delightful with three galleries, elegant quatrefoil piers and a decorative apse. An alabaster monument to William Brooke, a local Woolmaster (see *Armitage Bridge*), is on the sanctuary North wall. It depicts a weeping willow and urns. Said to be the highest pulpit in Yorkshire. Near the church in well-kept and spacious grounds is the late Georgian Honley House, ashlar with Doric porch, once a home of the Brookes. [20]

HORBURY Plain mill town north of the River Calder and standing above its much used sandstone quarries. It possesses the best Renaissance church in the county, by John Carr, the famous Yorkshire architect who was born here in 1723. In 1791 he built and paid for St Peter and St Leonard's Church with its wonderful tower and spire which can be seen along the Calder Valley. What makes a church so noble? The principal south elevation shows the long face of an octagon but is fronted by a tall Ionic portico with four attached Doric columns. A big pediment overreaches the roof. Pedimented South door with big arched windows between the columns – half

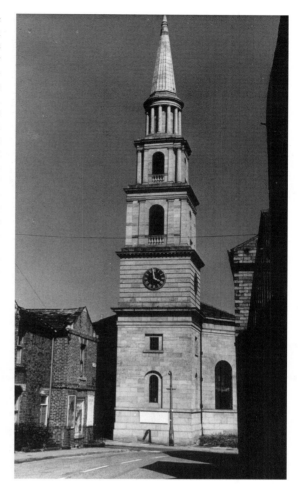

ST PETER AND ST LEONARD, HORBURY.

storey windows above. The proportions and focus of the building across the traditional axis create a tension worthy of Wren. The tower, rusticated above the cornice, has further diminishing stages rising through Doric arches before reaching a rotunda and fluted spire. In the church the west of the octagon is an apse; and through a double-square chancel is another apse at the East end. Corinthian columns screen the nave from the entrance portico and restore the conventional orientation. Carr spent £8,000 out of his fortune of £150,000 on this memorial church. He is buried here and no more fitting monument could be devised. On some summer Saturdays and before Christmas a tawdry market creeps out of the street into the churchyard up to the portico, a stark contrast to this beautiful house. [21]

Opposite: HOLMFIRTH.

97

CORINTHIAN SCREEN, ST PETER AND ST LEONARD, HORBURY.

HORSFORTH Leeds suburb but with dominating J. L. Pearson church on a high eminence. St Margaret, 1883, although surrounded by new housing is tall and starkly black, radiating aggression from the big, inelegant broach spire and high clerestoried roof. A tremendous monument to an age. Down towards the river Low Hall was the home of the Stanhopes from 1565; New Hall, 1710, displays a ridged front with mullioned and cross-transomed windows. Walter Stanhope was fined by Charles I for refusing to attend his coronation. [9]

HUDDERSFIELD In the Upper Colne Valley is in a grand situation and still produces textiles and clothing. Enclosed by wooded hillsides rising to the moors and astride the River Colne, it has been a settlement since Norman times. A market town for upland farmers, it became a centre for wool weaving and cloth in the

seventeenth and eighteenth centuries. Early mills used water power, and a number of mill leets and weirs remain. Its unusual claim to fame is an early railway station so grandly designed it was called a 'stately home with trains in it'; John Betjeman said it was the 'most splendid station façade in England'. Textiles have been the lifeblood of the town. The Lord of the Manor, Sir John Ramsden, was a key figure early in its development and the university a more recent contributor to its success. Here the Luddites were a considerable danger when new machinery was installed in the early nineteenth century. One thousand soldiers guarded a population of 10,000; Rawford's Mill was attacked, and William Horsfall, a mill owner, was killed. From the mid-nineteenth century steam power was used burning local coal, hence the forest of chimneys. The planners have reacted positively to mill closures to keep the shape

Left: Bankfield House, Halifax:
the Saloon ceiling and fireplace.
HW.

Left and below: Harewood
House, Leeds: the State
Bedroom and Gallery.

Dewsbury Minster: Medieval glass showing farming. WG.

Below left: Bolling Hall, Bradford: the Ghost room. WG.
Below right: Halifax Minstry: 'Old Tristram' poor box. WG.

Wakefield Bridge and *Chantry Chapel* (1793) by Philip Reinagle, The Hepworth Wakefield.

Pontefract Castle (c.1620–40) by Alexander Keirinx, The Hepworth Wakefield.

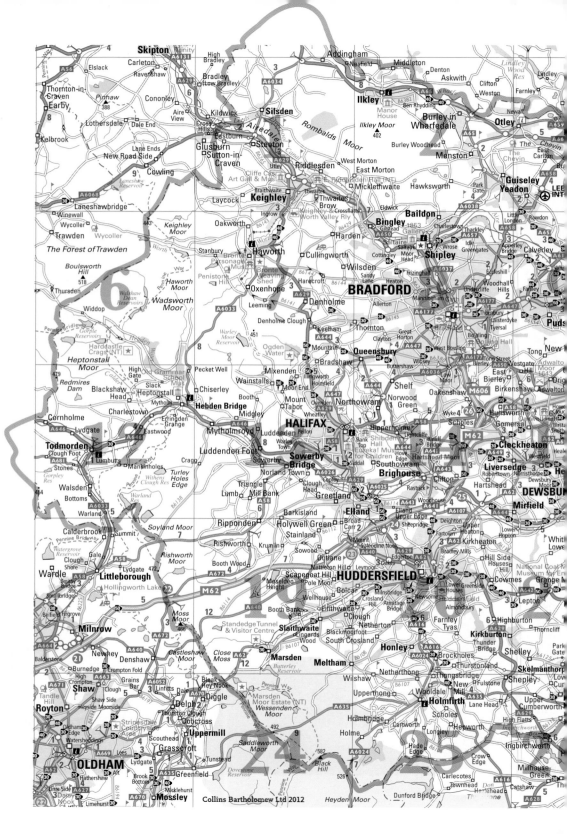

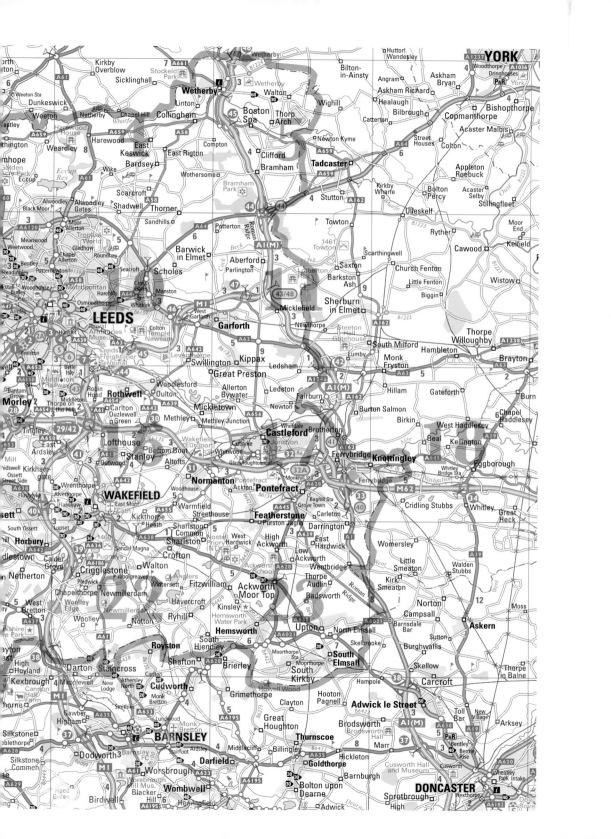

Halifax No. 2 by John Piper,
Calderdale Metropolitan
Borough Council.

Bowling Dyke by Claude
Muncaster, Calderdale
Metropolitan Borough
Council.

New Bank by Tom
Whitehead, Calderdale
Metropolitan Borough
Council.

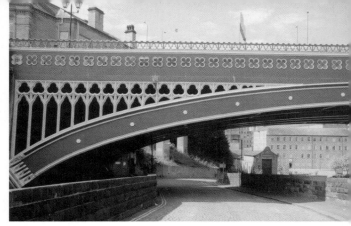

Clockwise from above: Halifax: Gothic cast-iron North Bridge, 1871, by J & J Fraser. WG.
Halifax Minster: the East Window by George Hedgeland. WG.
Cliffe Castle, Keighley, Pre-Raphaelite glass: Tristram and Isoude drinking the potion by Dante Gabriel Rossetti; Tristram and the Harp, and Recognition of Tristram by la Belle Isoude, both by Edward Burne-Jones. HW.

Clockwise from above:
Junction of Rochdale Canal. WG.
Welcome to Batley. WG.
Bargee and boy statue at the
Lock Beam, Sowerby Bridge,
Halifax. WG.
Weaving and dying at Roberts
Mill, Keighley. HW.

of the town – some have been converted to flats, and a portion converted by Huddersfield University. Old mills have been refitted for new use and new buildings have been put up in the style of mills, copying their fenestration and stone-built mass. [20]

Huddersfield Town Centre – walk 1   The visitor may well begin a walking tour at the railway station. It is no slight on the town to say it is the most distinguished building here – like a country house with large Corinthian portico and single-storey pavilions linked by arcades to the station. Designed by J. P. Pritchett in 1847, it could front rolling parkland. The platform canopies are mean, but the extravagant and colourful arms of the original railway companies – the Lancashire and Yorkshire Railway, the Huddersfield and Manchester Canal and Railway Company on the front – are not. The station presides over *St George's Square*, wide and cobbled; in reality the centre of the town. One of its sons, Harold Wilson, stands proudly in front of the station in bronze.

On either side of St George's Square are stone build-ings in a variety of Victorian styles. Directly ahead is the Huddersfield and Bradford Building Society, 1856, a big Italian palazzo – many similar buildings were put up in Rome at this time. Its windows are arched, rusticated and with keystone heads of the ancients; its first floor incorporates alternate triangular and elliptical pediments; a strong cornice is supported by corbels carved with garlands; above that is a balustrade with urns also showing Britannia and the Royal Arms. To the north is the George Hotel, 1849, a classical railway hotel with strong cornice incorporating circular motifs and lively rusticated ground floor. To the right is Arthurian Gothic – EE style, pavilion roofs, octagonal cones, shafted windows, turrets and (originally) six weather vanes. Directly opposite the station is Lion Chambers: coupled-arched windows, 1853, with a dramatic Coade stone lion on the parapet. Then directly ahead but downhill on Northumberland Street is the Mechanics Institute – much more modest than Leeds – with two large Venetian windows and a bold projecting cornice. Institutes were set up to advance working people in the nineteenth century by non-conformist churches, often being opposed by the

HUDDERSFIELD STATION, 1847.

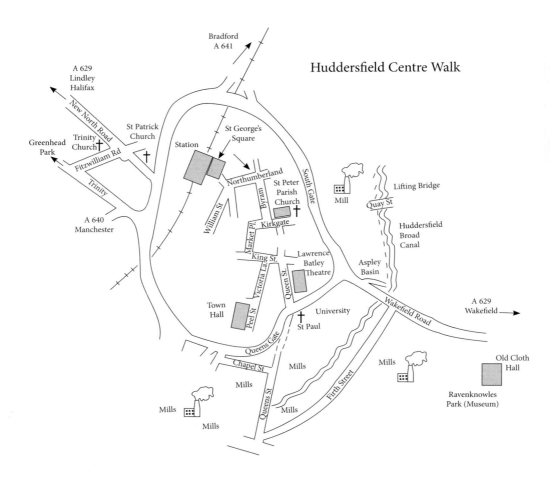

established Church. In Byram Street the small covered market is typical of 1878, with cast iron frame, glass roof and pillars with mixed capitals; the rams signify the source of Huddersfield's prosperity.

Byram Street south brings you to *St Peter's Church* via a welcome green square made from the former churchyard. The best view of the parish church, however, is from the far side in Kirkgate, and indeed lower down in Kirkgate entering off the ring road. From here the church looks lordly with its big gabled South transept of three transomed Perp-style windows and embattled parapet. The West tower is also Perp but the buttresses step in five times making it too dainty, certainly by Yorkshire standards. The crenellated parapet is pierced and fancy. Surprisingly the architect was Pritchett, 1846, who built the station, a far stronger design. The church stone has worn badly. Inside remain three galler-

ies and over the altar a slightly incongruous classical baldachino with angels. Opposite the church are early stone classical houses with sashes and large elliptical pediments. Turn right up Kirkgate to Market Place, still possessing its market cross – a fluted column with ball finial – but much restored. Then east down Cloth Hall Street where the Georgian Cloth Hall once stood, to Victoria Lane, Peel Street and the overwhelming *Town Hall*, 1875. Behind but all of a piece is the Concert Hall, 1878. It is on a cramped site and the strong classicism of J. H. Abbey is too loud – exaggerated elliptical pediments tower above you as corner pieces, the windows are Venetian, the cornice is very big and overly rich in carved Italianate devices. It is the poor relation of Yorkshire town halls and cannot be viewed with relish. At Victoria Lane is the Art Gallery. Then King Street leads to Queen Street with evidence of the late Georgian period. First a terrace of late Georgian houses, stucco with Doric porches. Next is the late Georgian 'Court of Requests' – pediment over five bays, four-columned portico with Royal Arms, 1825, latterly the County Court. Next is the former Wesleyan Methodist Church, 1819, a bigger Georgian building with five bays showing off a central Venetian window and porch of fluted Doric columns. When it was a chapel it had seats for 1,500 but is now converted into a theatre. It forms part of **Queen Square**, set behind railings and between two three-storey brick Georgian houses which face each other.

Continue south over the ring road into Lower Queen Street past St Paul's in a well-balanced EE style of 1829. Now a concert hall, its spire is prominent, and inside is an EE-style blank triforium with tall piers. It is by the renowned Grecian architect, Joseph Kaye, who was a native of Huddersfield and designed the Infirmary on New North Road, now the Technical College. Here are Huddersfield's mills and wool warehouses close to the centre. Divert for a moment west up Chapel Street to the junction of Manchester Road and the ring road to the Huddersfield Co-op built in 1893, but the 1936 extension was novel for its date – the windows are lodged in vertical bands and the entrance frontispiece has full-height cascading ribs on the corner rather like a cinema. Then back to *Queen Street* where many mills have recently been made redundant, but most are listed and efforts to preserve them are being made. First is Bates Mill with its big blackened stone chimney, 1855. Grand entrance under a six-storey tower crowned with a water tank. Then at Firth Street turn northeast where more mills and warehouses lie between the River Colne and the canal. Then Priestroyd Mills, 1869, five storeys of rectangular windows; then Priestroyd Ironworks, 1835;

LIFTING BRIDGE AT TURNBRIDGE MILLS, HUDDERSFIELD.

then Commercial Mills with a big, two-storey, classical cart entrance and projecting soffit; then canal-side development for the university of imitative warehouses as a hall of residence. The *University* lies between here and the town forming an excellent campus of distinctive modern blocks. The Huddersfield Canal enlivens the mill scene and after passing under the Wakefield Road leads into a pound at Aspley Place filled with gaily painted narrow boats. Follow the canal east to a quaint nineteenth-century lifting bridge which raises the road for barge traffic at Turnbridge Mills. Currently in use, the mills have an Italianate tower with twin arched windows, rise six storeys and retain a handsome octagonal chimney with strong corona.

About half a mile east down Wakefield Road is *Ravensknowle Park*, a nineteenth-century former residence of the Ramsdens, Lords of this manor, which is now preserved as a museum. Italianate with arched windows and big corbelled soffits. The intriguing stables have a tower and Flemish bell-shaped dome. Close by are remnants of the former Cloth Hall: its central clock tower, cupola and weather vane, and parts of the arcaded wings and Tuscan columns have been partially rebuilt. The plaque states 'Erected by Sir John Ramsden 1766'. It was originally sited by Market Place.

Huddersfield west suburbs – car or bike Just north of the centre is Huddersfield Technology College: the main building is Grecian, with big Ionic pillars. It was built by Joseph Kaye originally as the Infirmary. On the *New North Road* is St Patrick's Catholic Church in Regency Gothic – lancet windows but the West end has Perp-style windows, pinnacled turrets, embattling, 1832. West from here in Fitzwilliam Street are good early nineteenth-century ashlar terraces with Doric porches. Going out of town up Trinity Street, Trinity Church is on the right, 1816, by Thomas Taylor – dignified, big lancets with intersecting tracery, big buttresses between each window and a tall clerestory, all embattled. The tower also is very big and pinnacled, the bell storey with intersecting tracery and transom – this strange combination is also in the East window. The churchyard slopes away prettily to the south with rhododendron, holly and birch trees. Immediately west of the church is a unified terrace of late Georgian houses in ashlar with a central pediment, comfortably set back from the road. Opposite is Greenhead Park surrounded by well-to-do Victorian and Edwardian villas. On Trinity Road rising west, parallel with the park, are more good ashlar houses with Doric porches built between 1830 and 1850. At the summit of the hill is Gledholt Methodist Church, 1908, lavish and rich with a neo-Baroque classical tower, octagonal storey and dome: a considerable departure from the strictures of John Wesley.

Travelling west up New Hey Road the terraces become more Italianate as the nineteenth century progresses. Amid the palatial stone mansions of *Edgerton* on Halifax Road (go via Globe Street), castellated Gothic was favourite to express the profitability of your mill. Edgerton was west of the smoky chimneys but only a few minutes by horse and trap down to the factories. Here also is a fine Grade I listed Arts and Crafts mansion by Edgar Wood, 1899. It has a long frontage of à la carte Jacobean features – mullioned windows in gables – but different articulation, for example Art Nouveau-

CLOCKTOWER BY EDGAR WOOD, HUDDERSFIELD.

Opposite: OLD INFIRMARY BY JOSEPH KAYE, NOW TECHNICAL COLLEGE, HUDDERSFIELD.

HEATHCOTE, 1906, EDWIN LUTYENS, ILKLEY.

hooded entrance door in a gable slightly tapered; its first-floor cross-mullioned window has single window companions either side. Hopefully it will not receive the Leeds treatment of building speculative new houses in the garden to destroy its character. It is a private house but visible through trees. Turn left via Holly Bank Road to the pleasant stone-built suburb of **Lindley** where stands a large and glorious Art Nouveau clock tower – stone with diagonal buttresses, again by the Manchester architect Edgar Wood.

The Parish Church of St Stephen is in a leafy churchyard: Regency Gothic, 1829. The stubby tower has gabled pinnacles; the nave big lancet windows divided by buttresses, rather leaden under the trees. The villas and terraces have the pleasant ambience of a fashionable suburb. Further north and higher still is access to the M62 which runs along the ridge between the valleys of the River Colne and River Calder to ascend the Pennines. Where the A629 ducks under the motorway a huge and surprising view opens through an arch to show the industrial landscape in the Calder Valley around Halifax.

ILKLEY A commuter town in Wharfedale with its own railway line to Leeds. Trees, gardens, promenades and bandstand. The Malvern of the North, they say. With its back to the proud stands of firs on high Ilkley Moor, which glows gold and purple with the seasons, the town looks across the Wharfe towards the invigorating moors. The Romans had a fort here, Olicana, under Agricola in about AD 79. Doubtless like chilly Buxton, the waters were the attraction although they were cool. Dr Richardson summed it up in 1709, 'Ilkley is a very mean place, chiefly famous for a cold well . . .'. The first baths erected in 1760 up on the moor were known as the White Wells; they can still be seen, white-painted cottages in their chilly isolation. Stables were kept for donkeys to haul up the infirm. The town, rising to the moor, has many Gothic and Italianate houses. It was hydropathy that founded Ilkley's prosperity in the early nineteenth century when patent baths, compresses and pressure baths brought relief to the manufacturing middle classes. Huge hydro hotels were built, like the Ben Rydding (demolished) with its own railway station for invalids. Remaining from that era are Wells House

Hydro (now Ilkley College) by **Cuthbert Brodrick**, 1856, arched windows and zealous rustication – almost as heroic as the Grand Hotel, Scarborough; and Craiglands Hotel, originally the Grove Hydro. Among the Victorian villas and hotels is St Margaret's, 1878, a comfortable rich church by Norman Shaw. Very indulgent Perp with elaborate panel tracery, in places crocketed. The rood and Perp choir screens are oak. The grand throne-like canopy over the West font with its modern painting of the Madonna and Child is by Graeme Wilson. The Madonna is shown accompanied by a sheep farmer on the hills behind Ilkley. The reredos by J. H. Gibbons, 1925, shows Christ appearing on Easter Day – elaborate gilded vines frame the carving.

Of the old town the Elizabethan Manor House remains (now a museum). A handsome, gabled and mullioned house recently restored from multiple occupation, it contains locally found Roman exhibits. The medieval **Church of All Saints** hides the manor from the road; the church has an excellent thirteenth-century doorway with dog-tooth decoration; the tower is Perp, but much of the chancel and nave were rebuilt in the nineteenth

century. In the North aisle chapel is a well-preserved effigy of a knight; in the North aisle is a Jacobean pew screened with fat, turned balusters; south of here is the font with Jacobean cover. Under the tower are three Anglo-Saxon crosses carved with vine scrolls, beasts and figures; on the largest, Christ and the Evangelists. To the north a park leads down to the River Wharfe which here is wide and pebbly; in summer its shore is a beach for children.

West down Addingham Road is the restored old Grammar School of 1637 with mullioned windows. South is Middleton Lodge, 1600 – rather keep-like – with gables, oriel window over the doorway and mullioned and transomed windows. It was built by William Middleton whose family held the Lordship of Ilkley from 1484 to the early twentieth century. It adjoins Middleton House, a seventeenth-century farm to the east and a chapel to the west, and is protected by its own grounds. Some old cottages remain in the town, one with a richly carved doorway, Boxtree Cottage, but which has otherwise been tastelessly altered. Nowadays the prosperity of the place depends on Bradford and

Leeds commuters for whom this is the railhead and whose houses, Victorian and modern, line the hillside between the town and the moor. In King's Road is a noteworthy house designed by Sir Edwin Lutyens in 1906: 'Heathcote', now a company HQ – not his romantic broad-gabled Tudor like Berrydown House, but highly mannered Palladian. It has a hipped roof with red pantiles, a variety of window mouldings: cambered, arched and squared; a roofed string course; bevel-blocked basement; while to the south are pyramidal pavilions with Doric screens and insolent round-eyed windows. The huge chimney stacks are banded. Built of gloomy yellow stone its appearance is arresting; the flavour is Edwardian Cuthbert Brodrick. Not the customary Lutyens. [2]

ILLINGWORTH   On a bend of the A629 as it descends from the horrible blackened stone country of Denholme – a true Wuthering Heights of bleak, apparently unregulated development. Obviously the area is not abandoned because there is a large fire station, but the sad case of St Mary's Church may occasion tears. This eighteenth-century church has two storeys of arched windows and stands high above the zigzag of the main road in full view now that its supportive neighbour below has been demolished. It is a classical box of 1777 from which the removal of galleries has left little save for a huge two-tier brass chandelier (candles) shedding branches where it stands. Thieves have taken the roof lead and water ingress on the northeast corner threatens the structure. The classical chancel, 1888, suffers from an absence of proportion and is ornamented like a shrine. It is both sweet and sad. The West tower is eighteenth-century Gothic after a Vanbrughian style; it is, however, buttressed by a domestic building put up against the tower. This awkward church has never been a jewel but would be a loss to the history of the place.

A diagonal path descends from the churchyard east to the busy main road where remains an old lock-up with the date 1823. It has round barred windows on the first floor and an inscription: 'Let him that stole steal no more but rather let him labour . . .'. If you walk west of the church to the hilltop a surprising view is revealed of a village called *Mixenden*. In a moorland valley below you is a colony of rendered houses configured like an army camp, seemingly an alien presence in these dark stone satanic uplands. [13]

KEIGHLEY   Once a prosperous mill town which generated neat Victorian and Edwardian parades of stone-built shops, it now largely depends on light trades and engineering although some wool trade survives. The Victorian church of St Andrew, 1848 by Robert Chantrell,

is rather grand in its churchyard of gloomy mossy-layered table tombs which spread down to the beck. The tower is coarse gritstone, stately, buttresses reducing by crocketed pedimented stages, and gargoyles at the summit. A neat clerestory has six Perp-style windows. Opposite the church are some old houses including the Commercial Inn of three storeys, tripartite mullions, eighteenth century. In Cavendish Square is a fine war memorial with statues of a well-equipped First World War soldier, and a sailor using a telescope. On a pedestal is a statue of Peace. Off Cavendish Square the former School Board offices have a grand neo-Baroque frontispiece of big oriel window, voluptuous carving and pediment with the Borough Arms, 1892.

On North Street adjacent to Cavendish Square is the library, asymmetric neo-Baroque with high dormer windows in the roof (to Albert Street); the main façade commemorates its opening on the Coronation Day of King Edward VII in 1902. It has restrained Tudoresque windows, arches and cartouches. The Mechanics Institute, 1868, was built in a style said to be both patronizing and aggressive Gothic but it was burnt down in 1962 and only a portion remains – insufficient to judge how aggressive it was. Further up North Street is the restored Picture House, 1913, in white faience tiling demonstrating a Tudor Arts and Crafts, still operating as the Picture House. Such is the demand for stonemasonry in this area that a commercial mason's yard operates in Bradford Street.

The mills are mostly silent now awaiting new uses but Dalton Mills, 1872, should not be missed – dramatic 40 windows in length on three storeys with square projecting turrets and bell stages under pyramid roofs; huge modillioned cornice. An independent range, similar in size to the Tower of London, lies east of the gatehouse with its own clock tower. Next to the Baroque gatehouse is an architectural fancy – a little rock-faced tower with cornice, blank pedimented clock space surmounted by a 'melon' dome. It is all quite fun but the mill chimney, aping a clock tower, has an unfortunate mid-height belly with its own projecting roof and brackets. Its proportions are exquisitely awful.

On Emley Street is a fine new mosque in local stone, expensively wrought with pear-shaped windows, divided by plain ashlar piers, green dome, date stone 2007 – 'This House of Allah stands here as testament to the founder of the Keighley Jamia Mosque and Keighley Muslim community'. The railway station is shared between British Rail and the preserved Worth Valley Line. The booking hall has a wide coving for the ceiling with a long lantern or clerestory – it gives onto a balcony overlooking the lines. To the road a glazed canopy sits on pierced brackets of stylized dragons.

Opposite: TORS ON THE PLATEAU, ILKLEY MOOR.

ALL HALLOWS, C.1200, KIRKBURTON.

The owners of the mills did not stint themselves when building their homes. There are many handsome houses and mansions in the northern suburbs, in particular Cliffe Castle, now a museum, was rebuilt in 1878 with castellated turret and decorative Jacobean gables. It contains a good collection of Pre-Raphaelite stained glass, and still evokes the feeling of a nineteenth-century manufacturer's mansion. Further along the shoulder of the hill at Utley is a fine mansion, Whinburn Lodge, built for Sir William Prince-Smith, a textile engineer, in 1897. It is a magnificent Tudor revival house extended in Arts and Crafts, 1913. The great Hall has a 15-light window, stone interior with vaulted roof, carved beams and beautifully cast fall-pipes with foliage and fruit. A handsome feast of the craftsman's art. [1]

KIPPAX Well situated in the east of the county astride a col descending towards the River Aire and almost overwhelmed by development, Kippax has about it the air of more rural and charming parts; its streets wind interestingly and there is the distinguished eighteenth-century Royal Oak Hotel with hipped roof and pedimented doorway.

St Mary's Church has a splendid Saxon/Norman exterior with herringbone masonry, Norman windows on the North wall and a Norman South door. Aisleless, the interior is big, lofty, whitewashed and simple. A piscina in the Southeast sanctuary has two bowls. The fourteenth-century East window has intersecting tracery. The tower is a whole 2ft out of square, its Perp belfry stage was recased in 1893. Memorial stones to the wife and daughter of an eloping incumbent the Revd Cotton Gargrave have been incorporated in a bench in the porch. The 1634 octagonal font has a contemporary cover of lantern-like panels carved with leaves, fruit and flowers; the corner finials and semi-circular arms reach to a further tier of open semi-circular arms. A whimsical early twentieth-century wrought iron organ screen has gilded branches and leaves. Fragments of an Anglo-Saxon cross are in the clergy vestry. Good memorials to the Blands, baronets of Kippax Park, an Elizabethan house demolished recently because of mining. Its gate piers survive between cottages south of the village. Manor Garth earthworks northwest of the church are an old motte and bailey fortification and give grand views to the Pennines and to Ledston Park. [11]

KIRKBURTON Stands high on the shoulder of a hill overlooking Fenay Beck where the B6116 winds down the hill to Fenay Bridge. The age-old prosperous church of All Hallows stands on a well-wooded hill, its churchyard amply punctuated with tall finialled monuments, and gives views towards Thunder Bridge in the valley below. The tall embattled tower is very thin and was not much rebuilt to judge by the vestiges of the former steeply raked nave roof. It may originally have had a defensive lookout purpose. Old masonry to the south side shows a lancet church of about 1300 with chancel roof at the same rake as the former nave. The EE South aisle has a panelled Perp window. The West doorway has two shafts and some dog-tooth decoration from about 1200. The arcades are EE as is the chancel arch, but the nave roof is Perp with carved bosses. There are some nice old stalls as well as seventeenth-century stalls with knobs. Part of an Anglo-Saxon cross with interlace has been brought indoors. A good early and stately church.

On the other side of the 'B' road is the former rectory, Georgian but with nineteenth-century alterations to the ground floor. Winding one stage down the hill is the Georgian George Inn with stone sashes but an early twentieth-century ground floor 'improvement'. Here at Church Green and Low Gate terraces go this way and that following the lines of the hill. Falling down a little valley from here is Low Town which leads across Penistone Road to Thunder Bridge, a good place to take lunch.

From the side of the hill a stately Georgian mansion can be seen on a tree-clad hill to the west. This is Storthes Hall in golden local stone – seven bays of unframed sashes with a low pediment over the centre three. The entrance has a broad elliptical pediment on Tuscan columns. Built in 1791 by William Horsfalls to replace an Elizabethan manor. In 1925 the estate was taken over by a hospital whose departments camped extensively in the surrounding woodland. They have now been cleared and the hall restored to a private house. Access is only by arrangement but it is prominent west of the A629. [20]

KIRKHEATON Occupies a hill above a steep dedivity east of Huddersfield. Whitley Beaumont was a gritstone house of the eighteenth century whose grounds were landscaped by Launcelot Brown. It was demolished following opencast mining in 1953. Its site is two miles east of the village toward Grange Moor on a hill to the west. Beaumont monuments can be found in the North Chancel Chapel of St John's Church, fifteenth century. Also Perp is the tower arch and part of the North Arcade. In the Beaumont chapel lies Sir Richard Beaumont, 1631, on a tomb chest with other Richard Beaumonts of later date. Much of the church was rebuilt in 1867. A column in the graveyard commemorates the loss of 17 children in a mill fire. (See also *Grange Moor*.) [20]

KIRKSTALL ABBEY The de-roofed abbey is of cathedral proportions and is relatively complete. The A65 Kirkstall Road divides the abbey from its guesthouse, which is now a museum. Once you could obtain a tranquil view from a seat under trees by the River Aire but communion with the ruins and river is now impeded by an iron fence. Outside the fence by the river is a romantic view of the central crossing tower and elaborate South transept. This Cistercian Abbey (daughter of Fountains) is Romanesque – Norman windows in the transepts and tower but an alien Perp storey was added to the tower in the early sixteenth century – most has fallen down and would that the rest might go.

From the river you see well-preserved remains of the monastic buildings, many still stand to roof height. On the left the *Abbot's Lodging*, still three storeys, built about 1230, looks as though the roof is just ready to be fitted. External stairs gave access to a first-floor hall; above that was a solar. Now walking round the East end of the abbey you see the massive walled *Chancel*. The transept chapels and nave aisles have been re-roofed with lead and oak. Each transept has three east-facing chapels. The East wall of the chancel itself had a huge Perp window, to judge by the remains of the tracery. Close to its corner the tower has a dramatic presence – the large Perp openings stand on mullioned Romanesque openings through which birds wheel in the wind. The gables of the chancel and transepts have Perp pinnacles, hollow boxes of stone tracery. Looking down the length of the abbey church from the East window the symmetry of the transepts and length of the *Nave* is impressive. There are two tiers of Norman openings on the transept walls, and down the North aisle where (save for a later large Dec window) all openings are small Romanesque ones. The clerestory, however, has big arched windows. Toward its West end the North wall has a large Norman door whose shafts are missing but with bold square zigzag. The huge Norman West porch has five orders, but shafts missing within a gable. Access into the church is through the restored Lay Brothers' Reredorter – the adjacent Cellarium floor collapsed 200 years ago but still shows an upper storey of Norman windows and corbels which once held the vaulted first floor. Through a doorway is the large cloister (adjacent to the nave) and opposite is the *Chapter House* through large Norman arches; within is an excellent twelfth-century vaulted space: ribbed vaults on clustered column with cushion capitals. Continuing anti-clockwise are the kitchens and remains of the Refectory, almost

NORTH TRANSEPT AND TOWER, KIRKSTALL ABBEY.

100ft long with tall round-headed windows and serving hatches to the kitchen. Here some of the original floor tiles, glazed in red, blue and yellow, from 1240 are still in place. Just before reaching the Abbot's Lodging once again is the Meat Kitchen built in the fifteenth century when the monks were permitted to eat meat three times a week – provided it was cooked in a separate kitchen. It was roasted before two large hearths here.

Although relatively plain the Abbey is a vast church, its arches all slightly pointed, the pillars noteworthy for wavy scalloped capitals. The Guesthouse was over the main road which, with the original round gateway arch, was once a farmhouse and then a mansion but is now a museum and tearoom. The abbey was bought by Saviles in the sixteenth century and then went by marriage to the Earls of Cardigan who sold it by auction in 1888. It was bought by Colonel J. T. North. Sir George Gilbert Scott had been asked to consider restoring the abbey in 1873. Scott believed that despite being in ruins for three and a half centuries it could be 'restored to its sacred uses'. Others thought the ruins should be preserved (like the Romantics who wished to preserve Haddon Hall as a ruin). The Society for the Protection of Ancient Buildings believed nothing short of putting a roof over the vaulting was good enough but the owner, the Countess of Cardigan, would only agree to patch the ruin up. Col. North made a present of it to the City of Leeds. Magically, English Heritage and Leeds have installed new roofs of oak and lead over the aisles and transept chapels to save the vaulting. The *Visitor Centre* is in the Lay Brothers' Reredorter southwest of the church; it has been a barn and the roof is eighteenth century. The latrine portals on the first floor can be made out. [9]

KIRKTHORPE A quiet village east of Heath above the scarp of the River Calder. A footpath leads down to Stanley Ferry. Until recently the immediate vicinity was dominated by mines with their spoil heaps and railways but it has returned to peace. The little Perp Church of St Peter has stone-roofed cottages for neighbours. Its much renewed windows are straight headed with foliated lights, the chancel a lower later addition. The Dec West tower is embattled, with pinnacles. Rather pretty quatrefoil piers within. The original crocketed pinnacles now form entrance piers in the churchyard which is pretty in spring with bluebells, rhododendrons and azaleas. 'Wakefield Seamless Gutters' are permitted to advertise here on a board but say 'Thank God for rain'. The old stocks are situated by the side of Half Moon Lane.

Just to the west of the church is Frieston's Hospital

CHAPTER HOUSE VAULT, KIRKSTALL ABBEY.

North Aisle, Kirkstall Abbey, 1147.

CHAPTER HOUSE ROMANESQUE ENTRANCE, KIRKSTALL ABBEY.

almshouses. An Elizabethan building with a pyramidal stone roof and storey of dormers containing mullioned and transomed windows to light a double-storey dining hall below. The pensioners' rooms were on three sides of the hall. It is now a private house. [16]

KNOTTINGLEY   For long a manufactuary of pottery and in recent times glassware – both dirty trades occasioning some dehabitation: some houses are abandoned and windows and doors boarded up in grimy streets. Moving east through the puthering gantries and the sweet carbolic sense of chemical works is Kellingley Colliery on the border with North Yorkshire, and beyond

that a further coal-fired power station. St Botolph's Church in Knottingley stands somewhat aloof from the grime with a white-rendered classical nave, chancel with lancets and pinnacled tower of limestone. It looks out from here like a lighthouse over the River Aire, the navigation branches west towards Leeds or Sheffield. The locks are controlled by traffic lights which do not seem necessary, but this modern navigation still carries timber, stone and oil. The old village by the church was demolished in the 1960s for development leaving the church isolated. [18]

Knottingley, Kellingley Colliery.

Knottingley Chemical Plant.

SAXON DOORWAY, LEDSHAM CHURCH.

LEDSHAM Pretty limestone village once part of the estate of Ledston Hall two miles to the east. Still agricultural, the lane winds 90° round the pantile-roofed barns of Manor Farm, seventeenth century; some original mullioned and transomed windows remain, as in the back outshot and east gable; but other windows have nineteenth-century transoms. Opposite Manor Farm and elevated up a little hill is the Saxon Church of All Saints – Perp tower top and short stone spire, but essentially Saxon. The South doorway of the tower has elaborate Saxon detail; it was restored in the nineteenth century when vine scrolls and rosettes were re-carved. The chancel arch is Saxon, as are two windows each carved out of large flat stones. Doubling of the nave by adding the large Perp North aisle upsets the West–East focus. Big Perp windows lighten the nave. Memorials are mostly of the lords or ladies of Ledston Hall, for example Lady Mary Bolles, 1662, carved in a marble shroud, face of a farmer's wife. Large and grand is the tomb of Lady Elizabeth Hastings, 1739, by Peter Scheemakers, daughter of the 7th Earl of Huntingdon who, though a famous beauty, never married. 'To love her is a liberal education', wrote Sir Richard Steel, she was 'most strictly virtuous without tasting the praise of it'. Ledston Hall came to her as daughter of the Earl of Huntingdon – the Countess was heir to Sir John Lewis. She was devoted to good works: in the village she built the school with its cross-mullioned windows and a little turret; also the Lady Betty Hastings's Orphanage just east of the church – like a grand rectory – on the same hill as the church. This house of 1721 (looks late seventeenth century) rises grandly through three storeys, has seven bays of mullion-cross windows and octagonal chimneys. A little path west of the church tower reveals the side of the orphanage, and leads to a long row of mullioned almshouses of 1670 founded by Sir John Lewis. They have been modernized with brick additions behind and fixed up with generous timber-gabled porches. The Chequers Inn remains closed on Sundays in deference to the wishes of Lady Mary. [17]

LEDSTON HALL   The mansion is a Baroque delight of gleaming Permian limestone looking out from the summit of a scarp over its village to the Aire Valley and Ledsham. It is a very big house mostly of the seventeenth century with parades of Jacobean gables, flanked by ogee-capped towers like Hatfield. Seen from the village below, the garden front peers high over a brick garden wall with irregular gables and towers like a fairytale castle. Climb the hill by the lane to the distinguished entrance gateway – built on a diamond plan the lodges are linked by a pedimented arch. Look through it to the formal East front which is symmetrical. Six big Dutch gables with pediments have 'O' windows inserted in them. Sir John Lewis's mullion-cross windows were replaced with sashes to the ground and first floor in 1730 by his granddaughter Lady Betty Hastings (see Ledsham). A courtyard is formed by the outer pavilions stepped well forward. The house is of medieval origin and was a grange of Pontefract Priory. The undercroft of their

ENTRANCE FAÇADE, 17TH CENTURY, LEDSTON HALL.

chapel remains together with some windows and stairs of that period. At the Dissolution the house was bought by the Witham family: they made the parlour, dated 1588, now known as Lady Betty's Room from her later occupation but which displays Elizabethan plasterwork. In 1629 the hall was bought by the Earl of Strafford and his son sold it to Sir John Lewis in 1653. The stables are mansion-like, with cross-mullions and gables of the seventeenth century. English Heritage has safeguarded the mansion's roof but this important house is looking for someone to love it. The hall grounds are open to the public during summer months. [17]

Above: LEDSTON HALL FROM SOUTH, 16TH, 17TH AND 18TH CENTURIES.
Right: OLD LEADED IRON WINDOWS, LEDSTON HALL.

LEEDS A place of standing since Saxon times, it prospered by producing wool and cloth. Commerce was begun by Cistercian monks at Kirkstall Abbey in Norman times and the first bridge over the River Aire was built in 1372 – the 'bridge' entrance to Briggate. Cloth was displayed for sale on the parapet of the bridge. John Leland in 1536 described 'Ledes on Aire River is a praty market . . . the toun stondith most by clothing.' In 1727 Defoe believed the cloth market could not be equalled in the world. The Industrial Revolution brought cloth production to mills powered by water and then steam. Today Leeds is greater than a commodity capital: it is the commercial centre of Yorkshire.

Briggate, the original main street, was crossed by the T piece of The Headrow, later broadened to form the modern city centre. The old centre was on the north bank of the River Aire between Briggate and medieval St Peter's on the river strand, the Calls. Rich nineteenth-century buildings populate the city centre (but fight for life under modern development). Robust EE styles can be seen at Britannia Buildings; Venetian Gothic at the General Infirmary by G. G. Scott, 1862; baronial Gothic at the Victoria Hotel and Old Masonic Hall in Great George Street; Romanesque within the Municipal Buildings in Calverley Street, 1878, with grand foliated capitals on round marble piers. George Corson in particular was a prolific Gothic architect – a style popular with industrialists. Gothic clothed swimming baths, theatres and even non-conformist chapels. [9/10]

Leeds City Centre – walk 1 (about 90 minutes)

Start at City Station. The former booking hall is spacious 1930s Art Deco, plain and tall, with internally projecting concrete ribs, built by the LMS railway. In *City Square* the Queen's Hotel, again LMS, presents a massive Portland stone elevation to the square – plain ashlar crowned with pedimented roof pavilions – the 1930s parody of classicism. Projecting angular stair turrets rise into big lanterns. There are good 1930s Art Deco interiors. Opposite is a more dynamic façade, the former GPO, 1896, with a roof of double-stack chimneys and prominent classical clock tower. In City Square the famous Art Nouveau statues by Alfred Drury of *Morn* and *Even* – nymphs clad only in flowers – bear torches. Famous local persons are represented on the North side by statues: Dr Hook, James Watt and Joseph Priestley etc.; why is Watt here? An equestrian Black Prince seems out of place. The former GPO provides restaurant facilities which spread out continental fashion by the fountains.

Mill Hill Unitarian Chapel, 1848, successor to the chapel of the Reverend Joseph Priestley, 1674, is resolute Gothic: big crocketed pinnacles and over the West entrance a large 'mixed Gothic' window in the symmetrical front. It even has a mosaic of *Christ the Prophet* by Salviati like the apse of St Peter's. And like St Paul's in New York it is now seriously overbuilt. Make east past the Black Prince 'upholder of the rights of the people in the Good Parliament' with sculptured panels of fighting at Crécy, to *Boar Lane*. In face is the grandly classical former Midland Bank with a green dome and giant Corinthian columns built in 1899. From the corner of Mill Hill going east is a parade of 1870s Gothic buildings by Thomas Ambler. The old Griffin Hotel is a bizarre EE-style in brick with stone dressings and oriel windows; the window shafts and pinnacles lean out between storeys.

After New Station Street is an arcaded Norman/classical building – big arched openings are glazed, the cornices heavily moulded, and windows have ball and rope or egg and dart moulding – its busy cornices and capitals make it seem to totter as you look up. Further east on the north side is a Wren-style church of 1722, *Holy Trinity* by William Etty. Lady Elizabeth Hastings of Ledston Hall promoted it for local cloth merchants who wanted a proprietary church, that is, not open to the public. Nave windows have alternate segmental/elliptical pediments. It is not delicate; big Tuscan pilasters, thick entablature and balustrade with urns. Inside

Leeds Walk 1

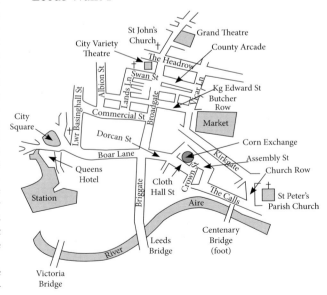

the apsidal sanctuary suggests a basilica. There is good plasterwork around the sturdy Venetian East window with delicate seventeenth-century-style wood carving. The narrow aisles have flat ceilings but the nave has a shallow vault between Corinthian arcades. The first tower and spire by Etty blew down and was replaced by the present effete classical structure by Robert Chantrell in 1839, adding two tiers. Some memorials were brought here from Park Square when St Paul's was demolished in 1905.

Crossing Briggate into Duncan Street is the Yorkshire Building Society, neo-Baroque in ashlar with oriel windows and a deep cornice faced in terracotta tiles. Opposite is a red-brick Italianate building with stone dressings and French mansard.

One's eye is then taken by the **Corn Exchange** – an Italianate oval amphitheatre with two tiers of arched windows, by Cuthbert Brodrick, 1861. Tuscan-columned entrances, the walls of diamond-faced stone blocks create a building of formidable personality. Inside the oval-domed roof spars fan out elliptically from each end with arched and latticed supports – to dizzying effect. The dome produces a clapping echo. Trading in corn is finished but the merchants' offices on the first-floor gallery have been made into little shops. The merchants used to promote their seed here from samples in cases like bookmakers' stands.

Close by in Cloth Hall Street is **White Cloth Hall**, 1775 – single storey of large arches and pediment with a cupola over. The façade only remains of a quadrangular market hall where undyed white cloth was sold. Coloured cloth was sold on Park Row in Coloured Cloth Hall (by City Square). White Cloth Hall transactions were restricted to two days a week and began at the signal of a bell for one and a quarter hours – trading outside these hours resulted in a fine. In nearby Assembly Street is the façade of the *Assembly Rooms* with a tall Venetian window, 1777. All may now assemble in the wine bar there. It was once *the* meeting place for Leeds merchants and local gentry, with card rooms and a grand ballroom. These are remnants of the Georgian town centre.

South of the Assembly Rooms and under the railway bridge is **the Calls**, a still-partly cobbled street where gentlemen's mansions and gardens once bordered the river; *callis* means a beaten path. Here the deep and navigable River Aire (a more compact Pool of London) is bordered by eighteenth- and nineteenth-century warehouses now mostly converted to flats and hotels. Many retain warehouse doors and cranage rising up to six storeys.

HOLY TRINITY, BOAR LANE, LEEDS.

From Langton's Wharf the Centenary Footbridge crosses the river giving views west to the nineteenth-century cast iron Leeds Bridge and east to Crown Point Bridge. North of the footbridge is a rear entrance to **Leeds Parish Church** through the churchyard. St Peter's is ashlar of 1839 in a fourteenth-century style rebuilt by Chantrell to 'purify' the original church. Parts of the South and West walls were retained, refaced, and a new West window formed; the North wall was built off old foundations. But a new chancel of equal length to the nave was ordered by the vicar of Leeds, Dr Hook, for 'the ample and proper administration of choral and cathedral services' – a daily habit which still operates. Dr Hook, in a strongly Dissenting town, declared he 'would have a good service even if he went to prison for it'. He was in the vanguard of the traditionalist fight-back against Dissenters – promoting true Gothic buildings and choral services.

The new order and liturgy combined with Gothic decoration, crocketed pinnacles, window tracery and embattling were designed to confront the Dissenters – with conspicuous success. The once-blackened stone church has three decks of roofs; the tall tower was repositioned midships in the North aisle facing Kirkgate. It makes a good civic entrance. Chantrell achieved intimacy within by many galleries – fulsome Gothic furnishing with cusped tracery panels and crocketed pinnacles. Over half the seats are in the gallery. Some parts are more theatrical than real as, when money ran out, panels and pinnacles were made of iron and plaster. Looking from the entrance a wooden organ screen fills the South transept opposite with fifteenth-century gabled buttresses and tracery painted black, no pipes on show. S. S. Wesley was Hook's organist. The raised, apsidal sanctuary has a glinting mosaic reredos of *Our Lord in Glory with Saints* by G. E. Street; above is a fan-vaulted roof. Southeast in the chancel is a Saxon cross which had been used as filler masonry in the previous church, a modern glass screen in the North transept shows *Jacob's Ladder* by Sally Scott, 1998. The font is thirteenth century with a nineteenth-century crocketed cover, and a later font is by William Butterfield, 1883. Monuments from the previous building are in the South chancel and Lady chapels by John Flaxman, G. G. Scott, Richard Westmacott Jnr and include Chantrell's Gothic 'demonstration piece' which commemorates the Leeds antiquarian Ralph Thoresby. Victorian stained glass, for example by Wilmshirst in the apse, adds to the warm comfortable glow of the interior; though there are seats for 2,000 the church has a wonderful intimacy. It will make a warm cathedral as a focal point of the new Yorkshire super-diocese.

From the parish church *Kirkgate* takes you to the cen-

CITY SQUARE NYMPH, ART NOUVEAU, LEEDS.

tre of town. Here Kirkgate Chambers is part of a large Edwardian building placed adjacent to the **Market Hall** (1857), by Leeming and Leeming, 1903. It is a massive confection of neo-Baroque features: steep mansarded roofs – balustrading on the ridges – octagonal turrets, domes, pyramidal mansards and ascending sets of classical gables. At street level cherub caryatids support each and every shop front. Inside this gigantic iced cake is the 1857 market hall, a cathedral of cast iron and

Oval roof, Corn Exchange, Leeds.

Opposite: Corn Exchange, Cuthbert Brodrick, Leeds.

Overleaf, left: St Peter's Parish Church, Leeds.
right above: Market Hall, 1857, Leeds;
below: Grand Arcade, Leeds.

THE GRAND ARCADE

County Arcade, Leeds.

ustrades. Halfway up *King Edward Street* one of the famous Leeds arcades, *Cross Arcade* (Frank Matcham, 1900), bisects Queen Victoria Street and *County Arcade* at right angles. Queen Victoria Street itself is another neo-Baroque fantasy, roofed over in recent times; where it meets Cross Arcade are gloriously decorated arches with glaze-tiled arcading and balustrading. The date, 1900, is depicted in an Olympic-style linkage of figures. The third parallel street of neo-Baroque, County Arcade, 1900, is the finest, also by Frank Matcham. Neat shops are set between scagliola Ionic columns and Jacobean arches in green, orange fruit tiles decorate the roof balconies; the roof is supported on trussed arches embellished with fruit. Where Cross Arcade meets County Arcade at a central dome allegorical figures of Industry, Justice, Agriculture and Peace mark the crossing.

Emerging into **Briggate** another flurry of neo-Baroque shows the western ends of these unusual streets. Then west of Briggate is the Gothic *Thornton's Arcade* of 1877 with marble colonettes, its tall roof supported on cast iron columns. The façade fronts Briggate, which is itself handsomely pedestrianized. There are buildings of excitement and interest throughout this street. Going north turn left into Swan Street for the *City Variety's Music Hall*, 1865, where Victorian variety performances are held. Its balcony tiers run the full length of the auditorium on cast iron Corinthian columns to a proscenium with Royal Arms. The theatre was rebuilt from the White Swan Coaching Inn Singing Room by Charles Thornton – promoter of the Arcade. It is recently restored.

Up *New Briggate is the Grand Arcade* where enclosed twin streets of shops descend to Vicar Lane. The entrance portal is glaze-tiled Art Nouveau. Next door is the **Grand Theatre and Opera House** – fairytale Gothic. The Grand owes its magnificence to George Corson, a committed Gothic architect, and his assistant, Watson, who knew the best European theatres. A skilful blend of Gothic and classical marks out the interior – memorably the fan vaulting and clustered shafts of the proscenium. Fan vaulting at each corner supports a huge oval moulded ceiling divided into segments and encrusted with plaster medallions; the tiers on cast iron supports curve forward to bowed out boxes – all encrusted in plasterwork reminiscent of the Second Empire in France. Recent restoration has revealed a wealth of original Burmantoft tiles in black, brown and beige with roses and fleur-de-lis, to make a 'hard sound box'. The decoration of deep green, red and gilding is opulent. A full orchestra pit was constructed in 1974 when the Grand became home to Opera North. Next door is the Howard Assembly Room restored and brought back into use in 2009 from the Plaza Cinema, that is, restored to its original form with

glass, open on its east side. Halls radiate from a central octagon where a massive iron clock used to stand – as remains the case in Halifax. The cast iron piers have dragon corbels and the spandrels of the arches contain painted cast iron Leeds Arms with quizzical owls.

Now north up Vicar Lane is a profusion of lavish Edwardian neo-Baroque building. The turreted ends to **King Edward Street** foretell a complete road of neo-Baroque – it is too little celebrated. Every device known to classical seventeenth-century architecture is moulded by terracotta into domes, bulbous oriels, carved pediments, pediments with double ellipse, pyramids and balan oak barrel-vaulted ceiling found behind the Plaza's plasterwork.

St John's Church off New Briggate, 1634, is still Gothic but spatially novel. It was built by John Harrison, a cloth merchant who also endowed almshouses and provided a new grammar school. His portrait is in the church. Standing in a little oasis of green in the city centre the planners have so far avoided overwhelming it. The aisles and windows have embattled cusped lights under flat heads; the tower was also embattled and used to have a Jacobean round-arched entrance with strapwork in the spandrels. No chancel, but double rectangular naves are divided by an arcade where angel corbels support oak roof-trusses. The ceilings are moulded with unpainted seventeenth-century strapwork and animals – rather like pargetting. The East end is marked by a large Jacobean carved-oak screen with Renaissance devices – tapering pilasters, carved tulips, vine leaves and animals. Above are the Royal Arms of James I and Charles I. The pulpit has tiers of Renaissance devices with the Eagle of St John carved on the backboard. Rather surprisingly the original axis was north–south through the arcade until 1807 when it was reordered. The magnificent pews have seventeenth-century bench ends with bulbous finials and carved panels. Outside the sundial reads 'so teach us to number our days that we may apply our hearts unto wisdom'. Norman Shaw was invited to report with a view to rebuilding St John's but he thought it should be restored. The trustees turned to G. G. Scott who was asked to paint it 'black enough' by the architect-in-waiting. But Scott could not destroy 'so singularly beautiful a church'. The President of the RIBA supported Shaw and Scott. The churchwardens, defeated, said its preservation was only 'to gratify the morbid taste of [those who admired] the debased architecture of the seventeenth century'. So they cleared it out, removed plasterwork, put the Royal Arms on the West wall, cut down the pulpit, etc. But later Dean Scott (relative of G. G.) and Shaw reinstated most of what had been removed in 1868.

West of the churchyard is a building with a large window of intersecting tracery. This was Harrison's Charity School, 1815, which trained 80 poor girls whom it dressed in blue ready for domestic service. South into *Lands Lane* is Thornton's buildings, 1873, brick with stone Norman arcading and rich capitals; here is the West portal of Thornton's Arcade, date stone 1877, picked out in gold. Pass *Queen's Arcade*, a touch of Arts and Crafts with cast iron foliated balconies, to *Ship Yard* followed closely by *Angel Yard* and a flavour of nineteenth-century alleys; to the polychromatic brickwork of the **Church Institute** on the corner of *Albion Place*. Here five tall plate-traceried windows under polychro-

County Arcade, Leeds.

matic arches reach into gables alongside a steep roof crowned by a central pinnacle. This was Dr Hook's Anglican education and community care work HQ for the assault on the non-conformists. West in Albion Place at No. 3 is the *Leeds Club*, grandly Italianate (T. Ambler, 1863), it was once immutably black, arched windows at ground floor and elegant four-columned Ionic porch. Inside a string of three coal fireplaces used to warm the

Overleaf, left: St Paul's House, warehouse, Thomas Ambler, 1878;
right: Grand Theatre, Leeds.

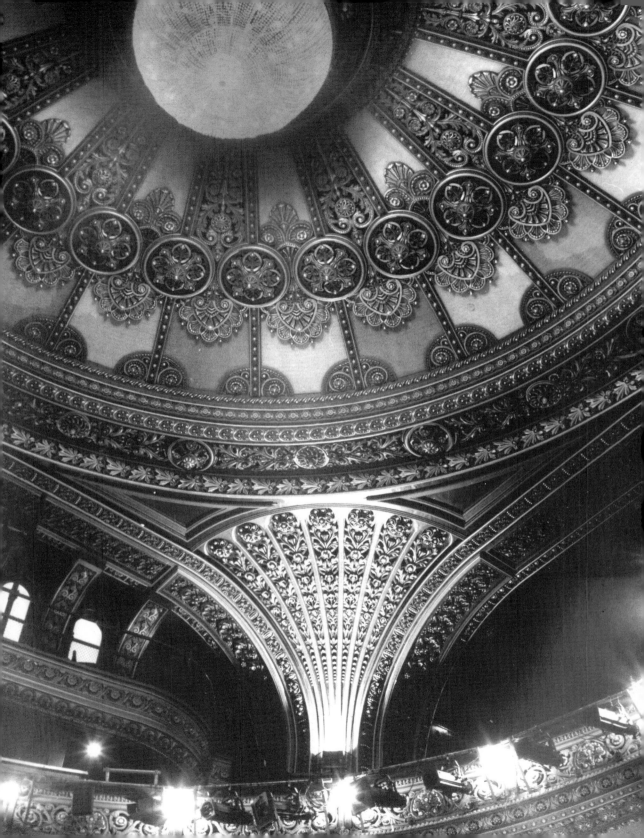

SIC·DEVS·DILEXIT·MVNDVM

CHRISTOPHER BRAMLEY

woolmasters as they chatted. A grand staircase with cast iron balusters rises to a ballroom and billiard room. Next door at No. 1 is the eighteenth-century pedimented town mansion of William Hey, 1794, Chief Surgeon and a founder of Leeds General Infirmary. Opposite is the former County and High Court, 1870, brick with stone appointments. West are neo-Baroque offices in ashlar sandstone. They extend around the corner into *Albion Street* where stands the onetime Leeds & Yorkshire Fire Assurance, a fortissimo Italianate building of 1852: its attached columns have capitals with ram's head volutes. Projecting cornices are carved with garlands of flowers and heads from antiquity. Looking down **Commercial Street** east is the *Leeds Library*, 1808, Grecian, stucco with attached Ionic pilasters. Still going as a proprietary library it was founded in 1768. The first-floor reading room has nineteenth-century iron galleries and spiral staircases. It is quite a survivor. Go west into Bond Street then south down Lower Basinghall Street giving a side view of the former GPO in City Square, to the well-buttressed Mill Hill Chapel and so return to the station.

Leeds City Centre – walk 2 (about 4 hours) Begin at City Station and City Square. From the Queen's Hotel adjacent to City Square along *Quebec Street* is the spectacular **Leeds and County Liberal Club**, neo-Baroque friezes in ruby terracotta; arcades of intricate moulded tiles on piers, 1890. The Liberals dominated Leeds at this time. Inside, a grand circular staircase is lit by arched stained glass windows showing the arms of Yorkshire boroughs. On the front of the building is an octagonal tower and balcony from which Lloyd George spoke. It is now a hotel. Cutting through to *King Street* is the rear of the Metropole Hotel, another spectacular red neo-Baroque building of 1897 in terracotta, the rear door is surmounted by a Leeds Arms – very beady-eyed owls. At the front are bulbous oriels of cross-mullioned windows; there is prolific foliage and cherubs; its entrance is in a big drum-like bay. The cupola was taken from a former Cloth Hall built on this site in 1868. The *fin de siècle* ballroom is arcaded and has a tunnel-vaulted ceiling, 1899. Also in King Street is the former Bank of England, 1969, but now offices; a satisfying modern design of granite facing and bronze, with storeys jettied out as they ascend. Turning north over Quebec Street and in *Infirmary Street* is the Gothic and extremely grand former **Yorkshire Penny Bank**, 1894. Behind iron railings on the ground floor is an arcade of big arched

Opposite: St John's Church, Leeds.

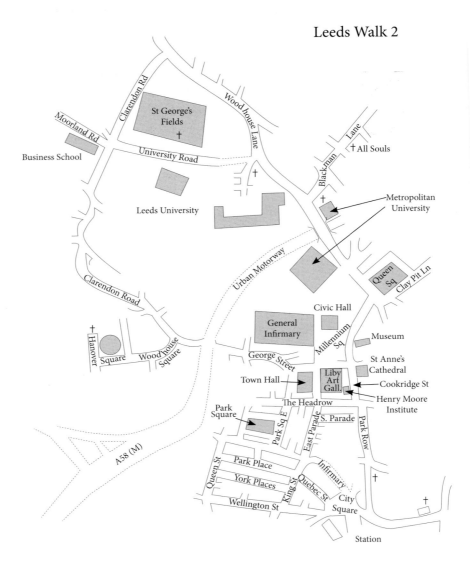

windows, then two floors of cross-mullioned windows and sharply gabled dormers; on the first-floor balcony are four large carved gryphons, each a singular personality. Right of the bulbous Romanesque doorway are more emblematic gryphons; gryphons support the letters 'YPB'; gryphons fly from the entrance arch, and gryphons fly from the tower balcony. Elegant cylinder chimneys are banked six or three or quatrefoil, reminiscent of Burleigh. Resuming north from *King Street* into *East Parade* is the neo-Norman Britannia Building, 1840, with arcades of round-arched windows, shafted, carved capitals. Next door is East Parade Chambers, 1899, with ivory faience tiling, gently Norman in theme,

big wooden bays of windows. Then a row of red-brick Georgian houses with stone Doric porches and a pedimented town mansion – rebuilt in new brick. Then a Venetian Gothic house of three narrow gables with big arched windows. Opposite in *South Parade* at No. 6 is an Art Deco building with symmetrical pedimented doors in marble. At the end of South Parade in **Park Row** is Park Row House, fairytale light neo-Baroque, delicately composed of brick and ivory faience-tiled windows; it is a lighter Alfred Waterhouse design originally for the Prudential. Also in Park Row is a building that looks Post Modern but was built by Waterhouse in 1898 – striking bands of grey stone, red brick and yellow terracotta; modern openings in the mansard. Just to the left is the original nineteenth-century Bank of England in Yorkshire, 1862, late classical, very grand porches of big modillioned cornices over Doric columns – the main entrance is to Park Row.

Further north and crossing The Headrow into Cookridge Street is the **Roman Catholic Cathedral of St Anne**, J. H. Eastwood, Arts and Crafts Gothic, of 1904, intriguingly built with chapels off the aisles of the short nave. The East end rises theatrically to an altar behind which is the Bishop's throne and gallery of choir stalls. The reredos shows the 'Coronation of Our Lady' in gilded carved figures. The window tracery is rather coy with label stops of fruit in the Lady Chapel. Excellent Art Nouveau doors. A cathedral in a small space. In the Lady Chapel is the reredos from the former St Anne's designed in 1842 by A. W. N. Pugin. The altar comes from St Mary's, 1794. There is a shrine to St Urban whose relics were brought here from Italy in 1904. The three-stage tower with belfry rises directly from the street on the north side.

On the corner of Great George Street and Cookridge Street is the Electric Press, a large Italianate former printing works, big arches and a grand cornice. Directly north in **Millennium Square** is the former *Mechanics Institute* now the *Leeds City Museum*. It is a starkly repellent building by Cuthbert Brodrick, 1868, said to be of French inspiration and was once the Civic Theatre. Fat rusticated pilasters support external first-floor balconies, heavy cast iron balustrades to each window. Windows rise into a scalloped arch with plain stone before a huge cornice. Cuthbert Brodrick is never warm but this bold essay is extreme. The museum has returned the former theatre to the original lecture hall format. The square itself has become a successful outdoor venue of bars and cafés.

On the north side the *Civic Hall*, 1933, is on an awkward site but the thin columned portico seems unsatisfactory. Its pinched look is accentuated by gold-painted clocks on brackets either side of the building. Two towers of reducing classical stages rise like graveyard monuments to obelisks surmounted by golden Leeds owls. The architect was E. Vincent Harris who also designed Sheffield City Hall. An irregular building on an irregularly proportioned site (east and west differ as well as north and south) forces one's eye to question an ostensible classical composition. The banqueting hall, however, is 'regular', made up like a Georgian hall with oak panelling, fluted pilasters, overdoors and galleries: a comfortable dining room. The council chamber is tiered like a lecture theatre. Continuing north up Cookridge Street and across Woodhouse Lane is eighteenth-century **Queen's Square**, cowering under new development. On

LEEDS METROPOLITAN UNIVERSITY, THE 'RUSTY PIN'.

the west side is a choice Georgian street of brick houses with stone Doric porches – the middle ones (of two and a half storeys) have elliptical pediments flying between the capitals of the door columns. The rest of the square is mostly two storey. It retains nineteenth-century gas lamps.

Walk from here to the universities up *Woodhouse Lane*. The former BBC studios in the Friends Meeting House of 1868 has Tuscan columns and pediment, and is now part of the *Metropolitan University*. Close by is the *Rusty Pin*, an idiosyncratic sky scraper of 23 storeys by Feilden Clegg Bradley, tawny-red and asymmetric in

ROGER STEVENS BUILDING, LEEDS UNIVERSITY.

outline from large angular bevels in its corners. Then up the hill on the right are multifarious Georgian brick houses, some two some three storeys, many with altered door casements – one of rather alarming proportion. Down Blackman Lane to the north is a large G. G. Scott (EE) church, All Souls, 1876. One of his last churches and very impressive. The adjacent vicarage is like a palace. The Sunday School is massive – no expense was spared. Very much in view and the eye catcher of **Leeds University** is the Parkinson Building, 1950 (but designed in the 1930s). It is a monument in Portland stone with a 1930s combination of flat geometry and classical adornment. Alternate first-floor windows have a pediment; the grand portico stands above steps and has large fluted Ionic columns. Its big tower is square and capped by a 'bell' storey with classical decoration. *Emmanuel Church*, next to it, with rigid rows of EE windows looks joyful by comparison. West of here the original *Yorkshire College of the Victoria University* is by Water-

house, 1877, in brick and stone Gothic. The Yorkshire College of Science became part of Victoria University in 1887 and became the University of Leeds in 1904. The original buildings behind *Parkinson* face south over lawns and trees and are more user friendly than the windswept frontage to Woodhouse Lane. Not easily accessible behind the Parkinson is the Brotherton library. It lies under a massive concrete dome supported by concentric circles of columns; the bronze capitals display nominal acanthus. The outer circle is of Swedish green marble, slightly lurid. Waterhouse's more traditional Great Hall shows a gable with big Perp traceried window; banded stone and brick above the window and in the flanking towers; pinnacle shafts corbel out of the tower angles and rise above the roof line. The towers have slated pyramid roofs. The Great Hall forms part of the courtyard of *Cloth Workers' Court* where the School of Textiles is situated – endowed by the Cloth Workers' Guild in the City of London. The unity of the Gothic terrace is maintained by a further tower, west (1912), also with a slate pyramid roof, big window four storeys high and showing the Arms of the university – by Waterhouse's son Paul. His grand staircase is lined with green tiles. As elsewhere this university is composed of disparate styles ranging from Gothic to erratic concrete. A modern building of note is Chancellor's Court, which progressively steps out; conjecturally it might express freedom and academic liberality (1969/70) but the truth is that it is merely the obverse concrete shell of a series of lecture theatres. Other buildings of interest are the sinuous steel and glass Marjorie Arnold Ziff Building and falling tiers of concrete in the Roger Stevens Building. Further west opposite Lyddon Terrace – a street of good Georgian houses all within the campus – is a large green open space, formerly the **General Cemetery**. There are Victorian monuments and a mausoleum with Greek Ionic columns. In the Beatles' *Sergeant Pepper* album we learned 'The Hendersons will all be there, late of *Pablo Fanques* fair' – the words came from an antique poster for the fair – Pablo Fanques was buried here close to the mausoleum. A Grecian gateway to the cemetery of thick Doric columns and pediment is now adjacent to the back door of the Engineering Departments and leads to bottled gas stores.

Going west again is the former *Leeds Grammar School*, 1859, designed by E. M. Barry in a rather elegant EE style. Arched windows rise into gables and protrude from the steep slated roof. It is now the University Business School. Opposite is Woodhouse Moor, a park, once the only Leeds park, where a statue of the Duke of Wellington stands. He was first put in front of the Town Hall in 1855, later joined by Peel to be consorts to a statue of Queen Victoria. They were moved here in 1937 when The Headrow was widened. A small extension to the walk takes you to Hyde Park Picture House, 1914: an early cinema with Ionic columns in faience tiling, terracotta frieze and a Dutch gable. The mosaic floor and ticket kiosk are original, also the low lighting in gas which always burns to ensure modesty in the auditorium. It has an Arts and Crafts staircase and good moulded plasterwork. Houses nearby, for example Pearson Grove and Terrace, demonstrate robust early back-to-back terraces, very prevalent still in Leeds.

At the corner of the university on Clarendon Road is The Library, a serious neo-Baroque building, once a police station, now a public house and a dubious alibi for the work shy. Clarendon Road to the south passes a number of buildings now within the university. Little Woodhouse Hall off cobbled Hyde Terrace is a good mansion of 1741 with canted bays. Inside is a wonderful circular staircase with cast iron balusters under a dome of swirling crossing tracery. Access is difficult. Spring-

MAJORIE ARNOLD ZIFF BUILDING, LEEDS UNIVERSITY.

field Mount Priory, Tudor brick-collegiate by Temple Moore from 1910, was a theology students' college for the Mirfield Community of the Resurrection. *Fairbairn House* is a brick and stone Grecian villa, 1841 – fluted Corinthian columns and a balustraded roof. Built by Mayor Sir Peter Fairbairn, a textile engineer, who entertained Queen Victoria here in 1858 during the opening of the Town Hall. Clarendon Road contains Georgian houses and new in-scale university buildings of brick and stone appropriate to this conservation area. At the

Overleaf, left: GRAND THEATRE, CARSON'S GOTHIC, LEEDS.
right: GENERAL INFIRMARY, GEORGE GILBERT SCOTT, 1863, LEEDS.

foot of the hill Woodhouse Square is a mid-nineteenth-century terrace of brick and painted stone. A bronze sculpture dated 1868 commemorates Sir Peter Fairbairn. North of the square is a row of nineteenth-century terraced houses built in the large garden of a pedimented mansion, Claremont (1772), by Corson for Dr Heaton, a founder of the university. From here along Denison Road is Hanover Square, Leeds' largest square. Denison Hall, 1786, by William Lindley (a pupil of John Carr) is a grand Georgian mansion of bow windows, garlanded pediment over the central three bays divided by Ionic pilasters. Its park was developed during the nineteenth century.

Signs to the 'Clarendon Wing' of the General Infirmary show the way over the A58(M) by bridge to Great George Street and *St George's Church* by John Clark, 1836. In ashlar with tall lancet windows it stands on a basement crypt which opens to a terrace. It was a church refuge for the unemployed in the 1930s. Steps to it rise from the street. The West door is set under a flamboyant ogee-crocketed arch. The painting over the altar is *He liveth to make intercession* by C. W. Cope, 1841. The tower parapet, pinnacles and lead spire have all been replaced recently after destruction in a gale. Behind the church is the former Leeds University School of Medicine, in Arts and Crafts Tudor, 1894. Immediately east is *Leeds General Infirmary* in G. G. Scott's Venetian Gothic, 1863. Mostly brick, its pointed windows are banded with brick and blackened stone. The prominent portico has banded arches on marble shafts; there are arcades of shafted windows and towers with little French pyramidal roofs. Scott advised the committee that a hospital should have medieval architecture, but a contemporary thought his styles of the thirteenth to fifteenth centuries were 'mingled with a boldness which must astonish the scrupulous adherents of precedent'. Its medieval look belied a modern plan of wards off a central court. Passing Oxford Place note the Methodist Church which is as Baroque as an Italian Catholic church; the original chapel of 1835 with round-headed windows is subsumed within.

Following Great George Street to the back of the *Town Hall* is the exuberant Victoria Family and Commercial Hotel, 1865 – Gothic shafted marble entrance and first-floor windows. Inside the stair balustrade is wood and cast iron; rich Victorian furnishings include old tiles in roomy wood-carved booths; a bar backstand has stained glass, and two massive spiral columns extend from the bar to the ceiling. Further east the Leeds

School Board building, 1880, by George Corson flanks the Town Hall. It has good Italian detail and carving but the first floor strays to Beaux Arts. On Calverley Street is Corson's Italianate Library and Museum, 1878. Inside is a spectacular Byzantine staircase with lively carved dogs. Calverley Street leads to *The Headrow* where the immense theatrical creation of Cuthbert Brodrick's Town Hall (1852–58) is overwhelming. The money and success of Leeds in cloth wanted to shout. Brodrick's refined lengthy colonnades of Corinthian columns, bold cornices and proportionate urn-capped balustrade, won the competition. It was a lot of building for £35,000. The tower was not included until 1857: it is like a town hall (or mausoleum) in itself – a colonnaded storey with six Corinthian columns and balustrade repeating what lay below; then the crowning clock storey with classical pinnacles and melon-shaped dome. Ruskin wanted to 'crucify the snobs or charlatans in architecture who could put such an abhorrence as that tower upon a Town Hall of fair Roman composite architecture'. Brodrick's success came from his manipulation of mass and form to create dramatic tension; his daring handling of form, like Wren, was his genius. Buildings in Australia, South Africa and America copied it, including Philadelphia City Hall crowned with a statue of William Penn. Inside, Leeds Town Hall is hugely grand and rich in a Roman way: giant arches spring from attached columns under a barrel-vaulted ceiling; capitals on the columns display the Leeds owls and woolpacks.

East along The Headrow is the Henry Moore Centre for Sculpture which displays and researches sculpture. The blank black granite face put on this old building does not seem appropriate, but that may be the point. Further east The Headrow has big 1930s blocks by Sir Reginald Blomfield. As chairman of the design competition he had rejected the local contenders before taking on the commission himself. West of the Town Hall go south into Park Square East. *Park Square* is a well-maintained Georgian square, houses built between 1788 and 1810. It was the site of the medieval park of Leeds Manor – and was set out for professional homes. Houses are brick, of two or three storeys, some with pediments: the bold elevations and tower of the Town Hall rise above them. St Paul's Church on the south side of the square was demolished in the early twentieth century and its memorials taken to Holy Trinity. To the southwest is St Paul's House, 1878, by Thomas Ambler, built as a warehouse and cloth works for John Barran, designer of mass-produced clothes. He was Mayor and Liberal MP from 1876 to 1885. Ambler's Moorish design with red-tiled architraves and window heads of terracotta is complemented by red brick. The fourth-floor arcades are Arabic with corner minarets. The

Opposite: LEEDS TOWN HALL '... THAT ABHORRENT TOWER', RUSKIN.

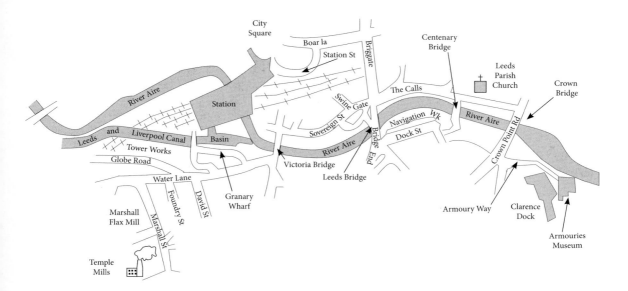

entrance arch is 'pinked' and formed of moulded tiles. It glows red in the evening sun. South of here in York Place and Park Place are more Georgian houses, Gothic houses, Gothic warehouses and Georgian town mansions, for example 18 Park Place, 1788, brick with flat Ionic pilasters and prominent pediment. Go south to **Wellington Street** where there are some lavish Gothic warehouses. No. 58 Wellington Street is Waterloo House, 1868 – Italian Gothic in stone and red brick with polychromatic brickwork and stout pink granite columns. Although the mansard windows are a recent spoiler below them is a continuous arcade of round-arched windows. It is quite spectacular. At Apsley House, 1903, George Corson engineered a baroque warehouse – arched windows, pilasters and canted bays – all in brick and terracotta tiling. Off Northern Street to the south is the *Truck Lifting Tower*, 1846, built to transfer trucks between the railway systems in Leeds which ran at different levels. It is of stone and rises 32ft. Now looking lonely, it is disconnected from any railway – its purpose is a mystery for many people. From here the return to the station is only a step.

Opposite: KING EDWARD STREET ENTRANCE, NEO-BAROQUE, LEEDS.

Leeds City Centre – walk 3 (about 2 hours) Industrial Centre. Turn east out of Leeds City Station on New Station Street. After the bridge over Neville Street follow the railway arches by descending steps. Shortly, facing you on **Briggate** is a good early Georgian mansion built in two halves which have settled unevenly. The central bays with bevelled quoins project forward; good rubbed-brick arches with stone keystones. To the left is a little Art Deco shop, then well-modelled neo-Baroque examples. First the Yorkshire Metropolitan Housing Association with stylized central tower (but restored in GRP). Then more Jacobean neo-Baroque with triumphal attic storey: big dormer with rounded pediment and five ball finials. Then a brick house of 1894 – nice carving over the first-floor window of what appears to be a Mr Punch figure, his wife holding garlands; in the wide pediment at the attic storey further carving of arabesques etc.; the carving is on tightly jointed red brickwork. Opposite this on the west side of Briggate an unusual building, once a jeweller's, displays two clocks and a weather vane, the *Time Ball Buildings*, 1865. The 'hours' of the clock describe 'John Dyson 25 and 26' – it is very large. To its left a large oriel window divided and filled with stained glass ascends three storeys to a dome. The dome has a pole with a 'Greenwich ball' which used to drop at 1 o'clock. A fine original Victorian interior of etched

and stained glass partitions and cabinets was formerly for the sale of clocks. At the rear is a baroque gallery under a coved ceiling of gold-painted arabesques. Restaurant.

Walk south under the railway bridge and on the corner of Swinegate is an old Victorian hotel, the former Golden Lion Hotel, with strong Italianate elevations of bracketed arched windows, polychromatic stone and brick, and very strong modillioned cornice. The interior has been pulled out but the iron staircase remains. Going south on Bridge End to **Leeds Bridge** brings a view of riverside warehouses. The bridge has a cast iron parapet of concentric and intersecting circles centred on white Yorkshire roses which shine like diamonds in the sun; six old lanterns on the parapet still illumine your way. In the centre of the east side is a deeply profiled cast iron Leeds Arms.

From the bridge the often fast-moving River Aire reflects tall balconied warehouses with St Peter's Church tower rising above Calls Landing. The river was made navigable by the Aire Navigation Company in 1700. Immediately south of the bridge is Leeds Bridge House, 1875, whose corner frontage has wavy string courses between tiers of arched windows with novel top balustrade – corbelled-out. It was built as a temperance hotel. Fronting the river itself is a Georgian building whose plaque records the Band of Hope Movement (teetotal) founded here in 1847. Louis le Prince also made the world's first moving pictures here in 1888. Now return to the north end of the bridge and go east by the river. At Call Lane (for the Calls) turn immediately right to the towpath, which is precarious in places. Through gates is a fine six-storey warehouse built over barge entrances in the basement. You must then temporarily leave the river. The next warehouse is *Calls Landing*, followed by a rake of gables with a projecting timber hut four storeys high – to guide the warehouse cranes. Then cross the river by the Centenary Footbridge from The Calls and go east by the river to Brewery Wharf and the **Royal Armouries Museum** at Crown Point Bridge. The bridge, widened in the twentieth century, has layers of iron lattice in its spandrels and a cast iron parapet, fine engineering; into Armouries Way and the modern complex around *Clarence Dock*. This has been redeveloped with balconied flats in the Docklands idiom. Pleasure boats occupy the dock which is connected to the river. Here is another modern footbridge over the Aire and some large red-brick former flax mills are to the east with banks of windows. The new octagonal lock keeper's tower in grey brick mirrors the adjacent glass and stone octagonal tower of the Armouries Museum, by Derek Walker, 1996, to show armour stored in the Tower of London. Its large, banded, grey marble tower plinth contrasts with red brick warehouses; there are six storeys of glazed octagon showing pikes, swords and staves fixed to the tower's white octagonal core. A visit here should allow a further two hours. Returning via the towpath west are fine views of river-front warehouses with Chantrell's towers of St Peter's and Holy Trinity at Boar Lane riding above.

Opposite Centenary Bridge (1992) is the old coal wharf, replaced by flats in 1991. By **Crown Point Bridge** is Turton's Provender Mill built on the site of Crown Point Oil Mill in 1876. Keeping on the south of the river, Dock Street takes you west past nineteenth-century housing and warehousing to the Adelphi Hotel at the south end of Leeds Bridge. The Adelphi Hotel is neo-Baroque and retains a good Edwardian interior. Another route along Navigation Walk closer to the river brings you past the Aire Navigation Company's flyboat warehouse – a wide elliptical arch close to the water where the flyboats were kept. These were fast passenger craft towed at some speed by horses in the eighteenth century along the new navigation. Going over Leeds Bridge transfer to the north towpath of the River Aire past more converted warehouses – noting the fine gabled warehouse with transit doors up its entire six storeys. Cross south over the elliptically arched stone Victoria Bridge to **Granary Wharf**, an eighteenth-century stone-built warehouse of four storeys with mullioned windows and arched transit openings. It was built in 1777 as the Terminal Warehouse for the Leeds and Liverpool Canal for smaller vessels to cross the Pennines. The pound is often full of narrow boats. At the head of the pound is a stone arched bridge and an early Canal Office, also in stone. The bridge carries a sign under the Motor Car Acts 1896 and 1903 prohibiting Heavy Motor Cars. To the north over the embanked railway the skyline of Leeds appears almost entirely modern, but a sad intruder in the curtilage of the pound is a large circular modern tower which is disproportionate and alien.

To the west, three towers remind one of Italy. One is a tall square chimney. Another with polychromatic brick arches and octagonal lantern is also a chimney – built in 1864 after Lambertini Tower in Verona. The third, with tall arched windows within blank arcading, was based on Florence Cathedral campanile, built in 1899, and is actually a dust-extraction shaft. They were part of *Tower Works* off Globe Road. Now take Water Lane to the south, and in Marshall Street are eighteenth-century brick warehouses and Marshall's Mills, a seven-storeyed, pedimented flax mill. To the left *Temple Mill,*

Opposite: TIME BALL BUILDINGS, 1865, LEEDS.

TOWER WORKS, LEEDS.

a flax-spinning mill designed by Joseph Bonomi, 1838, is a copy of the famous temple at Edfu, Egypt. The two buildings have battered profiles and enormous coved entablatures – one with lotus-leaf capitals on engaged columns and the other with a loggia of columns with papyrus capitals – there was originally a chimney in the form of Cleopatra's Needle. The mill covered two acres. The roofs are shallow brick arches on cast iron columns and covered by soil as insulation – the grass on it was grazed by sheep. Bonomi spent ten years studying temples in Egypt; Egyptian architecture had a small vogue at this time, compare cemeteries in Sheffield and Bradford.

Return to the station via Water Lane. Foundry Street represents the former hamlet of **Holbeck** and early industry in Leeds. Only fragments of the foundry of 1797 remain today – most of the machinery installed in Leeds

mills came from here. The plaque dedicated to Matthew Murray (1765–1856) commemorates the pioneer of flax-spinning machinery and steam engines. There should be a statue of Matthew Murray in City Square rather than Watt, who was not a Leeds man. The gabled building dated 1797 is the oldest surviving engineering works in the UK where all components were made and assembled. The Dry Sand Foundry has three arches on Doric stone pillars; the original open roof has kingposts. It is home for the Tourist Board for Yorkshire. Behind it is a warren of brick courts. Park Mills, the first mechanized cloth mill, 1792, is close by. A gothic experience

Opposite: TEMPLE MILL, BONOMI, LEEDS.

ARMLEY MILLS MUSEUM, LEEDS.

to regain the station is to walk under it through an undercroft of rushing water from the weir of the River Aire which is known as the Dark Arches.

Car tour of Outer Leeds Taking the Bradford road, A65, from the city centre turn left up Viaduct Road at a huge stone railway viaduct of 21 arches across the Aire Valley. The road crosses the Leeds and Liverpool Canal by a fine cast iron balustraded bridge, then turn right to *Armley Mills*, an industrial museum and preserved factory of Benjamin Gott. Of stone, four storeys high, it was built with iron joists on cast columns to reduce fire risk. The mill was powered by a water wheel for fulling; it was rebuilt in 1805 as a wool mill. The tall tapering column of a chimney was for steam power brought in 1840. The steam engine shown is called Fiona – a horizontal, tandem compound-steam engine built by Wood-

house and Mitchell of Brighouse about 1887. The power was transmitted by a system of shafts and pulleys throughout the mill. Now a museum, it shows wool making on an industrial scale: first, sorting wool by a carding machine – great spikey rollers draw the wool fibres out uniformly ready for spinning. Richard Arkwright's original Spinning Jenny was developed by Samuel Crompton into a mule; but a further mule called a Slubbing Billy was used throughout Leeds. The mules could be up to 150ft long with as many as 1,300 spindles all producing yarn. The cast iron power looms then wove fabric by raising the healds and lowering alternate threads (the weft and the warp) to allow the shuttle to fly through the gaps alternately. That was followed by burling and mending, carried out by women and girls in a well-lit room at sloping mending tables to pick out burrs and knots. There is also an exhibition of multiple tailoring developed in Leeds by Montague Burton. The remains of the water wheels are in the basement and there the smell of hot oil leads to Fiona. The buildings here are connected by a steam railway which operates from time to time and shows locomotives produced by the Hunslet Foundry in the early nineteenth century. The manager's house is open and furnished for the 1860s. (Allow 2 hours for the museum.)

Returning to Viaduct Road, immediately ahead is a neo-Baroque mill of 1888. Turn right past *Armley Canal Road Station*, left into Armley Road and in a mile right for *Armley Prison*. The picturesque castle of 1847 by Perkin and Elisha Backhouse, prominent on the hill west of Leeds, belied its function. Castellated octagonal towers and groups of arched windows lead to a symmetrical entrance with battered towers and projecting parapets. The Leeds Arms signifies it was once the town gaol. The severity of the architecture was doubtless meant to induce a certain chill. Also prominent on this hillside is the Parish Church of *Armley, St Bartholomew*, 1872 (on Wesley Road). It is EE on a grand scale with a clerestory of twin lancets twice the height of the aisles; the West tower is shouldered by gables four storeys high – more lancets and a rose window in the gable. The tower is truly enormous with a big 'bell' lancet stage showing green louvres (no bells in the belfry). The pinnacles grow at the corners from below the bell stage rising to conical pinnacles; the short spire is leaded. With shafted EE doorways it is like a major chunk of a cathedral. Tremendous coherence and power. Built at the height of industrial prosperity, it replaced a chapel which was adjacent. It is equally lofty within. Faced in limestone with quatrefoil piers it is grandly furnished: the font with red and black marble arcading, a pulpit of alabaster and marble, and a terrific organ case for the largest UK Schulze organ filling the North transept. The organ was built for Thomas Kennedy at his bizarre mansion, Meanwood Towers, where it was so large it had to have its own 'shed' in the garden. It came here to the largest church in Leeds via St Peter's, Leeds. Benjamin Gott, the owner of Armley Mills, who died in 1839, is commemorated – taking his ease reclining in a rather comfortable old suit.

Now returning along Armley Road you will see remnants of old mills and chimneys in Armley together with terraces of rosy red back-to-back houses with blackened lintels. Benjamin Gott's mansion is in the middle of the golf course, gained by turning right at Armley Ridge Road; and today is a slight disappointment as the first of many manufacturers' Grecian mansions in West Yorkshire, for example, Roundhay and Gledhow. Robert Smirke added the Ionic portico to the former house together with wings whose removal makes it look mean.

Humphrey Repton advised on the site and was impressed with the 'panoramic stare', it looked up the Aire Valley towards Kirkstall Abbey (then recently painted by John Turner). But it was not only a romantic view but included the Gott factories. Later nineteenth-century pictures show the valley thick with mills and chimneys. From Gott's Mansion return to Stanningley Road, continue west into Lower Town Street, *Bramley*, for St Peter's church, left, up Hough Lane. The steeple remains with an unusual clock storey of gables on the tower below the spire, 1861, by Perkin Backhouse. The nave and aisles are chopped short – a tiled roof like a pyramid covers the now square building. From here travel straight over Lower Town Street into Waterloo and continue along Outgang Lane to descend the hill to the River Wharfe. Here an elegant tower of blank arches and brick chimney stands at the foot of the hill. This was the *Kirkstall Brewery*, 1860; it has ceased brewing and is now part of the campus of Leeds Metropolitan University. From here it is only a short distance to *Kirkstall Abbey*, described elsewhere.

From the Abbey Museum you can visit a late (1935) W. D. Caroë church on the Hawksworth council estate by extending west up Spen Lane, left into Cragside Road. It is a cut above the quality of the housing and is faced in knapped flint. The spatial organization by progressive narrowing toward the East End under a single-pitched roof is clever. A gable-roofed belcote like a chimney is at the southeast where the vestry might be. From Kirkstall turn east on the A65 and B6157 via Kirkstall Lane to *Headingley*, passing the famous Yorkshire County Cricket Club grounds on your right before coming to the village of Headingley at the junction with Otley Road (A660). This well-treed area with grand houses was much favoured by Victorian industrialists. Here is a mighty church by J. L. Pearson, 1884, St Michael. The thirteenth-century Gothic of Truro Cathedral is used. Tall, with a clerestory rising high above the North aisle, its steeply pitched red-tiled roof contrasts with ashlar gritstone; the tower is capped by a tall spire with the architect's characteristic pinnacles. EE porch with shafts and saints in niches in the gables; West door with dog-tooth and West window in plate tracery. Verticality is emphasized in the tower by tall thin buttresses and lancets. The nave and chancel are of equal length; although plain within it is bold and lofty, knit together by transverse stone arches over the nave below a wooden roof. Gilded reredos by Temple Moore; the pulpit and font are richly carved in marble and alabaster.

Follow the A660 north for a few hundred yards before turning east on the B6157 to Meanwood. Holy Trinity on Church Lane is a big church of 1849 by William Railton: many tall lancets, crossing tower, the broach

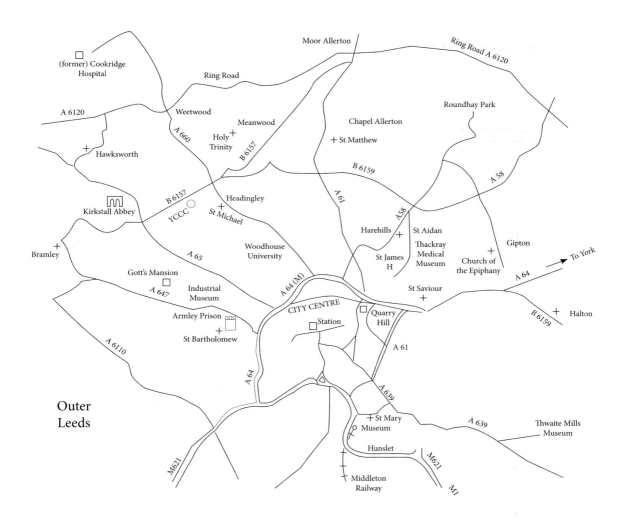

(former) Cookridge
Hospital

Ring Road

A 6120

Weetwood

Moor Allerton

Ring Road A 6120

Roundhay Park

A 660

Meanwood

Chapel Allerton

Holy
Trinity

+ St Matthew

B 6157

B 6159

Hawksworth

+

B 6157

Headingley

A 61

A 58

Kirkstall Abbey

YCCC

+
St Michael

A 58

Harehills

St Aidan

Gipton

Bramley

+

A 65

Woodhouse
University

St James
H

Thackray
Medical
Museum

Church of
the Epiphany

To York

Gott's Mansion

A 647

Industrial
Museum

A 64 (M)

St Saviour

A 64

B 6159

+ Halton

Armley Prison

+
St Bartholomew

CITY CENTRE

Station

Quarry
Hill

A 61

A 6110

A 64

A 639

Outer
Leeds

+ St Mary
Museum

A 639

Thwaite Mills
Museum

M621

Hunslet

M621

M1

+ Middleton
Railway

Opposite: Schulze organ, St Bartholomew,
Leeds.

spire sits on a pinched-in tower and seems ill-at-ease – compare especially Thomas Rickman's spire at Oulton. The steeply raked nave roof displays trusses. It was financed by the Becketts of Meanwood Hall who have a mausoleum in the churchyard – it has an Eastern flavour – pyramid roof and gabled niches. The Hall in Woodlea Park, north, was built by Thomas Denison (same family) in 1762, but was given heavier classical embellishment in 1834 for Christopher Beckett. The porch has fluted Ionic columns and cornice. Its status was demeaned in the popular mind when it became a mental hospital; now its park has been developed for housing which forms a maze around it. Meanwood Towers, just to the east, is now also imprisoned by houses but surprisingly still exists as a flamboyant Gothic tower built for a textile engineer by E. W. Pugin in 1867. Traceried oriel windows, gables, tall mansard roof with spikey dormers, and offensively tall chimneys display the mid-nineteenth-century Leeds taste for Gothic. Within is a marble staircase, stained glass and Gothic fireplaces. Then at Tannery Square in Meanwood is the Beckett Institute, Arts and Crafts mullioned windows, built by William Beckett. On Church Lane is the Tannery itself which has luckily ceased operations. Stone built with cart entrance, the tanning drying floors are now flats.

From Green Road go east, doglegging over the B6157 via the B6159 to the A61 for the premier suburbs of Leeds. Turn left for *Chapel Allerton*, right at Stainbeck Lane and left into Harrogate Road. Once described as the prettiest village in Leeds, it hosts many manufacturers' mansions around Allerton Park. Off Wood Lane is a church by G. F. Bodley, 1897. St Matthew's has a detached tower with an emphatic slender stair turret in the midst of one elevation. The crenellated tower has a conical roof. Verticality is emphasized by flat, thin buttresses framing the tower throughout its height. Conventional tall Dec arcades in the nave and chancel are not distinct. The Art Nouveau Dec windows sacrifice tracery in the centre lights to emphasize height. The roof is a timbered barrel vault – over the chancel screen is an organ loft. A capacious yet intimate interior is modernized with a semicircle of choir stalls west of the chancel. It is an arresting modern church in a traditional mould. Back at the junction of Harrogate Road and Town Street is one of many Leeds neo-Baroque libraries, and on Stainbeck Lane a pub, the Mustard Pot, an early Georgian house has the coat of arms of *Henson* above a bolection fireplace. The overmantel frame has a picture of the room as a private house. Nearby Allerton Hall dates from the eighteenth century but has spread somewhat unevenly since.

Then south down Harrogate Road to the junction with Harehills Lane are a number of nineteenth-century classical mansions for manufacturers. With slight exaggeration this area is known as Little Switzerland. To the north is Gledhow Grove, a large Grecian house well sited on a hill – handsome two-storey Ionic portico, pilasters at the corners and a deep cornice. It was built in 1840 by John Clark for a flax manufacturer, John Hives. Not only neglected but its garden has been stuffed with new housing in a most disrespectful way. What excuse do the planners give? In Potternewton Park, a little further east, is another Grecian house built for a wool merchant, James Brown, in 1817; gloomy, ashlar, tall windows, it has a semicircular porch on Ionic columns; balustrading over the cornice to hide the roof, now called Potternewton Mansion, again neglected. Returning to the junction of Harrogate Road and Harehills Lane take Gledhow Lane to the east; it drops through *Gledhow Valley* (a linear park which follows a deep wooded valley and stream). At the far side of the valley one comes to Roundhay Hall on Jackson Avenue, another Grecian mansion, 1841, with an Ionic portico; it is now a hospital but was built for a 'stuff' merchant. The disproportion between the Corinthian portico covering a single doorway is rather suburban. Then it is but a short distance to *Roundhay Park* and its mansion (which is mentioned on page 149).

Now south on Gledhow Lane via Roundhay Road and Amberton Road to *Gipton*. Amid council housing in the Wyke Beck valley is the 1930s *Church of the Epiphany*. It has received much praise and is listed as Grade I; with its plain thin piers and curved and modelled interior it is expressive of a 1930s move from the geometric. Tall, brick with thin rectangular windows, curvaceous ends to the aisles and drum-like East nave, plus an apsidal chancel. Its architectural importance no doubt lies in the big curtain wall approach with slot windows, all reminiscent of a contemporary cinema; designed by N. F. Cachemaille-Day in 1938. Then south down Roundhay Road toward *Harehills* where amid very red-brick back-to-back housing, tightly laid around St James's Hospital, is the grand Italianate *Church of St Aidan*, 1891, also ruby brick. Aisles, and clerestory of little Romanesque windows for the nave, the South chancel chapel is grander with tall shafted windows. The West towerlets have conical caps. The exterior is slightly industrial but inside are some wonderful Arts and Crafts depictions by Sir Frank Brangwyn. Finished in 1916 they illustrate the life of St Aidan in vividly coloured mosaics. Sturdy Romanesque stone arches form the arcades; a grand Romanesque chancel arch has the rood beam before it. The timber-lined roof has kingposts standing on collar beams – this daring feat of engineering must have steel in it.

From here go east to Harehills Road via Elford Grove

or the Bayswaters: streets of narrow, crowded back-to-back houses which in other cities would have been thinned out or rebuilt. At Beckett Street is the **Thackray Medical Museum** in an old part of St James's University Hospital where primitive facilities and techniques are on show. There is a surprising appetite for this. The original hospital buildings were a workhouse for men and women built in the middle of the nineteenth century in Romantic Jacobethan – shaped gables and octagonal stone turrets with ogee-capped roofs. A tall 16-light Jacobean window in the men's workhouse is labelled 'Moral and Industrial Training Schools AD1848'. The women's workhouse is also grand – shaped gables, strong central tower and ogee-capped turrets, each with gold-painted weathervanes. Forward is a Romanesque-style chapel in red and blue brick with stone dressings, twin doorways, and a Gothic clock tower with pyramid roof. It is a local authority draughtsman gone mad. Opposite is Beckett Street Cemetery, the first municipal cemetery in England.

Continue south down Beckett Street and Burmantofts Street into Marsh Lane and a view of *Quarry Hill*. Until recently it was a gulag for the poor in a huge walled enclave of 28 acres of municipal housing. It was the largest council estate in England, its walls opened west onto the A61 through elliptical arches, which busy road divided it from town. It was designed in 1935 and caught the fascist mood of the time. Although not unsanitary it gave strong negative vibrations to Leeds which demolished it, citing structural problems. People do not like its huge replacement, **Quarry House** (1999: The Building Design Partnership), which is a government department. But the site requires a dominant building and Quarry House is sufficiently monumental. Its high central hall is flanked by broad ashlar stone piers, glazed in dark glass, while massive sheds either side have big stone-latticed windows giving an engine house impression – in reality they are floors of offices.

Then a little further east via Marsh Lane and Richmond Street to another hill where *Mount St Mary's Catholic Church*, 1857, was built by the French Order, Oblates of Mary Immaculate, for Irish Catholic workers. E. W. Pugin added the chancel and transepts in 1866. Overwhelming French lancets in the apse reach over the vaulted roof 83ft high. The pulpit is crowned by a huge pinnacle and the reredos is faced with variegated marbles and enamels. The rigorous Catholics have closed it but people would like to see it again: the striking Pugin architecture should be shown, but permission has been obtained to demolish it in part. Also nearby on the same hill is **St Saviour's**, 1845, a famous Anglican church, one of 21 promoted by Dr Hook, the Vicar of Leeds. It was paid for anonymously by Mr Z (Dr Pewsey), its archi-tecture pioneered the Ritual Revival and the return to medieval form. Its tower is bold and low but the transept and East windows are tall with EE geometric tracery. The spire, planned to be modelled on St Mary's Oxford, was not built. Glass in the North aisle and North porch window is by *Morris & Co*; other windows by Pugin have pre-Raphaelite colour and vigour. Not everyone wanted the Ritual Revival. Trollope's Mr Slope inveighed against Pewseyites and high pitched roofs. The Bishop of Ripon did not like candles, nor would he consecrate it 'Holy Cross', so it had to become 'St Saviour's'. The Pewsey Chapel and reredos are by Bodley, 1890. The vicarage by William Butterfield, 1847 with tall Gothic chimneys, and church, are enclosed by a wall planted with glass against this desperate area. Access is on Sunday mornings. Southeast of here East Street leads to the new crossing over the river and links with the motorway.

On Church Road in **Hunslet** is *St Mary the Virgin*, the tower and tall stone spire alone remain of a distinguished EE building, 1864. The tower has setback buttresses and a big cusped entrance with shafts. The elegant tower and broach spire must have saved it from demolition; the odd looking new nave in stone with rounded corners is lit from high continuous windows. Then go up Beza Street to the M621 roundabout where Moor Street leads to the **Middleton Railway**. This historic railway ran from Middleton Moor Colliery where coal was mined in a series of bell pits and brought into the centre of Leeds from 1758. It had horse-drawn wagons at first, replaced by *Blenkinsop's* rack railway in 1812: engines made by *Matthew Murray*, builder of the first commercial steam locos. Engines and equipment are on display at the *Moor Road Station Museum* in the modern Engine House adjacent to the station. From here short trips are made by steam to Middleton Park, still an open area with ancient woodland. A link to the main line permits noble itinerant steam engines to visit the railway.

From Hunslet, Beza Street runs to the A639. Take Thwaite Lane to a water-powered industrial mill, 1832. The valley is wide here and the River Aire appears to flow in two channels, the closest portion is the Navigation and a strand of land divides it from the River Aire. The Transpennine Trail follows the strand back into the centre of Leeds. *Thwaite Mill* is also on an island where the river is dammed behind a weir causing a head of

Overleaf, left: BODLEY REREDOS, ST SAVIOUR, LEEDS;
right: ST SAVIOUR, LEEDS.

water to flow under it. Built of brick in 1832 it has conspicuous ventilators which rise over the roofs. It originally ground flint to make glaze for Leeds pottery products and latterly chalk for putty, but in 1975 the weir was destroyed by floods and this put it out of business. Now it is efficiently run by Leeds Museums and the waterwheels turn once more, but now grinding nothing at all. The manager's house is of the same period in brick with a stone porch; it is furnished for its period, that is, mid-nineteenth century. Small steam-powered ships off-loaded at the jetty here until the early twentieth century and a quayside steam-powered crane still works on bank holidays. From here you may return to the centre of Leeds, take the motorway north or south, or the M62 east or west.

LEEMING Ascending Black Moor and Thornton Moor from Oxenhope to Denholme stands a small mill village in blackened stone with its iconic round stone chimney. The breeze and the reservoir add to the flavour. [7]

LEPTON High above the Fenay Valley and Fenay Bridge on the Huddersfield to Wakefield road. Among low eighteenth-century mullioned cottages St John's Church, 1868, EE, stands well. A Southwest embattled tower and West end have neatly shafted lancets. The rood screen is finely carved. A sympathetic modern hall is alongside the nave, like a chapel. [21]

LEVENTHORPE HALL Eighteenth-century mansion by John Carr, 1774, says the inscription. The main interest on the front façade is the canted bay in the centre with pedimented doorway. Its side pavilions have been demolished. Situated between Oulton and Swillington. [16]

LINTHWAITE High, high up the Colne Valley south side with roads called Pennine View etc. The broach spire of nineteenth-century Christ Church is a landmark for miles. The large mill was aptly known as *Titanic Mill* but is now apartments. Linfit Hall is of 1600; the cruck barn which is now a garage is reduced from five crucks, that is, tree-sized supporting pillars. [19]

LINTON Of mellow Tadcaster limestone, this higgledy-piggledy village clings to a bluff over the River Wharfe. Some roofs are red pantiles, others stone slate. There are several cottages in a folksy idiosyncratic style like a Yorkshire Portmeirion. [4]

LIVERSEDGE At the foot of a ridge road to Halifax rising from collected industry in the Spen Valley and up to breezy High Town Heights, the town straggles out along the roadside. There are seventeenth-century houses with gables and mullioned windows interspersed with modern development. The parish church is off Church Lane from Knowler Hill between the Halifax and Bradford roads. *Christchurch* lies below the ridge but aloof on a little knoll above the Spen Valley. A footpath from Halifax Road to the church is the best access, via the Parish Centre. It is entirely surrounded by housing but has views north to hills. Late Georgian Gothic, 1812, by Thomas Taylor the church has a robust Dec tower with 'Y' and intersecting tracery at the bell stage. The aisles have big windows with stylized Dec tracery. The East window, oddly, has transoms across ogee-headed lights but anti-vandal screening spoils the effect from the exterior. Below the East window are heavy doors conjecturing a massive crypt on this hillside site. The headstones in the churchyard are all gabled and to the same design by order of the Reverend Hammond Roberson who built the church in 1812 at his own expense. He was Mr Hellstone in Charlotte Brontë's *Shirley* whose rectory was envisioned as nearby Healds Hall. From the crossroads at the foot of the valley, up the Leeds road on the left is Healds Hall, a Georgian two and a half storeyed house with straight corniced windows, now a hotel. It was actually a boys' boarding school when imagined as Mr Hellstone's rectory. [13]

LONGWOOD By a dramatic gritstone escarpment running west out of Huddersfield. St Mark's church is an EE design of 1877. [20]

LOTHERTON Near Parlington and Aberford in the gentle northeast of the county where the Gascoigne baronets were squires and coal owners. Lotherton Hall is a late Victorian house built around a Georgian core and has a Norman chapel for company. It was the junior part of Parlington Park. Sir Alvary Gascoigne left it to Leeds in 1968 who use it as a gallery but also show a portion appropriately furnished from the Edwardian era. It has an irregular front of quoined and arched sash windows – one gabled bay, one round bay and one hip-roofed bay. The walls are pebble dashed, very twentieth century, against which grows a handsome tree-size *Magnolia grandiflora*. The awkward porte-cochère on tall Tuscan columns was designed in the estate office. Colonel Frederick Gascoigne converted the house to its present appearance between 1896 and 1902: the dining room has his portrait over the fireplace, 1896. The morning room was finished in 1898 followed by the hall and East drawing room. The chimneypiece in the hall comes from Huddleston Hall and is seventeenth century; the chimneypiece in the sitting room was brought from Parlington which he abandoned after 1905. The well-kept gardens were designed by Colonel Frederick's wife Laura. With Voysey wallpaper and Pugin furniture it is possible to imagine Edwardian house parties arriving. Today anyone can be in a house party and take guided walks through the estate woods, explore the gardens, the house or play games, many of which are designed for children, and take tea. In the grounds and close to the house is a little twelfth-century chapel with Norman double-roll moulding to its North door, leaf capitals and two original windows. There is a sweet little gabled belcote. The original twelfth-century chancel has lost its arch; the rood is by Sir Ninian Comper; there are memorials to Gascoignes. The only other part of the former village to remain is the Old House just west of the Hall, once the home farm it is now workshops and accommodation for the estate. It is a tall irregular Jacobean house with mullions, some blocked, and a good seventeenth-century staircase with turned balusters. [11]

LUDDENDEN Has the atmosphere of a Yorkshire fishing village quaintly set round the rushing Luddenden Beck; particularly reminiscent of Robin Hood's Bay. St Mary's Church, 1817, by Thomas Taylor, on a bow of the stream in a gorge, has the schooled elegance of Regency Gothic: tall Perp-style windows with compressed intersecting tracery – originals remain on the North side only; octagonal turrets divide the bays; clipboard Perp detail to the tower. In 1866 an ill-matched Dec-style chancel was added. The tracery in the South aisle windows was converted to Dec but looks awkward. A little bridge leads beyond the church to an idyllic valley burial ground around the stream – peaceful, well-wooded and rural except for Murgatroyd's Mill, whose intrusive black windows peer down over the shoulder of the hill. The tall nineteenth-century vicarage stands above a cliff and waterfall, gothic in detail and situation. The rushing stream can be heard perpetually. Opposite St Mary's in the steep and winding village street is the Lord Nelson Inn, a cosy mullion-windowed pub dated 1634. Horatio Nelson used to stay with Lady Mary Horton up at Howroyd Hall, Barkisland, but he would have felt near to the coast here. [13]

LUDDENDEN FOOT Where the Beck from pretty Luddenden Dean meets the swift Calder in a valley bottom crowded with little mills, chimneys and terraced houses. On the hillsides stand isolated blockish terraces and the conspicuous Parish Church of St Mary with its octagonal spire and unusual triangular dormer windows. A grand classical chapel is on the main road with central clock tower and pedimented wings (now apartments). Attractive cast iron river bridge. On Luddenden Lane is an excellent Jacobean mansion, many gabled,

LUDDENDEN CHURCHYARD.

shaped finials, large mullioned and transomed windows, projecting porch and a Yorkshire wheel window on the first floor (cusped lights). On the summit of the valley a crown of purple heather spreads in August. [13]

MARSDEN Frontier town at the westernmost part of the Colne Valley. From here the ancient packhorse route to Lancashire and western ports ascended the rugged hills and moors of the Pennines. Even today the name *Marsden* conjures endurance hikes in the most severe conditions of weather and terrain. *The Pennine Way* almost calls at Marsden, descending from the peaty morass of Black Hill via Wessenden Head and the Wessenden Valley. That brook flows down to Marsden via a number of little reservoirs enlivened with rhododendron in spring, but the Pennine Way branches off west at Wessenden Lodge (where jugs of hot water for your tea could once be purchased). If you follow the path down into town the contrast from high wild hills to a sudden townscape of mills with close gathered houses is dramatic.

West Yorkshire's products for long crossed these hills via little packhorse bridges – there is one by the church and another one and a half miles west. In 1794 a canal was built along the valley and in 1811 Telford and Outram dug the longest tunnel in the UK for the canal to reach Diggle in Lancashire. Recently restored by British Waterways and the Huddersfield Canal Society you can visit the eastern portal. There is no tow path: the horses went over the hills. Bargees had to 'leg' boats through by treading the tunnel roof. Water laps ominously at the low front of the portal, the entrance to over three miles of grim travelling. The neighbouring railway tunnel (1894) communicates with it; in the days of steam the shriek of the whistle, the flurry of sparks and fire would burst into the silent world of the bargemen with a shock. You can sample this claustrophobic world by taking a glass-roofed observation boat into the tunnel from the Georgian warehouse by the British Waterways basin. Water for this high pound of the canal is supplied by the nearby reservoir whose sparkling, stepped overflow can be spotted high up the A62. There is a Canal Visitor Centre in the Georgian canal-side warehouse and an old navvies' pub by the tunnel.

Marsden had its own small classical town hall which remains, although local government now operates for Kirklees. The big Victorian church of St Bartholomew (1895) is a Perp design, the tower more bulk than finesse. It replaces an earlier building on the old trade route. Opposite the church is a memorial to Enoch Taylor whose factory made sledgehammers and shearing frames, and where Luddite riots occurred. The sledgehammers were known as 'Enochs' and thus the Luddite call was 'Enoch made them and Enoch shall break them'. [19]

MELTHAM AND MELTHAM MILLS Two adjacent upland towns situated in quite a hostile environment but whose prosperity was determined by mills now mostly turned into apartments. The older of the two villages is Meltham where the church of St Bartholomew was in existence in 1651. The present building dates from 1786; the Georgian nature of the nave, six bays of straight-headed windows in two storeys, reflects basic mill design. The West tower also is classical (1835) with urns for pinnacles. The proportions do not really satisfy and the chancel looks particularly odd in neo-Norman. [19]

MENSTON Below the escarpment of Rombold Moor and almost in Wharfedale. It is on the Leeds–Ilkley commuter line and thus a village suburb of substantial villas, but the old centre is not without charm. There are two good houses surviving from the seventeenth century, Grange Farm, 1672, a typical manor house with a projecting two-storey gabled porch, and a round window in the gable, mullioned windows throughout and dripstone course between the storeys; said to have been the court house. It is said to be linked by underground passage to nearby Old Hall, also with gables, and whose mullioned windows have arched heads. There is also a bay of transomed windows. Its porch was removed to Farnley Hall in the nineteenth century. St John's church just to the east is Victorian lancet style, 1871. Here also was the notorious High Royds Asylum, institutional Gothic in stone, 1888. A vast area of wards is linked like a fishbone. Tall, pyramid-roofed water towers heighten an air of angst. Here patients were restrained for life, some with only minor complaints, until the late twentieth-century sea change in psychiatric treatment initiated by Minister of Health Enoch Powell. Many would wish this ugly building razed to the ground. [2]

METHLEY East of Leeds in an isthmus formed by the rivers Aire and Calder. The collapse of mining has left surprisingly rural charm. A mansion of the Earls of Mexborough stood at Methley Park but, worn down by mining encroachment, taken over by the Americans in the Second World War, it was abandoned by the time Pevsner called in 1959. He described its outer porch door as 1500; the inner door was Sir John Savile's work of 1595. Elizabethan octagonal towers flanked the porch and there were four storeys of transomed windows: compare Heath Hall, Wakefield, and Barlborough Hall in Derbyshire. It was demolished in 1963 – but its ghost still intrigues the imagination. The earls continue elsewhere.

St Oswald's church, however, brings history to life. A Perp porch, Gothicized clerestory and fine nave roof with angel corbels add to a thirteenth/fourteenth-century building. It has good reticulated Dec windows, and Dec corbel heads inspired by the Book of Revelation. The alabaster monuments make it worth seeking the church key (best to write first): in the South chancel chapel are Watertons and Saviles gone by. Sir Robert Waterton and Lady are carved in alabaster (1425) under an elaborate cusped arch in the chancel/chapel wall. He with curly pointed beard, in armour, and a jewelled turban like a Turk; his wife wears a headdress and gown. On the south side of the chapel is Lord Welles (1461) whose wife was the Waterton daughter and heir. He commanded Lancastrians in the Wars of the Roses and

SIR ROBERT AND LADY WATERTON, 1425, METHLEY.

was killed in the nearby battle of Towton where much blood stained the snow. Splendidly preserved, he carries a sword and wears elegant articulated armour; his wife has a horned headdress – wafting angels attend. Next chronologically is Sir John Savile, d.1607, and his son Sir Henry and wife, all three elevated on a grand tomb chest of black and white marble in the South aisle by the porch. Sir John also wears armour but his son is in academic cap and gown. Sir John was Elizabeth's Baron of Exchequer; buried in London but his heart is interred here. Two carved babies lie at the foot of the east side of the tomb. In the Waterton Chapel reclines a marble Charles Savile, d.1741, in classical robes, mourning wife seated at his feet, carved by Scheemakers. Then the first Earl of Mexborough, John Savile, d.1778, by Westmacott. He seems pleased with his elevation, wearing ermine with ruffed lace sleeves, coronet placed on a table.

He points hopefully upward. The tower has a corbelled out parapet, is much restored and lost its spire in 1937. The old rectory is neo-Jacobean by Anthony Salvin; the new rectory in brick is next to the church rooms.

The Elizabethan font was rescued from a poultry yard in 1898, the contemporary spired cover is operated on a weighted cantilever. A worn medieval sculpture of St Oswald was brought inside to a place by the chancel arch. The vestry is divided by an openwork screen of Jacobean turned balusters. In the East window of the South chapel fifteenth-century stained glass from other windows was reassembled to make eight saints. An impressive lectern with big American Eagle exhibited in Philadelphia in 1867 stands on a continental nineteenth-century base. Henry Moore attended this church as a 7 year old with his aunt from Castleford, said to have been fascinated by the carved corbel heads. [16]

COMMUNITY OF THE RESURRECTION, MICHAEL TAPPER, A POWER STATION METAPHOR, MIRFIELD.

MICKLEFIELD A pleasant linear village now bypassed by the A1 with old limestone cottages and farmhouses. The Parish Church of St Mary the Virgin is a high-roofed Victorian chapel, rock-faced, rather mean Dec style windows and belcote. Old Micklefield runs south into an industrial quarter whose terraced houses are built of limestone. [11]

MIDDLETON Colonized by Leeds Corporation's pre-war grid-pattern council housing with broad streets and dull houses. On the site of the former Middleton Hall a park has retained some open land. St Mary's church overlooks the park, a neat EE-style of 1846 with double lancets and a Southwest tower over the porch. Quite pretty. There is an occasional steam railway service to the park from Hunslet which is the successor of an early hill wagon-way carrying coal from a multitude of pits to a jetty on the River Aire. Blenkinsop made it into a rack railway in 1812; steam trains visit from other companies. [16]

MIDGLEY High up the north side of Calderdale a straggle of old stone houses and cottages overlooks the River Calder from a dizzy height. Weavers' cottages and older, mullioned farmhouses line the main street and a classical, gable-ended chapel faces proudly down it. Good views are seen west through the hills towards Lancashire under a setting sun. With a slight autumn mist below you, it is like standing on a ridge in the clouds. [19]

MIRFIELD Famous as the home of the Community of the Resurrection – an Anglican teaching community which has an outpost in Africa and which trains Anglican priests. It is the only such institution in West Yorkshire; the Community moved here in 1898 from Oxford to be involved in industrial life. A church was built in the spacious grounds of a Gothic industrialist's mansion – its thirteenth-century style marble-shafted doorway is surmounted by shouldered-lintel windows. The 1911 Community church is grand Romanesque by Sir Walter Tapper. Not for him delicate Arts and Crafts Gothic but sturdy, fat-pillared arches: double-arched screens to the East, North and South of the altar at the crossing. The aisles are tunnelled passages against the nave walls lit only by pokey Norman slits and the nave only by a clerestory of round lights. The brothers' stalls are set collegiate-style in the nave. Sir Walter's building was given further mass by deploying polychromatic red Cheshire sandstone with limestone. The West nave by Michael Tapper (son) is in brick; this has an emphatic power-station feel with a great wall of brick rising to two squat towers. Studiously bizarre, the barrel-vaulted roofs, crossing dome and tower caps are in copper but,

within, the church lacks unity and seems to lack the visual stimulation which must have been intended. It has recently been modernized and given a softer look. [15]

MORLEY Hilltop town southwest of Leeds whose fortune was built on cloth. Although many streets are mean brick or stone terraces there is a spectacular Town Hall. Clearly the wool towns of the West Riding competed with each other. Dominating portico of six circular columns, elaborate Mixed Capitals and modillioned pediment. Under and in the pediment are carved figures of *Industry* and *Weaving* presided over by *Justice*. Stepped back from the portico are balustraded wings. The hilly site is used to good effect with a spread of stone steps rising to the arched entrance with richly carved pilasters; a Venetian window and small balustraded balcony. A dominating but not unfriendly building. The tower with pedimented clock storey and melon-shaped dome is said to imitate Leeds. The interior is equally rich. The main stair displays a bust of Herbert Asquith, the Liberal Prime Minister and the town's most famous son. The town is rich in classical buildings whether chapels or small warehouses. South, at Town End, St Paul's is Victorian Dec but with chancel of a slightly earlier church. On Commercial Street is a warehouse with a carved beehive crest in the spandrels of the arch. Nearby is the Baptist Tabernacle, 1897, twin castellated towers of rock-faced stone with symbolic classical adornment – meagre pediments and pared-down neo-Baroque. North is the former Sunday School and parish hall, an unusual classical design of three arched windows over symmetrical Sunday School doors and a broad elliptical pediment. Weekday use of the premises spawned the Morley Technical School which later became the Grammar School. Opposite is Morley Library, plain neo-Baroque in ashlar with flanking pediments 'erected through the generosity of Andrew Carnegie of Skibo Castle Scotland 1905'. The vestibule is decorated with glazed-tile Art Nouveau Ionic pilasters and a tiled frieze illustrating English authors from Chaucer to Tennyson, also *Learning* and *Labour*.

Outside the library stands an incongruous gate pier moved from Chapel Hill on the demolition of the Old House, an early eighteenth-century mullioned farmhouse. Smith's *History of Antiquities of Morley* describes the Old House as the residence of Samuel Clark, a dry salter, who 'received his neighbours with roaring fire where sundry flitches of bacon, oaten cake and hard wheaten breach burdened the hooks and creels of the kitchen ceiling'. Morley Hall was built in 1683. Much altered, there remains a wing with mullioned windows and drip mould. The front was Georgianized with a castellated cantered bay. It stands on a knoll by Dawson

MORLEY TOWN HALL.

WEAVERS' COTTAGES, 18TH CENTURY, MYTHOLMROYD.

Hill with the park sloping away from it. On another knoll is the Church of St Mary's in the Wood, much enclosed by trees, now redundant and in need of attention. In 1650 a lease was granted to local Presbyterians for 500 years; they became Congregationalists at the turn of the nineteenth century, the name reverting to St Mary-in-the-Wood more recently when it became the United Reformed Church. It is the only example of an ancient Episcopal church not returning to Anglican at the Restoration. The present building is in high slate-roofed EE, mid-nineteenth century and is in need of rescue. It has retained its earlier Charles II arms painted on boards; also seventeenth century is an odd mausoleum in the graveyard, 1688. On Station Road an early mill of 1790 – Crank Mill – was named from its steam-powered outdoor flywheel and crank. The Anglican Church of St Peter is a few moments away on Rooms Lane. It is very

plain with lancets deeply inset and an octagonal stone spire rising directly from the corbel table; the jarring awkwardness of this is mitigated by broaches chamfered in from the corners, by Robert Chantrell 1829. The chancel, 1885, exhibits later flamboyant Victorian window tracery. Morley now counts as a suburb of Leeds but retains its own distinctive town identity. [15]

MYTHOLMROYD Calder Valley mill village at the foot of Cragg Brook. The old village is south of the river and railway where opposite the classical Methodist Church is a good Jacobean farmhouse with a five-light transomed window in the gable. Weavers' cottages line the road east to Sowerby beneath a wooded and craggy hillside. The Parish Church of St Michael, 1848, impresses with military rows of gravestones but otherwise appears undistinguished from outside. Blackened Dec, it has a South chapel and castellated tower which forms the entrance porch, and a small stone spirelet. In front of the church is a new public space or little square with a new village cross. It is a revelation to gain entry to the church. In the sanctuary are extensive mosaics by Whitefriars of London; around a white reredos on the East wall are mosaics of the Godhead illustrated with seven lamps – the rainbow 'like unto an emerald' – then the crystal sea. The *Ascension* displays a green orb for the Earth with the trace of Christ's footprints – angels carry him up. On the North wall are the Apostles with their emblems – St Peter with key and book, St James with a club, and St Matthew with his money bag. On the South wall are northern saints from not far away, St Aidan from the Isle of Iona, St Hilda the Abbess of Whitby, St Oswald King of Northumbria, and St Cuthbert of Lindisfarne. Whitefriars also made four of the stained glass windows including one illustrating Boy Scouts. The present East window inserted in 1900 has William Morris colours. The former window is displayed in the West gallery with some Art Nouveau glass in a finely carved wooden tracery screen.

On the main road opposite the canal bridge at Bridgend is a good eighteenth-century house with Venetian windows. The main street consists of weavers' cottages. Up Midgley Road are banks of weavers' cottages standing four storeys high next to a mill that makes clogs. Stacks of wood are seasoned here in an ambient temperature. [13]

NETHERTHONG Overlooking the Holme Valley south of Huddersfield, distant views towards Farnley. Stone houses and weavers' cottages gather around All Saints Church. No. 147 Town Gate has a six-light window in the gable watching over the churchyard. The church is Regency, castellated west end flanked by turrets; ogee West window over the porch which is like a castle with embattling and smaller turrets; the window has a swaggering carved stone plume above the ogee, 1829, by Chantrell. The clock and Victorian belcote show the bell mechanism. Four gargoyles at the corners. Some good memorial stones are in the churchyard. [25]

NEW MILL Deep in leafy Wooldale south of Huddersfield, where dams on the quick stream powered the first factories there remain some big stone mills and their cottages. Above the road Christ Church stands lordly, a broad William IV church; big lancet windows in the nave have panelled tracery; West tower with crocketed pinnacles; some excellent churchyard memorials. Above the church is an eighteenth-century mill on Sude Hill once used as a knitting factory – four storeys, stone. Picturesque stone cottages and houses settle in the val-

ley, many from seventeenth and eighteenth centuries with rows of square mullions to give light for weaving. Moorbrook Mill has a tall stone chimney. Some recent sympathetic stone houses infill. The road to Denby Dale climbs high up the Pennines from here with spectacular views to the north and lonely groups of weavers' cottages on the hillsides.

On Holmfirth Road is a charming Unitarian Chapel of 1695, the arched windows and tower with cupola are later, 1748. The ball finial is a natural ironstone sphere found locally. Manse to the west is Victorian Tudor. Further west is an early flat-roofed building, the Sunday School, designed by Edgar Wood of Arts and Crafts fame. [25]

NEWMILLERDAM This pretty hamlet on the main road to South Yorkshire (A61) lies just south of Wakefield. A crook in the road suddenly reveals a lake extending south up a wooded valley; a Gothic boathouse is at the eastern edge and the village retains eighteenth-century cottages. The woods by the lake now form a country park with access round most of the lake. This was part of the estate of the Pilkington baronets who lived at Chevet Park, a now demolished house which was east of the lake. Their memorials are in Sandal Magna church. The village adjoins Pledwick where, turning west off the A61 up Kettlethorpe Hall Drive, you reach a fine early Georgian hall, curvy pediments on the ground-floor windows, and an Ionic frontispiece with a hood-pedimented doorway. The roof with central chimney stack looks bare without a balustrade. [22]

NORMANTON A colliery town grafted onto an old agricultural village. All Saints is within a churchyard the size of a large sports ground where gravestones seem to go on into the distance. Until recently the pithead gear looked over the roofs of the parallel lines of red-brick miners' houses. All Saints is medieval: Perp with a broad five-light East window; the nave windows are straight headed (the plate glass appearance is anti-vandal screening) and the arcades are earlier. The South arcade has octagonal piers and North arcade EE piers with attached shafts giving a wavy profile (compare Bradford Cathedral and Sandal Magna). Now modernized, the axis of the church has been changed across the nave North–South with the altar and font on a rostrum. Of particular interest is the well-preserved Dec font with crisp motifs combining Gothic tracery and spinning wheels. At the East end of the North arcade is a monument to John Frieston, 1594, the benefactor of Frieston's Hospital at nearby *Kirkthorpe*: it is a 7ft-high stone table tomb with coupled Ionic columns at the corners. [17]

Nostell Priory in the winter.

NOSTELL PRIORY, MIDDLE LAKE.

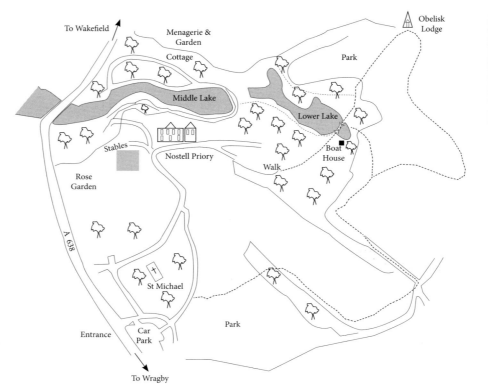

Nostell Priory

NORTHOWRAM Village above Shibden Hall astride a col descending from the blackness of Queensbury and Black Dyke. The road here from Coley is through a cutting lined with high blackened stones in a dramatic fashion, as in will they collapse soon? They are an extant brother to the now removed Walls of Jericho at Egypt (near Thornton).

St Matthew's church is an exciting early twentieth-century Gothic – the tower is independent, placed north of the chancel whose East window faces the road. It is Arts and Craft Gothic: little oblong windows symmetrically placed in the tower; huge battlements with just a sliver of light between, pinnacles *below* the corners of the tower; and massive bell-stage lancets wearing aggressive baffles. By Walsh and Nicholas, 1913. A tour de force.

Pretty elements of Gothic design are freely placed in the church, for example, below a low transom bar on the East window are small foliated lights. The clerestory likewise is a long run of double foliated window lights. Inside, clean Gothic arches in the arcades have no piers or capitals and are similar to those in the East end of Bradford Cathedral by Sir Edward Maufe, 1958. The wooden ceiling is flat but recessed with a chamfer. Re-ordering of the interior allows half the nave to be used for meetings but opens out for large services. The former heavy rood and screen have been broken down to make a more intricate screen east of the choir to divide off a small chapel. The former rood cross entirely fills an arched niche in the chancel. [14]

NOSTELL PRIORY One of West Yorkshire's great houses with wide parkland views to the east. The original St Oswald's Priory was founded in the twelfth century and the last Prior built the church just off the drive to the house. At the Dissolution Sir George Gargrave,

STAIR HALL ROOF, NOSTELL PRIORY.

Speaker of the House of Commons, bought the Prior's lodging and the Winn family bought the house in 1654. The present house was built in 1735; nothing of the Priory remains. A tall imposing portico looks over a park newly restored by the National Trust. It is famed for its collection of Chippendale furniture made for the house. The pediment encloses the Winn Arms and rests on six semi-circular Ionic columns. Below is a wide terrace with double curved balustraded staircases. Originally planned by a friend, Colonel J. Moyser, James Paine took over the building. In 1765 the 5th baronet commissioned Robert Adam to complete the interiors; he also added a family wing on a quadrant to the right of the house – rather like Kedleston – which is still used by the Winns, but the other three quadrants were never built. In fact the family wing was only completed internally by 1st Baron St Oswald in 1876. Co-operation between the National Trust and the family allows some private rooms to be shown. The Trust has recently taken over a large swathe of parkland from Lord St Oswald and is

now able to show attic rooms with some original furnishing. Until very recently the Winns ran the house on behalf of the National Trust.

The arrangements within the house are quite symmetrical with two internal staircases. Visitors enter under the terrace to a low hall on Doric columns where shooting parties were entertained. Here is a large and arresting picture of Sir Thomas More showing Tudor family life with children and pets, original by Holbein. The Roman marble statues in alcoves are Bacanti and Silenus. North and South stairs have three decks of landings, wrought iron banisters, the steps cantilevered out of the walls, and Rococo plasterwork by Paine. Glazed lights over the stairs are reminiscent of an eighteenth-century frigate. 'Top Hall' on the first floor is in the centre of the house and opens out east to the terrace; its plasterwork is by Adam, executed by Joseph Rose the Younger, copied from Hadrian's villa at Tivoli. The Saloon to the west is accessed through adjoining apses in each room. The Breakfast Room (to the south) was burned out by

DINING ROOM BY JAMES PAINE, NOSTELL PRIORY.

Top Hall by Adam, Nostell Priory.

PYRAMID LODGE, NOSTELL PRIORY.

an electrical fire in 1980 and refurnished with a Paine Rococo Gothic fireplace taken from a bedroom. This leads to the Crimson Room, also Paine, with a Rococo four-poster bed. Here is Hogarth's *Tempest*, the earliest painting of any Shakespearean scene. Then facing south with big Venetian window is the State Dressing Room, furniture by Chippendale, 1771, listed as 'dome Bedstead Jappane'd Green and Gold'. The fabric is new following the fire next door. A grander bedroom follows with Rococo decoration in the coving and a painted ceiling of putti playing instruments. The Palladian chimney piece by Paine is heavy. The furniture is again Chippendale and chinoiserie coverings and curtains were given by English Heritage. Then comes the State Dining Room, lavish Rococo by Paine with plasterwork by Rose and ceiling painting of Ceres with putti gathering

in the harvest. Two huge portraits of Winns are in gilded frames.

The house route shows the Saloon opposite the Top Hall next. Like the Top Hall it was revisited by Adam who installed a deep coving and Grecian cornice. The medallion in the centre is by Zucchi – Apollo's horses watered by the Hours. The Adam chimney piece is unflamboyant with honeysuckle and urns; the furniture is also Adam. The Tapestry Room is so called from the Flemish tapestries bought by Charles Winn, 1824. Here are statues of Flora and Zephyr – a naked male with wings. Gillows settees and armchairs with gilded serpentine legs and rests are newly restored in striped Regency material woven from original remnants. The Library has an Adam ceiling and a magnificent Chippendale desk made for the room. There is a picture of the 5th baronet and his wife painted a year after the library's completion. East is the Drawing Room, part of Lord St Oswald's suite, designed by Paine as a family bedroom and therefore the plasterwork is modest. Here is a self-portrait of Angelica Kaufmann, 1791, hesitating between music and painting – apparently she could not decide whether to be an opera singer or painter. The Small Dining Room facing east has a ceiling by Adam based on frescoes found at Herculaneum. The ceiling panels are by Zucchi. The decoration on the cove was painted on paper, cut out and then applied. Stairs to the second storey bring you close to its ornate ceiling, and rooms occupied by the late Dowager.

The stables are big and with the gatehouse are by Adam. They have been restored to form a catering and hospitality centre. On the south side of the stables Adam built a Garden Room and Banqueting House (1770) – a tall bow-fronted structure, now with a rose garden. The park has a lovely walk through woods and wild flower meadows to Featherstone Lodge. By Robert Adam it is a pyramid – fronted by a pedimented arch through which a carriage can drive. The gardens are to the north and occupy a valley made into lakeside walks. An ornamental five-arch bridge (1761) carries the Doncaster/Wakefield road over the Upper Lake; the Lower Lake has a boathouse – all are surrounded by rhododendron and azaleas providing delightful walks. A path from the lakeside to the north takes you to a discrete dell where a Gothic gardener's cottage remains – though boarded up – called the Menangerie House. The central portion with intersecting traceried windows and Rose plasterwork was by Paine, 1765; the side wings by Adam, 1776. More could be made of it. The naturalistic look of the Park – clumps of trees, lake cascade, walks – dates from 1820 when an old plan by Stephen Switzer was executed by James Hank. The National Trust has restored the lakes and paths following mining depredation, and in 2002 took over the park from the Winns, restoring it and providing walks over to the Pyramid (Featherstone) Lodge. Winns kept deer in the Park until 1975. [23]

NOTTON Rather smart agricultural village now for commuters, some old mullioned cottages, spacious housing and laid-out village green. The road to Nostell rises through fields of corn. [22]

OAKWELL (See Birstall)

OAKWORTH The church of Christchurch is a chunky lancet style of 1845. Just east of the church on Providence Lane is the old hall with deeply set mullioned windows, 1702 – two of the door lintels are decorated with

a motif of semi-circular hollows – compare East Riddlesden Hall. Above the village are some good terraces of eighteenth-century weavers' cottages in stone with stone roofs; indeed all the village is stone, and from the Colne Road are outstanding views to the south across the Worth Valley towards Haworth. In the centre of the town is the bizarre Holden Park, a gift from and memorial to Sir Isaac Holden whose home has now gone. The Grecian gate piers to the park remain; they are mounted by statues of almost nude Africans, but in swimming costumes. The boundary of the park is marked with stone grottoes – they entirely surround the bowling green. Scots pines, a monkey puzzle tree and rhododendron complete the unusual effect. Between the Great War Memorial and the bowling green is a huge memorial tabernacle to *Holdens*, incorporating their crest within an elliptical pediment. Sir Isaac must have been an unusual person. The park now comes under Bradford and the Council has fixed a notice prohibiting use of the bowling green 'for any other purpose'. The Victorian railway station is at the foot of a very steep hill descending past stone cottages which appear to stagger down the road. It is part of the private Worth Valley Steam Railway. [7]

OSSETT Wool town on a hill near Wakefield which prospered in Victorian times on the rag end of the trade. It has a handsome proportioned neo-Baroque Town Hall, 1906, in local light golden sandstone. Well rendered architectural themes from the usual Renaissance sources include a central balustraded balcony supported by classical female caryatids – one bends a knee to the left the other to the right – perfect for a town hall. The two gabled wings have massive semi-circular pediments carved with dragons. Over the porch the Borough's Arms show the wealth of the town: a carved coalmine, a factory, a sheaf of corn and a woolpack. A white classical tower and clock preside from the roof. The large square in front is pedestrianized, and seeming to fix the Town Hall with a baleful stare is a Great War Soldier on the war memorial. Clearly the late nineteenth century was a prosperous period because Holy Trinity Church, 1865, is very, very big – its EE crossing tower and spire are visible for many miles; it rises clear above the hills west of the M1. Designed by W. H. Crossland, a pupil of Sir George Gilbert Scott, Holy Trinity spire is 226ft high. A big clerestory is composed of twin lancets and plate tracery. The arcade piers are of polished granite. Prosperity is further demonstrated in the churchyard where there is an excellent collection of expensive Victorian memorials to woolmakers and cloth merchants of which Hammer Films would be proud. [15]

BLACK BULL IN MARKET, OTLEY.

OTLEY Old market town in Wharfedale at a crossing of the River Wharfe in a glorious situation. A medieval bridge with ribbed arches takes the B6451 via the Washburn Valley to the North Yorkshire Dales; to the south steep tree-clad hills rise 600ft to the Chevin. On the north side of the river there is a little promenade facing calm water before a weir. At the south end of Kirkgate amid more old stone cottages is the Norman and medieval *All Saints Church*, in a churchyard of yew with a great serpentine willow tree. Norman chancel windows and a North doorway have vestiges of waterleaf on the capitals. The West tower is plain, Dec with Y-shaped

Opposite: 17TH-CENTURY GRAMMAR SCHOOL, STATUE OF CHIPPENDALE, OTLEY.

tracery; some Dec windows appear heavy restorations. The transepts and East end maintain height on sloping ground. Transepts have very tall Perp windows, including a big Perp five-light East window. Here the gritstone masonry is unsawn, rather like field walling stone. Inside the church are fragments of Anglo-Saxon crosses marking the importance of this settlement at a crossing of the Wharfe. The communion rail is seventeenth century with fat balusters. Also of that period are memorials with strapwork, and eighteenth-century memorials to the Fawkes family who lived nearby. Close to the churchyard is a large memorial to navvies killed digging nearby Bramhope Tunnel in the form of a stone model of the tunnel, 1849. The old-fashioned Market Place is at the north end of Kirkgate. At the junction with

Market Place is a house with a little Venetian window which peers over the cobbled square. At the west end of the market is a nineteenth-century shelter on cast iron columns with benches for sitting and chatting. Here is a stone memorial with clock tower in cast iron – commemorating the Transvaal War. Market Place has some seventeenth-century three-storey houses with mullions; the Black Bull was mullioned but now has little sashes; it was reputedly drunk dry by Cromwell's troops on the eve of Marston Moor. Boroughgate shows the nineteenth-century expansion of the town to the east. There are strings of stone terraced houses for those who worked in the mills. In Boroughgate, adjoining Market Place, little ginnels lead off, for example Bay Horse Court, and there are good Georgian houses including one with a big Doric columned porch next to the house of Dr John Ritchie, the apothecary who hosted John

Left: St John, Oulton, muscular Early English; *below*: Mould stop grotesque, St Oswald, Methley.

Wesley during his visits here. Opposite in Market Place is a gabled Georgian house with canted bays, cornice and tripartite semi-circular window over.

Kirkgate has some good houses: opposite Market Place is a 1704 house with alternate triangular and segmental window pediments, in the centre an oriel window – it is the front to an even older house. Other three-storey Georgian houses include the Yorkshire Bank in ashlar.

Walking towards the bridge, on the corner of Kirkgate and Westgate is the Black Horse Hotel – a nice essay in neo-Baroque, 1901. To the north Barclays Bank in Manor Square once presided over the town as the White Horse Hotel – nineteenth century, three storeys of arched windows, Italianate, heavy porch with iron balustraded balcony and tall corner lamps. Before the bridge is the *Grammar School*, founded in 1611 – three gables of mullioned windows and a very big transomed bay window in the centre rising through two storeys. A statue of Thomas Chippendale, born here in 1718, stands in the forecourt. Bridge Street has some tall three-storey cottages with square mullions and Courthouse Street one with four storeys of sash windows. Laithe House is a Yeoman's homestead of the seventeenth century where house, farm buildings and barn are under one roof. Here the jumble of stone cottages with stone roofs, showing vestiges of old fenestration, makes a singular show of organic development. [2]

OULTON A graceful large Victorian church with handsome Italianate mansion of 1851. The village has some good examples of vernacular buildings. A timber-framed house of 1610 with herringbone gable stands opposite the church, and along Foster Lane are some attractive cottages including a stone seventeenth-century house with partially blocked mullioned windows.

St John's Church is all turrets and pinnacles which, especially round the polygonal apse, enlivens the often dreary lancet style. But this building has a crisp elegance with good proportion of aisle to clerestory windows. The tower pinnacles are linked by flying buttresses to the lofty spire. Within a ring of bare trees and before a winter sunset its silhouette is dramatic. Its large size, stylistic perfection and isolation induce a sense of threat close to. The architect was Thomas Rickman. It was originally within the grounds of Oulton Hall, an early nineteenth-century classical building, with station-style chimney pots and broad porch on fluted Ionic columns; tripartite windows in stone with sashes. A golf course preserves the park, originally designed by Repton. The hall is now a hotel. [16]

OXENHOPE In the Worth Valley, nestling under moors which remain wild even as a luminous summer green spreads to their windy heights. Not entirely hidden in the valley behind to the south are the flashing sabres of modern windmills. Oxenhope is the terminus of the preserved Victorian steam railway from Keighley; its original station buildings still use gas lamps. You can walk to Haworth via The Goit: the path crosses an old packhorse bridge. Oxenhope is divided into Upper Town and Lower Town. St Mary's Church in Upper Town is by Ignatius Bonomi, 1849, the Egyptologist of Temple Mills fame. His academic essay is erudite Romanesque but the proportions seem clumsy. A fat tower of defensive proportion incorporates the parish room. The North aisle has scalloped capitals on round piers, small Norman windows have splayed reveals and the reredos and screens have carved intersecting Norman arches. Yorkshire Saints, St Hilda, St Chad, St Cuthbert – and the Virgin Mary – are carved on newel posts. It has a good ambience. In Lower Town is a classic small mill with a tall round chimney still in place, but now apartments. Some good weavers' cottages. [7]

PARLINGTON PARK The house and park of the Gascoigne baronets. The house is no more. It was pulled down in the 1950s by Sir Alvary Gascoigne. It had been used by the military in the First and Second World Wars. Sir Alvary's father, Colonel Sir Frederick, never bothered with it, preferring to live at Lotherton Hall (see Aberford) after 1905. [11]

PENNINE WAY The long-distance walk from Edale in Derbyshire to Kirk Yetholm passes the length of West Yorkshire high in the west. Inspired by Tom Stephenson

BLACKSTONE EDGE, PENNINE WAY.

over 60 years ago, it mostly follows the eastern side of the Pennine watershed. The southern entry is a rigorous leg from the Etherow Valley (source of the Mersey) to Black Hill, 1905ft, a trial of wading through black peat swamp. Black Hill summit is firm, known as *Soldier's Lump* after generations of Royal Engineers who made the triangulation surveys. The survey of 1784 used the 36ft Great Ramsden theodolite now kept in the Science Museum. The Pennine Way descends towards Marsden slowly revealing industry and settlement on the valley floor. At 500ft down from the summit is the A635. Locals call it Skye Road, not because from Marsden below lorries appear to ride through the sky (which they do), but because the Skye Hotel once stood where the Pennine Way crosses the road. This is Wessenden Head. Below the main road the path descends Wessenden Valley on a good track, past reservoirs to Wessenden Lodge – a 1930s water board house. The valley begins to become wooded and in spring rhododendron line the reservoir. The Pennine Way crosses the Wessenden stream by a dam wall, past the waterfall facing the Lodge.

The Way lies west through Blakeley Clough to Black Moss Reservoir, over the old Standedge road, via a packhorse track to White Hill along the county boundary – again firm footing at the summit is surrounded by peat bog. From here you approach Windy Hill telecom mast above the M62 which is crossed by a dedicated bridge before tackling Slippery Moss and Blackstone Edge with views into Lancashire. The trig point here is atop a huge boulder. A reputed section of Roman road (going east to west) forms part of the route before reaching the White Horse Inn on the A58 road to Littleborough, Lancs. The Way then follows water board tracks and reservoir embankments high above the pass to Coldwell Hill above Todmorden. Here Stoodley Pike comes into view, conspicuous by a huge stone tower in the shape of a needle. It is 125ft high and celebrates the Allies' victory at Waterloo, 1815. A dark stairway leads to the tower top. Below the summit is the village of Mankinholes, a hamlet on the flanks of the hill with a welcome youth hostel.

From Stoodley Pike the Way descends into the Upper Calder Valley through Callis Wood. Apart from a possible stay at Marsden (if coming from Crowden Youth Hostel) this will be the first descent from the Pennine heights. Here the environs of Hebden Bridge are dramatic: high gritstone edges and crags break out over tree-clad hills in the twin valleys of Colden Water and Hebden Water. The official route ascends Blackshaw Head and down into Colden Water before again seeking high ground on Heptonstall Moor. It is, however, a far better route to visit Hebden Bridge and walk the charming Hebden Water – a remote tree-lined valley with grit-stone outcrops. After passing Hardcastle Crags the path ascends the valley to join the official Pennine Way at Walshaw Dean Reservoirs before crossing to Top Withen on Stanbury Moor. This is the reputed model for *Wuthering Heights* (see Haworth) but today is a broken-down ruin. After crossing Ponden Clough Beck to Upper Ponden the Way leads to **Ponden** Hall, home of the Heaton family until 1898. It dates from Elizabethan times and has deep mullions, partly rebuilt in 1801. A stone inscription is from the demolished *Old House*, also rebuilt in 1801, not the Hall. It is believed to be the model for *Thrushcross Grange* and is now a hotel. The Hall overlooks Ponden Reservoir, 1877. Below the reservoir, east, is Ponden Mill and Haworth, but the Pennine Way is to the west over Dean Fields to Slippery Stones, again seeking the high ground of Ickornshaw Moor in North Yorkshire before descending to the gentler fields of Lothersdale. [6–24]

POLE MOOR   An exposed ridge in the Pennines west of Huddersfield where the wind is always singing in the wires. It overlooks the Colne Valley and via Standedge over the moors to Manchester. Farmsteads shelter in the lea of Warts Hill, a rocky ridge over which electricity poles stagger. Its principal claim to fame is the radio aerial twin masts of latticed steel at Moor Edge. The towers rise over 500ft and the wires between them transmit on a power of 200kW. The boggy ground gives a good 'earth signal'. [19]

PONDEN   (See Pennine Way).

PONTEFRACT   Pontefract! An echo from history. The once massive 5-acre castle stood on a hilltop between the Rivers Aire and Calder. The rocky outcrops were augmented with seven massive limestone towers and curtain walling – it was the King's HQ in the north. Henry VIII lived here. Built by a Norman, Baron de Lacey, it went to the Earls of Lancaster and via a daughter, Blanche, to John O'Gaunt, to whom the duchy was restored in 1361. He entertained Chaucer here, who described it as the 'white walled castle'. Here Edward IV rested before the Battle of Towton where the Red and White Roses fought in the snow. Its dungeons were fed with prominent opponents of the Crown: James I of Scotland, the Duc d'Orleans after Agincourt, Richard II, Thomas of Lancaster and Earl Rivers. Henry VII married Richard III's niece for political unity here: their son Henry VIII made Pontefract his northern home. It was

Opposite: THE KEEP, PONTEFRACT CASTLE.

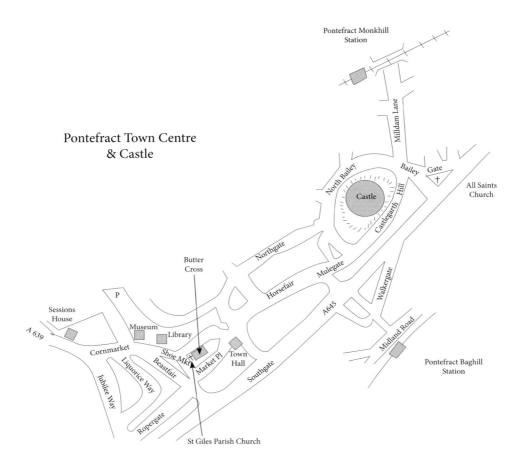

Pontefract Town Centre & Castle

Pontefract Monkhill Station

Milldam Lane

North Bailey

Bailey Gate

Castle

Castlegarth Hill

All Saints Church

Northgate

Mulegate

Butter Cross

Horsefair

A645

Walkergate

P

Sessions House

Museum

Library

A 639

Cornmarket

Shoe Mkt

Beastfair

Market Pl

Town Hall

Midland Road

Pontefract Baghill Station

Liquorice Way

Jubilee Way

Ropergate

Southgate

St Giles Parish Church

here that Catherine Howard dallied, fatally, with a courtier. A painting of the medieval castle in the museum illustrates the fairytale strength of this grim Tower of the North. In the Civil War it was a bastion for the Crown and held out even after the death of Charles I. So fed up were the locals in the adjoining town that after the Civil War they petitioned that it be slighted. Now only the stump of the once puissant trefoil-shaped keep demonstrates what once was here. Still owned by the Duchy of Lancaster, that is, the Crown, it is leased to the council who have landscaped the grounds around the foundations of its ring of towers – Gascoigne's, Consta-

ble's, Queen's, King's, Swillington's, the Pyx and the Round Tower (keep) which still rises some 30ft and may be climbed for a view. The outer bailey extended down the hill towards the town. Witness South Bailey Gate, the remains of the twelfth-century gate with portcullis grooves are still discernible.

From the castle's grounds look east through cottage chimneys to the ruined church of All Saints. Like medieval Coventry Cathedral and the Kaiser Wilhelm Church in Berlin these preserved ruins are a witness to our Civil War and the siege of Pontefract. In the first siege of 1644 Sir Richard Lowther garrisoned the castle for the King.

Sir Thomas Fairfax for Parliament breached the walls at the Pyx Tower with huge losses from an exploding magazine – but failed to capture it. Sir Marmaduke Langdale relieved the Crown but was eventually starved out. Then Colonel Cotterel and 100 men garrisoned for Parliament, but the Royalists retook it with a ruse and even Cromwell could not get them out till March 1649 – months after the King's death. Ordnance fired from St Giles caused its ruin, and from the castle the ruin of All Saints.

Today, from the castle entrance a good view of ruined All Saints enlarges as you walk down Beech Hill past council houses built up to the very castle walls. The church tower is bulky with two large Dec bell openings, crocketed pinnacles and Dec balustrade. Above the tower is an octagonal stage in perfect proportion – with crocketed pinnacles, embattled with pierced merlons. Walking round the church the mass of the tower is dramatic. In 1838 Robert Chantrell made some repairs to the transepts creating the shortest and widest church ever. A little apse was built into the ruin of the chancel. Here are fourteenth-century remains up to the roof plate. Rather cheekily, a new nave has been built in brick within the fifteenth-century nave which still rises above its new companion; its double clerestory windows contain forlorn tracery remnants. Well-worn octagonal piers support the aisles. The former large panel-traceried Perp West window is propped up against the North wall of the ruins – it is very similar to the North transept window. The brick nave was only erected in 1967; it may have been better to reroof part of the old nave – in line with current English Heritage thinking to preserve old stonework. To the north of the nave is the medieval two-storey porch – looking somewhat worn and opening into ruins.

Then into Pontefract, west via Micklegate, passing by nineteenth-century and recent houses one reaches the Georgian town centre via evocatively named Horse Fair. Here stands a spectacular ten-floor block of flats belonging to Wakefield District. It is a lunatic imposition on this Georgian town visible from Garrowby Hill near the East coast and from the Pennine watershed to the west. Unfortunately the names of the architect and chairman of the planning committee have been obscured.

The glory of Pontefract today is its broad eighteenth-century market place, cobbled and set with Georgian town mansions. It has shaken off the coal dust from its colliery days to reveal a Georgian gem of a town. Maybe this hibernation for 150 years saved it. Before coal the rich local soil was ideal for a discrete horticulture growing licorice, commemorated in many local names and also in verse by John Betjeman:

In the licorice fields at Pontefract
My love and I did meet
And many a burdened licorice bush
Was blooming round our feet;
Red hair she had and golden skin,
Her sulky lips were shaped for sin,
Her sturdy legs were flannel-slack'd
The strongest legs in Pontefract!

The light and dangling licorice flowers
Gave off the sweetest smells;
From various black Victorian towers
The Sunday evening bells
Came pealing over dales and hills
And tanneries and silent mills
And lowly streets where country stops
And little shuttered corner shops.

At the east end of the market place is the Georgian Town Hall, pediment on fluted Doric pilasters over three open arches. First-floor windows are grandly balustered: above is a white clock tower, cupola and weathervane. Behind, fin-de-siècle extension, 1882, neo-Baroque with a large gabled transom window rising through the cornice to the roof. Then, going west into the market place is a good Georgian house on the left by James Paine, 1776 – bow-fronted windows and blank arch rising to a broken pediment two and a half storeys up. It is presently Barclays Bank. To the right is The Liquorice Bush, a classical mid-nineteenth century house, now a pub. Then perhaps the grandest Georgian house here, The Red Lion, with a central tripartite opening marked by four Doric columns which rise from the ground floor to become Ionic columns on the first floor, with a very pretty frieze and balcony. Next door is the proportionately large market hall with big arched openings. The tall frontispiece is flanked by twin columns with mixed capitals; a huge modillioned cornice and arch rise above the roof and within a gable the Arms of Pontefract. Almost every other building is Georgian with yards and alleys leading off; most houses are penetrated by shop fronts, but Maud's Yard is of special interest having bowed windows on the first floor – the second floor is supported by Doric columns and oversails as though from an earlier age. Where the square widens to the west a tall Arts and Crafts corner building has timbered gables and a turret on its loft as though it was visited by Norman Shaw. Here also is the Buttercross, 1734, an arcaded stone shelter. To the north is St Giles, the pretty parish church with rusticated arched windows and geometric tracery. This is post-Civil War rebuilding and within are arcades of the medieval church blown up in that war. The classical tower rises by

reducing stages with urn finials then an octagonal clock storey with open stone cupola.

Carry on west past Shoe Market (by St Giles) and Beast Fair into Ropergate which has more Georgian houses including a splendid eight-bayed mansion with an off-centre three-bayed pediment and grand Doric pedimented porch. At the west junction with Jubilee Way is a faience-tiled former cinema of the 1920s. Then turn into Liquorice Way and east once more for Corn Market. Here is the late Georgian Sessions House built for the borough's quarter sessions by Charles Watson, 1807, a dramatically bold Ionic portico and Royal Arms within the pediment. Here also is another hotel, The Green Dragon, with Doric porch and triple bow-windowed bays rising up two storeys. No. 17 Corn Market is a grand symmetrical Georgian house with bolection moulding in its principal doorway and a strongly modillioned cornice. Another Georgian house is The Barley Mow, a grand three-storeyed hotel; opposite is a further Georgian three-storey brick house with two oriel windows (probably Victorian). Here Corn Market widens and in the centre is a war memorial to the York and Lancaster Regiment which used to be garrisoned in Pontefract. The Blackmoor Head is an Arts and Crafts pub of about 1920 with a green glaze-tiled front and timbering. In the museum behind the library is an oil painting of Pontefract Castle. Returning from Corn Market to the side of St Giles Church via Shoe Market it is easy to imagine the medieval layout of this town with different markets held in the various streets. It provides a very worthwhile visit at market times but, if just for the buildings, come on a Sunday morning when the churches are open. [17]

POOL Wharfside village at the intersection of the Wharfedale Road and the Bradford to Harrogate Road which swoops into the dale and off to Harrogate over a long bridge of seven arches. St Wilfrid's Church is diminutive with a small tower and small octagonal spirelet. Designed by Robert Chantrell in 1839. Its proportions are ruined by the addition of a later apse but which has Morris glass. [3]

BUTTERCROSS IN THE MARKET AND ST GILES, PONTEFRACT.

PUDSEY A comfortable stone-built town still incorporating old cottages. It occupies a hill between Leeds and Bradford bordering good country. To the south remains a precious oasis of farmland, woods and vales where flows the Tyersal Beck to Cockersdale. Like Bradford, Pudsey was famous for manufacturing worsted cloth. Everything of interest in the town centre is nineteenth century: the Town Hall is a poor exercise in random Gothic and Tudor on a cramped corner site; Trinity Methodist Church on Low Town is stilted Renaissance: Corinthian columns carry a three-bay pediment and a squared ogee dome sits on a gabled tower. Just off the main centre is the Parish Church of St Lawrence, rather grand with sternly buttressed West tower in a handsome rendition of the EE style by Thomas Taylor, 1821. Tracery is Y or intersected in the aisle lancets – divided by buttress with big gabled pinnacles. Inside is a lofty, ribbed plaster ceiling and three galleries. On the terrace

Opposite, above: MARKET PLACE, PONTEFRACT; *below*: ALL SAINTS – DAMAGED IN THE CIVIL WAR, PONTEFRACT.

hillside to the south of the town is the Moravian settlement at Fulneck. (See *Fulneck.*) Birthplace of Sir Len Hutton, former captain of YCCC. [9]

QUEENSBURY   A high breezy outpost in the hills west of Bradford where the sophisticated neo-Baroque Victoria Hall somehow seems a surprise in so high a place at 1,000ft. Stone terraces were for the mill workers who once worked the mill. Holy Trinity Church is a strained and ugly Dec composition with thick tower, narrow lancets and broad pinnacles. The body of the church is an aisleless attachment of the tower; double lancet windows and plate tracery in the West end. Robust Victorian memorials are in the churchyard. At the town's central crossroads is a well-proportioned Gothic Memorial to Prince Albert. The Black Dyke Mills are of terrifying mass with a tall blackened stone chimney. The former gatehouse is gabled with a clock and weathervaned cupola. [8]

RAWDON   High up above the steep north hillside of the River Aire and bordering Leeds/Bradford Airport, a home for wealthy commuters. St Peter's Church retains the dumpy Gothic-survival tower from Thomas Layton's church of 1706, but the present nave dates from 1864; the high, short chancel is restored to proper proportion within by a good early twentieth-century Dec-style screen. Rawdon Hall is across the A65, half a mile to the southwest. It is an L-shaped house of the seventeenth century with a seven-light mullion and transomed window. Built by Francis Rawdon in 1625 according to the initials and date inscribed on it. [9]

RIPPONDEN   Charming mill town lying deep in a Pennine valley and astride the fast-flowing River Ryburn, a tributary of the Calder. Its old centre, gathered round a cobbled and hump-backed bridge, is largely sixteenth- and seventeenth-century cottages. Turning down the B6113 from the main road presents a picturesque scene of stone roofs stepping down the hill to the river. The church of St Bartholomew was moved to its present leafy position here after being severely damaged by a flood in 1722. That Georgian church may be seen in a painting inside: it had arched windows and a pedimented entrance. It was destroyed, not by water, but by nineteenth-century Gothic zealots who gave us the present dark but elegant Dec church with a tall broached stone spire. The Dec tracery weaves unusual patterns, quatrefoil piers in the arcades. Up above the town to the west is Shaw Edge with splendid views over rolling hills to Lighthazles and Lumb and a pub from which to stare when the weather is fine.

Opposite: St Bartholomew, Ripponden.

RISHWORTH   Scattered Pennine village on the windy shoulder of Rishworth Moor overlooking the valley of the River Ryburn. Some good vernacular buildings of the seventeenth century, especially Cockcroft Hall well up into the moors. It is a rambling gabled mansion in two distinct halves linked by a transverse ridge. The right wing is older, 1607, and stepped forward with a big mullioned and transomed window. The long, low, left portion, 1672, has a similar window and a gabled two-storey porch. Descending the hill is a group of cottages collectively called *Upper Goat House* with mullioned windows and which gives the impression of a distinguished house. Opposite the *Goat House*, west, is St John the Divine on Godly Lane – Arts and Crafts, low, embattled tower, round-arched lights and a rose window whorl. Rishworth School, an eighteenth-century foundation, is off the main road. Its pedimented three-storeyed building has wings with pyramid roofs, 1820, which look over the Ryburn Valley and woods. Rishworth Mill in the lower valley is known locally as Rishworth Palace. [19]

ROTHWELL   Has a fine fifteenth-century church, Holy Trinity, with tower, aisles and nave all embattled, and a good original Perp nave roof with carved bosses. The arcades were rebuilt in the nineteenth century. The tower is similar to Woodkirk and with a corbelled-out parapet, in the Yorkshire fashion, looking quite military. There is a Jacobean font with a two-storey pierced cover and three-stage spire; fragments of Saxon monuments carved with creatures within arcading. Opposite the church, west, is a highly weathered remnant of the former castle, now scarcely more than a stoop. Formerly on this site was Manor Farm, a timbered house of the fifteenth century taken down to be preserved by the City Council. Where is it? [16]

ROUNDHAY PARK (LEEDS)   This big country estate to the northeast of Leeds which flows on into the countryside was bought in 1797 by Thomas Nicholson, a London banker who married into Leeds business. It is a large undulating park dipping down to the Waterloo Lake with banks of trees, where a little promenade follows the lake as though a seaside. It was bought by John Barran the clothing manufacturer in 1871 who resold it to the city, but retained parts for development. There are intrusions of big manufacturers' houses, though well wooded and not fatal to the large charm of the park. Indeed at one corner the busy town begins in an instant where the tramway used to deposit hundreds of pleasure seekers at weekends and holidays. The corner is marked by the Oakwood Clock Tower. Boats are available on the lake and it is a place for fun and relaxation. *Round-*

hay Mansion is up the hill to the north overlooking the lake and was built in 1816 by Thomas Taylor the architect for Nicholson's Union Bank in Leeds. It has a wonderful prospect over the park to the lake but is modest considering the size of the park. It is in grand Grecian style: Ionic portico with four giant columns; Doric pilasters at the angles; and full-height bay windows to elevations either side of the main façade. Now a function suite. The Stables, a little to the west, 1821, are conspicuous by a weathervane over the cupola and a pediment on the carriage house. Nearby estate workers' cottages also have a pediment and have been converted into a useful public house. A carriage drive through the park is now a road; rather like Chatsworth. It was made by Thomas Nicholson and also takes you to the lake and boathouse. It joins *Princes Avenue*, which was intended to be the start of a villa development in 1873 which luckily (mostly) failed to occur. The road bisects the estate so that the kitchen garden and conservatories are to the west. The largest conservatory was built in 1911 as Coronation House and is now the centre for *Tropical World*, a lofty home for exotic trees and shrubs, and open to the public. [16]

SADDLEWORTH MOOR   At the furthest west in the county on the M62 at its junction with A672 is exhilarating Windy Hill. The secrets of the west side of the Pennines are revealed from a viewpoint in the no-man's land between county signs: over bobbing cotton grass industrial Rochdale and Oldham appear below with views beyond to the Irish Sea. An old boundary post states 'Lancashire County, Milnrow Local Board'. Walkers on the Pennine Way following the crest of the Pennines lean in the incessant wind as they make for the dedicated Pennine Way bridge over the M62. On Windy Hill by the viewpoint is a tall latticed mast belonging to BT whose high and sinister can-shaped aerials silently relay cross-Pennine gossip while the wind roars through the wires of the fence. [West of 19]

SALTAIRE   The creation of Sir Titus Salt who established a massive factory extending to 14 acres outside Bradford in 1853. His father was a wool merchant from Morley. He travelled widely to buy wool and chanced his arm in purchasing an unwanted cargo of Alpaca wool in Liverpool – it has a long fibre and the Bradford worsted equipment was ideal for the purpose. His alpaca and mohair worsted with a lustrous sheen became highly fashionable and made Salt's fortune. His mill is like a five-storey Italianate fortress, its windows placed in sets of six, divided by a string course, and under a heavily corbelled cornice. In the centre of the façade twin towers rise above the cornice each with an arched

lantern storey. An obelisk-like chimney stands in front of the building – originally it had a big corona. The mill has storeys of iron beams on tiers of cast iron columns; between the girders brick arches support stone floors – a precaution against fire. This vast five-storeyed, two-hundred-yard long mill was all for spinning. In 1868 the 'New Mill', a dye shop, was put up. The new chimney is a copy of the Frari in Venice. The main entrance to the mill is down Victoria Street between the two buildings through a triumphal archway crowned with a Baroque arch.

A capitalist manufacturer, Sir Titus was Liberal MP, Mayor of Bradford and a notable humane employer. He set up his factory away from the unsanitary, dirty, back-to-backs which all drained into the Bradford Beck. Sir Titus's new estate was designed by Lockwood and Mawson, Bradford's nineteenth-century architects of renown; they built rectangles of houses, 16 in a row with gables and arched windows all with an Italianate flavour – there were no back-to-backs and everyone had a backyard. Sir Titus abhorred the evils of drink and so there was no pub, only the Institute for recreation; a hospital, alms houses (if you could not work), a park, boathouse on the river and tramway up the hill across the river to Shipley Glen, which still operates. This gave access to the hills and woods beyond. Although now demolished, there was a public washhouse with baths and early washing machines for clothes. At the company dining hall you could bring your own food and have it cooked or buy plates of meat and bowls of soup. The village had its own fire service. The four lions in front of the Institute garden are called *Vigilance, Determination, War* and *Peace* (T. Milnes). The Institute has a pyramid-roofed tower, five bays each side and statues representing Art and Science (T. Milnes) either side of the Baroque entrance.

Salt was a Congregationalist; he employed Lockwood and Mawson for his new classical chapel – tunnel vaulted with scagliola Corinthian columns, but furnished for preaching and Bible reading with clergy pews and organ. Still in place today are the huge ormolu gasoliers, that is, gilded gas lights. Above them are flower shaped grilles to allow the gases to escape. The Corinthian portico is almost circular and forms both tower and entrance to the church and, as the icon it has become, is best seen from Victoria Road. The first stage of the round portico supports a broad soffit, the circular roof is capped by a strong octagonal tower with Corinthian columns rising to a dome. The tower has a peal of bells (or at any rate six), one of only two Congregational churches so equipped. The original bells were used for

Opposite: SALTAIRE MILL.

SALTAIRE ON MONDAY.

munitions in the last war but a new set was given in 2003 by Maggie Silver to commemorate her husband Jonathon, who fought to preserve the mills commercially after they ceased production. The tenor bell is called *Titus* and inscribed 'Sweet is the work my God, my King'. This peal was cast by Eijsbouts in Holland; it has a distinctive Continental lightness of tone. A statue by T. Milne of Sir Titus in Carrera marble stands in the vestibule, brought from Salt's home at Crow Nest, Lightcliffe. As in Salt's Coat of Arms, the base of the statue depicts Alpaca and Angora goats; also representing that new and glorious period is a cornucopia of rich fruit descending on a symbolic Saltaire. The statue was given to Sir Titus by his work people and he in turn gave a garden party at Crow Nest for 3,000. The Salts are

interred in a mausoleum attached to the 'North' side of the church. Crow Nest is demolished.

The mill by Victoria Road has been turned into a dignified set of galleries – the ground floor is a Hockney Gallery; there are exhibitions of Hockney's opera set designs, the history of the building, carpets, suits, flowers, etc. The galleries are a powerful draw and enable one to see the huge space and interior of the mill. The old boathouse on the River Aire has been turned into a pub and the Shipley Glen tramway still operates at weekends. The local authority is endeavouring to preserve this conservation area, now in many hands. Although lost to the world of industry only in 1986, the survival of Sir Titus Salt's creation appears assured. [8]

Opposite: SALTAIRE CONGREGATIONAL CHURCH – SALT'S MAUSOLEUM.

SANDAL CASTLE.

SANDAL MAGNA An original motte and bailey castle of the twelfth century was replaced by a strong medieval castle in the fourteenth century – shell pattern keep with a circular outer bailey and moat with attached towers. The ruins have a small visitor centre and the keep on its little mound stands above the landscaped Pugney Country Park and lake. The castle ruins look spectacular from beyond the lake from the A61 with the rising sun behind them. On the former main road from the south to Wakefield is the Parish Church of St Helen. Mainly thirteenth century, with a crossing tower. The nave windows have unusual shouldered lintels, copied in the nineteenth-century extensions. The chancel has two Dec windows each divided into two lights; ovals within the inner ogee sweeps. The South aisle windows are straight headed, plain with arched lights. The East window is Perp. The crossing tower piers are spectacularly strong: each arch has trefoil roll moulding amplified by strong base sections. The moulding is like a series of attached shafts as at Bradford. Without doubt of the thirteenth century. Above the chancel arch notice the profile of an earlier nave, also the inconsistent masonry added above it.

At the East end of the South aisle are memorials to the Pilkingtons, baronets of nearby Chevet Park. The strength of mourning for Sir Thomas Edward Pilkington is amply demonstrated by an emblematic Corinthian column, fractured and covered by a marble 'shroud'. East of the crossing tower is a glazed-in portion of the chancel used as a meeting room. The oak screen to the South chancel chapel has a dado of carved vines; the patterned tracery in the carved heads of lunettes is more Dec than Perp but today has the sense of Art Nouveau. The roof also appears to be Dec. The retained vicarage opening off the churchyard is a stone-roofed Georgian house with broad sashes, quoins and string course – a Victorian addition has arched windows. Nearby are a number of former farms with stone roofs and cottages which, but for the traffic, would make Sandal with its trees a distinguished retreat. [22]

SCHOLES (Bradford) Victorian almshouses with gables and tall chimneys in a Tudor style. The church is Victorian Dec but the tower is modern with a triangular spire rising out of sharply cut gables. There are some old cottages and farms in the village around Towngate in this rural area.

Overleaf, left, above: DOVECOTE, SHARLSTON HALL;
below: SHARLSTON HALL;
right: ENTRANCE PIERS, SHARLSTON HALL.

SCISSETT In a Pennine valley near Denby Dale is St Augustine's church, 1839, with big lancets and a strangely small tower with pinnacles like chimneys. It has a spacious wooded churchyard. Southeast, uphill at Wheatley Hill is a twin-gabled farm, 1651; the West gable facing into the yard is timbered although the more handsome South front is now timbered only in appearance. From here may be seen the gantries of an operating coalmine which fastens itself to the hillside. Bagden Hall (hotel), 1866, is a mixed Renaissance mansion with Jacobean-style chimneys; over the Doric porch is an eight-light transomed window. Built by Sir Thomas Norton, from its elevated position it looks out through trees – above the coalmine and mills – to wooded hills beyond. From Scissett via Wheatley Hill and Lower Denby is a good hilltop drive to Upper Denby, two or three miles away, affording wonderful views of tree-clad hills. [21]

SEACROFT (Leeds) Although dominated by spreading concrete development and tower blocks which surround it, a broad green is preserved with cottages, the lancet-windowed church of St James, 1845, and to the north, Seacroft Grange. The latter is a rebuilt seventeenth-century mansion with Jacobean chimney stacks and a mixture of shaped and Dutch gables; the east elevation contains an array of mullioned windows, those on the ground floor all with transoms. [10]

SHADWELL Village north of Leeds Ring Road. In the High Street is a distinguished old stone cottage with continuous drip mould over door and windows (lintel dated 1637). Down Main Street are more cottages with drip moulding, one 1698 but with modern windows. The old hall, square on to Main Street, is a low Georgian affair with an arched end window. Just below is St Paul's Church of 1841 (R. D. Chantrell), neo-Norman, in the shadow of an excellent yew tree. It has tall, round-arched windows with shafts set in bays, the parapets are supported on corbels, a polygonal apse and belcote. The yew tree gives it credibility. Shadwell Grange has the Grecian air of the early nineteenth century: mini pediment and coat of arms over its west entrance. It is attached to Shadwell Grange Farm, an eighteenth-century range with pediment and blocked-in stone-mullioned windows. [4]

SHARLSTON COMMON A mining dormitory, especially New Sharlston. Turn off the A645 by the colliery monument and south to the Green, a common within an old farming community. Here is Elizabethan Sharlston Hall – low with rambling gables, mullioned windows, a projecting porch, wood-framed upper storey and over-

SKELMANTHORPE FROM EMLEY MOOR.

sailing gable of 1574. Grand Elizabethan gate piers have ball finials, and pedestrian gate piers obelisk caps. Picturesque and many gabled, it was once owned by the Earl of Westmorland. Go up the lane to further obelisk gate piers, oddly bearing the street number 60, to see the pretty timber-gabled porch projecting into a garden sheltered by multi-gabled wings. A large transomed window dominates others disproportionately. Behind you is a huge dovecote with 240 nesting boxes in a field. At the far corner of the front walled garden is a ruined gazebo, open to the south and west, on a flight of stone steps. On the main road St Luke's Parish Church, 1886, is big and rectangular like a barn, with Dec-style tracery. [22]

SHEPLEY Stone eighteenth-century weavers' cottages and Victorian terraces in the hills south of Huddersfield. The church of St Paul is 1848, with belcote and lancets. In the village is the Old Hall – Elizabethan, with mullioned and transomed windows of a primitive character.

To the street is a gate with a nicely carved Tudor arch. On the wooded hillside are cottages of seventeenth to nineteenth centuries, many with strings of mullioned windows. [25]

SHIPLEY In the Aire Valley where the Bradford Beck joins the River Aire. The congestion of railway, road and canal has forced a newly built centre into an introspective piazza with modern clock-towered market hall and bus station. The Parish Church of St Paul, 1823, enjoys a prominent isolation up the hill west of the town. It is quite rich Regency Gothic with tall transomed windows, intersecting tracery, embattled gables; the tower has fancy pierced merlons. Down the Bradford road (Carr Lane) is seventeenth-century Shipley Old Hall, the Conservative HQ. It has not been well treated over the years. The twin gables are from distinct periods: that to the left has remnants of diamond profile mullions under a drip mould, whereas the later right-hand gable has quoins and square profile mullions and transoms. Shipley is riven by busy roads but this does not affect the tranquillity of nearby *Saltaire*. [8]

SILSDEN On the north side of the Aire Valley above lush meadows between the River Aire and the Leeds and Liverpool Canal. Where the canal passes through the town, stone mills gather as evidence of past industrial achievement. Stone chimneys and gabled mills remain, converted to modern use. Waterloo Mill retains its cast iron loggia made of columns and girders. In the centre, old cottages from the sixteenth and seventeenth centuries gather prettily round the stream where ducks devoutly claim their rights. The Parish Church of St James is an eclectic mix of 1816 Dec with a tower and tiny spire of 1876 tending to Art Nouveau. It looks rather unsatisfactory, but once you know that its base is a broad, aisleless nave built in 1712 much is explained. North of the church is the hall: three gables of varied mullion windows with transoms, 1682. [1]

SKELMANTHORPE Hilly former mining village set in good unspoilt country of woods and green vales with a pub called The Chartist. The towering presence of the Emley Moor Transmitter – a tapering concrete tower of 1,084ft – which holds aloft a massive white anode – stands a mile to the north. Stone terraces and seventeenth-century farmhouses are in the village centre. The church of 1894 by G. F. Bodley is partially faced in stone, EE-style Y tracery windows. [21]

Opposite, above and below: ST PETER, 1763, SOWERBY.

SLAITHWAITE Small mill town in the Colne Valley, its compressed centre is shared with the river, railway and Huddersfield Narrow Canal. To the north, below Pole Moor aerials, is a feeder dam (for the canal) which seems to threaten the village clustered below the big stone railway viaduct. Mills and chimneys remain but are now mostly converted to non-woollen use. St James Church, 1789, has two storeys of straight-headed windows; a little like a warehouse itself, it also has a Venetian East window and classical tower. Opposite is a gem of an Elizabethan manor house with picturesquely narrow diamond-section mullioned windows – transomed on the ground floor – with that asymmetric casual style that so often spells picturesque. The handsome five-storey mill, Globe Worstead Co. Ltd, is by the canal, and Spectrum Yarns at Spa Mill. [19]

SOUTH KIRBY Old village with a distinguished Perp church. Much new housing but this former mining village has recovered and once again sits splendid among golden fields in early autumn. The tower of the limestone All Saints is particularly handsome, embattled – diminishing diagonal buttresses. The South aisle windows are typically Perp below a plain balustrade; the nave and aisle roofs have a shallow pitch giving the tower greater prominence. Within, however, round piers of 1200 support EE arcades. Carved roof bosses belong to the Perp period. The South porch is of two storeys, rib vaulted and displaying the arms of local families. There is a monument to John Wentworth, 1720, by John Rysbrack. West of the church on a little green is the statue of a miner on a black marble plinth. It commemorates those who worked and lost their lives in South Kirby and Riddings Mine, and Frickley South Elmsall Colliery. The sculpture is by Graham Ibbeson. [23]

SOWERBY On a steep col between the confluence of the Calder and the Ryburn, Sowerby contains some remarkable buildings. Near the church is Sowerby Hall, gabled, with odd finials, a lurching chimney, hipped roof and blocked-in mullions. West is Trinity Cottage and a collection of tiny mullioned windows. High on the blustery hill opposite the hall is a grand classical church, St Peter, 1764. The South side shows arched windows, an attic storey and balustrade embellished by ranks of Tuscan columns and large doorways with Gibbs surrounds. A slightly later tower tends to Gothic with coupled lancets but has other classical displays including unusual topiary-like pinnacles grouped four by four. The North front by contrast is bare of ornament like the back of a stage set. Inside, large Corinthian columns support integral galleries. There is no chancel as such but in the apsidal sanctuary is an elaborate Venetian East window, painted reliefs of Moses and Christ, stucco medallions and Royal Arms. The pulpit has combined Corinthian and Ionic columns. There is a portrait of Archbishop Tillotson, whose statue stands in an alcove behind the font, and who was born at Haugh End in the parish. The date of the statue, 1796, comes from its model which was kept in Field House, a nine bay classical house with pediment (1749) – south down Dean Lane.

Down the hill towards Sowerby Bridge (north) is Wood Lane Hall, 1644, an excellent Jacobean hall with a gabled front, transomed windows and a magnificent 27-light hall window. A gallery extends along three sides with turned Jacobean balusters. The fireplace supported on fluted Ionic columns has the largest mantel in the county. The ceiling is in fine contemporary plaster. The embattled two-storey porch has a Yorkshire rose window with cusped 'pears' around an apple. [13]

SOWERBY BRIDGE An industrial town with much remaining eighteenth-century infrastructure. Here the River Ryburn runs into the River Calder and there are mills either side of the river and canal. The main street has many former weavers' cottages and nineteenth-century prosperity is evident in ashlar commercial buildings and Christ Church, 1819, by John Oates. It stands on a bluff overlooking the main street and river. It is a large Regency Gothic church – West tower and exceedingly tall South aisle also embattled; large transomed lancet windows divided by buttresses with very tall pinnacles, galleried within. Across the main street is the Rochdale Canal and eighteenth-century canal-side stone-built warehousing. The main street is lined with mills and also the banks of the River Calder which here rushes over weirs to provide a canoe slalom course. Greenaps Mill (1792) was water powered with numerous waterwheels running 100 looms. Now made into flats it was the first integrated wool mill. Some of the stone mills are early with mullioned windows; the tall Carlton Mill (1850) whose stone chimney stack is bound with iron hoops was powered by steam.

On Town Hall Street just by the cast iron bridge (widened) over the River Calder is the grand former town hall, 1857, with an embellished front of elliptical pediments, tall bracketed windows, a balustraded round tower and dome reminiscent of Salt's Congregational Church. West up Hollingsmill Lane is a jumble of tall mills, for example Joel Mill with a vertical line of warehouse doors to each of five levels. Looking up at the junction with Carnegie Street opposite the library the effect of high gables and stone chimney stacks is quite dizzying. Between the main street and the river, old mills stand out into the water, some built on piers, and actu-

SOWERBY BRIDGE, WOOD LANE HALL, 1649.

ally standing on the main street is a theatrically placed octagonal chimney. A little east is the Canal Wharf – eighteenth-century warehouses including the Salt Warehouse used for trans-shipping goods from the Rochdale Canal (Manchester 33 miles) to the Calder and Hebble (Wakefield 21 miles), which here lie alongside each other. The two canals were engineered for barges of different lengths and depths. Today the Wharf is a busy marina but many believed the Rochdale Canal would never reopen, having been filled in and abandoned in a significant way. Volunteers and enthusiasts combined to reopen it in 2002. At the Wharf is a sculpture of a navigator and boy operating a lock beam. Two other eighteenth-century warehouses are here, one is now The Moorings (pub). The Navigation Inn was once the Moot Hall (c.16th) and then called The Chain because here a chain locked the canal on Sundays. By the Wharf is the Georgian canal manager's house now used to hire canal craft. The Rochdale climbs west through the town via Locks 1 and 2 passing under Tuel Lane to the west of Christ Church where Lock 3 is the deepest in the UK at 30ft. [13]

STAINLAND Stone Pennine village overlooking industrial West Yorkshire, it is all on one descending street. Opposite the ancient village cross is St Andrew's, a Georgian church with arched windows, a sun dial and two-stage octagonal tower with cupola. The classical chancel is of recent date. Higher up the village is a delightful sixteenth-century farmhouse with such a variety of mullioned windows and crooked chimneys that it might be an illustration from a book of nursery rhymes. [19]

STANBURY (OUTLYER OF HAWORTH) The Revd Patrick Brontë promoted Haworth's daughter chapel of St Gabriel, 1848 (Romantic Elizabethan); it was given part of Haworth's three-decker pulpit in 1910. Ponden Mill was built to spin cotton in 1792 but is now committed to wool products. Ponden Hall is partly Elizabethan (early 17th) and is a hotel enjoying wide views over Ponden Reservoir. (See *Pennine Way*.) [7]

STANLEY Half suburban, half rural, it lies just above the flood plain west of the Calder, north of Wakefield. Longstanding engagement with the sinuating and flooding river still shows in local place names like Bottom Boat and Stanley Ferry, but the ferry is now a bridge and the river bypassed by the modern sweep of the Aire and Calder Navigation. An 18ft canoe was discovered below here preserved in mud since the Bronze Age; it is now in York Museum. St Peter's, 1821, in Romantic Tudor Gothic, was rebuilt by W. D. Carӧe. It is unusual even for the Regency – very broad with many gables on the aisles and Perp windows. Because of subsidence it is likely to be demolished. From the churchyard are extensive views of the Calder Valley and, just across the road, a seventeenth-century partially Georgianized gabled farmhouse. [16]

STANLEY FERRY On a broad reach of the Aire and Calder navigation below Stanley. Here the canal crosses the River Calder by a cast iron Grecian aqueduct complete with fluted Doric columns and pedimented pavilions with Greek key moulding. The Aire and Calder is a commercial waterway and the old aqueduct has been duplicated with a wider concrete one. Nearby is a boatyard with chandlery located by a canal toll house also Grecian – pediment on Doric columns. Next door is the Old Mill House where the canal basin makes an attractive marina for moored pleasure boats. British Waterways has one of their two canal repair depots here. (See also *Bottom Boat*.) [16]

STEETON Situated on the south side of the valley above the flood plain of the River Aire are ranks of stone cottages which once housed the workers for Woodlands Mill – tall and standing high above the village, south of the B6265. The old village is down an unmade road gathered around St Stephen's Church, Victorian EE style – steep roofs, a tower with short spire and elements of broaching. Old cottages and Steeton Hall Farm are opposite, with High Hall dating from the sixteenth century with small diamond section mullions. Sandstone extensions in Yorkshire Jacobean look odd on a gritstone house. Steeton Hall is nineteenth century, pedimented and has a Doric porch (now a hotel). On the hillside north is a stone castellated tower built to celebrate Queen Victoria's Jubilee in 1887. At Currer Wood further west is an Arts and Crafts Pennine manor house built in 1895 for mill owner Sir Swire Smith. [1]

STONE CHAIR Terraces of blackened stone houses and the rump of a mill with its chimney. The church of St Michael and All Angels on the main road is a Dec-style chapel with aisles and belcote. The Duke of York is a seventeenth-century inn with massive chimney breast on its north side. It is stone roofed. On the road to Northowram is a cutting through a stone-lined ravine like the former Walls of Jericho at Thornton. [14]

SWILLINGTON A suburb village southeast of Leeds, somewhat forlorn but possessing a good fourteenth-century church with nicely patterned Dec window tracery. A tall arch leads through to the Perp tower which was refaced in 1884. Part of the exterior is gritstone which has turned really black, and part is in local limestone. The unusual nave roof is in steel, painted with anticorrosive coating and supporting corrugated aluminium panels; how does it sound in a storm? There are a number of monuments mainly to Lowther baronets; some old brasses in the South aisle; and in the North aisle a monument to Harpham Green, 1771 – marble screen with books, urn and flag, 'an honest upright sensible man, lived much estimed and died much lamented'. In the South wall is an Easter sepulchre. Tall octagonal arcades support the fifteenth-century clerestory. [10]

TEMPLE NEWSAM Close to the east of Leeds but still in open country this large if plain Jacobean mansion has played its part in British history. 'Temple' because it was once the property of the Knights Templar. After their suppression it passed into the Darcy family and Lord Darcy built a Tudor mansion in the early sixteenth century. The West wing with its diapered brickwork, massive oak beams, Tudor arched doors and fireplaces, remains – but the turrets, gables and chimneys have gone. Lord Darcy was executed for taking the side of the monasteries in the Pilgrimage of Grace; Henry VIII gave the house to the Earl of Lennox who married Henry's niece. The house was a centre of Catholic intrigue. Lennox's son, Lord Darnley, was born here in 1545 – he married Mary Queen of Scots and their son was James I of England. Darnley himself was assassinated in 1567 and the house was managed by an agent under Elizabeth I; but when James I came to the throne he gave it to the Duke of Lennox. It was then sold to Sir Arthur Ingram in 1622. He was a successful Yorkshire merchant and Controller of the Port of London. He retained the West wing of the Tudor house but rebuilt the North and South wings leaving the east side open to the wooded valley opposite.

For such a wealthy patron the house is surprisingly plain. New wings of brick were built to match the old west part with stone-dressed canted brick bays, transomed windows and a stone balustraded parapet. In the late nineteenth century Mrs Ingram made an Art Nouveau entrance in the West wing as you approach the house. Sir Arthur's entrance, however (which is used today), is inside the open U of the courtyard – a triumphal Jacobean porch in carved limestone of twin Ionic columns, cornices and the Ingram Arms under a broken pediment. A handsome 12-light window is above. After the Civil War Ingram was promoted to Viscount. Almost two centuries later the male line failed, and the house passed through the female line to Lady Hertford. The new-looking panels of the Great Hall are hers, also the plasterwork, the heraldic glass in the bay window (from a former chapel) and the pine panelling which was treated to look like oak. The Chinese Room has hand-painted wallpaper given to Lady Hertford by the Prince of Wales in 1806; the birds are cut from a book. The Dining Room has a Jacobean plaster ceiling – but the Elizabethan chimney piece was copied by C. E. Kempe from Hardwick Hall. Mrs Meynell Ingram made further dramatic alterations in the 1890s, removing the pedi-

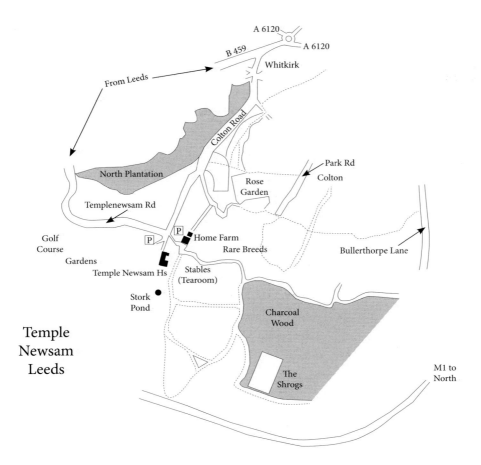

Temple
Newsam
Leeds

ment on the North front and Georgian windows; she unified the three wings restoring mullions and transoms. Kempe rebuilt the staircase for her on a Jacobean model (from Slaugham Place in Sussex) and old fragments of plasterwork modelled a 'restored' frieze in the Darnley Room. Devoutly High Church, Mrs Ingram instructed G. F. Bodley to convert the library into a chapel. When she died in 1904 the property was left to her nephew, the heir of 2nd Viscount Halifax. He opened a colliery in the park, he said, to save the estate. Politics ennobled him also as Viscount Irwin (2nd creation). He became Viceroy of India and later succeeded as Earl of Halifax, eventually becoming Chamberlain's Foreign Secretary. In the misery of the 1922 depression, however, he sold the park to Leeds City Council – the house passed for no charge. At first it was on show as an empty shell but in 1938 Leeds developed it as a country house museum of art. Lord Halifax returned many of the historic pictures,

and other chattels, for example tapestries, were re-acquired at auctions. Today the house is furnished as a home, once more expressing the art and history of the people who lived here. It is very successful.

Some rooms of note are the Edwardian library containing a Chippendale library writing table made for Harewood House in 1770. The picture gallery or ballroom was made out of the 150ft Jacobean long gallery; the 7th Viscount Irwin revamped it with two chimney pieces designed by William Kent, and Rococo plaster by Perritt and Joseph Rose Senior. The Georgian library was divided off in 1743. The bookcases are heavily framed by demi-columns and cornice, but Perrit and Rose's Rococo ceiling with flamboyant arabesques is outstanding. This room (converted by Bodley into a chapel for Mrs Ingram) reverted to a library in 1972 but is now promised to be a chapel again. The organ is still there. Of the Tudor house there remain parts here and

there: some massive beams, the West wing brickwork, in the cellars Tudor arches, the remains of circular stair turrets at the angles of the building, and beneath some Georgian panels are friezes and a concealed original ceiling. The arched doors and a fireplace with linenfold panelling in the Tudor Room came from Bretton Hall. The house is very extensive and half a day should be allowed to see it.

The elegant stables by David Garrett, 1740, are below the house occupying a hollow. They are also in brick with a brick pediment and white cupola sporting the Irwin's crest. Tea is in the stables. The grounds were laid out in the 1770s by Capability Brown retaining William Etty's avenues, bridges and ponds. He amplified the natural prospect with clumps of trees and lakes towards the valley. The formal gardens are to the west. The North entrance to the park is guarded by the *Sphinx Gates* – lead sphinxes sit on rusticated piers imitating those by Lord Burlington at Chiswick. Mining exploitation of the Aire Valley right up to the garden of the house usefully held back other development but a determined policy by the Council to protect the house has preserved its environment. Now mines and industry have receded and the gardens are restored. In spring, when azaleas and rhododendrons frame the lakes and classical temple, the effects of industrialization can be forgotten. The only reservation is that, although it defers a little, the M1 might have been hidden. Open daily. [10]

THONGSBRIDGE Weaving village of stone mills and houses gathered around a bridge in the Holme Valley outside Huddersfield. St Andrew's is a small Victorian chapel with exaggerated plate-tracery windows. [25]

THORNER A stone village northeast of Leeds surprisingly little affected by it. Sheltered by a gentle hill to the east, St Peter's Church is built into the gradient with the South chapel and chancel seeming uphill of the nave. The nave is only three bays, has an arcade of octagonal piers, and was rebuilt in 1855. The robust Perp tower stands west on a bank directly above the main street amid eighteenth- and nineteenth-century houses. A worthy rather than distinguished village, it has thus far successfully fended off the sprawl of east Leeds. [4]

THORNHILL Riding high on the southern slope of the Calder Valley on the B6117 where stone miners' terraces lodge above Saviletown. The Savile Arms Inn, seventeenth-century mullions and sign of painted arms, overlooks the Perp Savile church. Saviles lived in the manor house down the hill east of St Michael's. Their family chapel survives as the chancel chapel. The nave and aisles were rebuilt in 1877 in a rather coy Dec style.

Note the tracery in the spandrels of the roof trusses. The late Perp East window contains old glass given by Robert Frost who was Chancellor to Prince Arthur in 1499; it depicts a Jesse Tree but the colours have endured unevenly within the six lights: blues, reds and greens dominate. Heraldic eighteenth-century glass screens are in the Savile Chapel; its original roof has painted heraldic devices in the coving. Some excellent monuments include a cross-legged knight in chain mail with fine features. A tomb chest in alabaster for Sir John and Lady Savile has six panels of mourners, 1481. Then opposite, effigies of the next Sir John and his two wives are in oak, originally under a canopy with four posts, 1529. The ladies are a little severe. The most easterly arch between the chancel and North chapel contains effigies of Sir George and Lady Savile (1622), he in elegant armour, turned-down boots, ruff and helmet; she wears a lace-edged gown and reclines on embroidered pillows. The tomb arch has twin pillars with heraldic shields and figures; their two sons guard its foot, one kneeling, the

Opposite, above: JACOBEAN PORCH, TEMPLE NEWSAM; *opposite, below*: ELIZABETHAN LINENFOLD, TEMPLE NEWSAM;
below: ELIZABETHAN BRICKWORK, TEMPLE NEWSAM.

other reclining. What did this mean? Then against the North wall is an excellent alabaster monument to Sir George Savile with obelisks and wonderfully carved shields and heraldic achievement; the baby lying on its back and holding the font is not sinister, it is the second Lord Savile who went on to live for 77 years. Lord Savile last redecorated the chapel in 1952. In a glass case west of the North aisle are fragments of Saxon crosses.

Across the road in the park are the ruins of the Saviles' old manor house on a little island formed in a moat and picturesquely clothed by beech, ash and elm. Just east of the church is a handsome late Georgian rectory with bow windows. Thornhill Hall is in Hall Lane behind the old rectory – a modest gabled seventeenth-century structure with mullioned windows. Its farm has a truly massive stone barn with vents for a prodigious store of hay, south of the cart entrance. Mullioned windows on two storeys under drip moulds indicate past domestic use of part of the range.

Lees Hall off Ravensthorpe Road down in the valley is a timber-framed survival of Elizabethan manorial days although its situation is now industrial. Retrieved from the local council 60 years ago when it housed six families, it has been well restored from a ruinous condition by the family who still live there. Its sixteenth-century staircase opens to a low-ceilinged room with original plaster mouldings. The contemporary Gate House with mullioned and transomed windows is still in need of restoration. [21]

THORNTON On the south-facing valley side of the Pinchbeck rising up to the Pennines west of Bradford. The Church of St James is a very strong lancet style of 1870 with aggressively placed tower and broach spire at the southeast of the church. The nave and tower are both very tall and the clerestory has big emblematic rose windows. The churchyard is across the road to the south and at its foot is the old bell chapel – a ruin, of which is retained the East wall with Perp East window and cupola from the bell tower. That church was built in 1612 and was where Patrick Brontë was minister from 1815 to 1820, when Charlotte, Patrick, Bramwell, Emily and Anne were born on Market Street (a plaque commemorates the place). The font in which the Brontë children were baptized was moved to the new church and remains in use. Thornton Hall is directly below the churchyard with a terrace looking out over the valley; seventeenth century with six-light mullioned and tran-

somed windows – the east of the house can just be seen. Lower down the main road is Leventhorpe Hall (just before the brick grammar school), also seventeenth century, with stone roof and mullioned and transomed windows. Inexplicably, seventeenth-century outbuildings are half demolished as though vultures had picked at them. [8]

THORP ARCH All Saints Church is distant from the village situated on the north side of the River Wharfe. The tower with its sundial is Perp; the EE-style nave and chancel with red-tiled roofs were rebuilt in 1872 but incorporate earlier parts, for example the old chancel wall with piscina and tomb recess. The South chancel doorway may be original; the South nave door certainly is with fine Norman beakhead decoration. From the church gentle views are seen through trees over the Wharfe to the pyramid-roofed towers of Boston and Clifford, the tall tower of Bramham and its windmill; to the south the distinguished stone buildings of Boston Spa appear across a dip in the meadows. The hall is a low, classical building by John Carr, 1756, with centre block forward of pyramid-roofed wings; its park has been reduced by new housing cutting off its Gothic lodge. The village is set around a triangular green and linked with Boston Spa by a long narrow bridge of five arches, 1770, with attractive views both up and down stream.

Close by is the former War Office Munitions factory extending to a good square mile. It is now an industrial, retail and government estate with prisons, vehicle testing and British Library storage. After the closing of Woolwich Arsenal in 1934 as the main shell-filling site, new dispersed munitions sites were sought. This one was constructed in 1940 and was served by its own railway. It still contains a large number of Second World War buildings – huts and brick warehouses, as well as sections of rail disappearing into strengthened bunkers where trucks of munitions could be isolated prior to dispatch. Its roads are 1, 2, 3, etc., but it is not easy to find your way. Parts are waiting for someone to make a museum. [5]

THUNDER BRIDGE Below the A629 between Shepley and Huddersfield is a little hamlet severely constrained by wooded steep valley sides. When in spate the beck thunders under the bridge. Here is an archetypal row of weavers' cottages from the eighteenth century – some

with five mullioned windows in series, others with four, stacked three storeys high. Much of it is now converted to a comfortable inn, The Woodman. [20]

TODMORDEN   At the head of the Calder Valley and so far west that it seems to trespass into Lancashire. High in the Pennines this self-contained town crowds under the sheltering valley sides. The lofty Stoodley Pike can be seen distant from the town on a bare hillside; a 125ft-high monument on top of the hill commemorates the Allies' success at Waterloo, 1815 (rebuilt 1856). It is on the Pennine Way. The fortune of the town, founded on cotton, came early. In Hall Street is a seventeenth-century gabled residence with manifold mullions, 1603, for Saville Radcliffe whose arms are over the doorway. The drawing room is lit by a magnificent 18-light window and there is a contemporary carved-oak fireplace decorated with little obelisks.

The enlightened Fieldens prospered here in the eighteenth century by organizing outwork for cottage weavers and finishers from their 'takkin-in shop'. Joshua Fielden started cotton spinning in 1782 and his sons enlarged the lane-side mill to accommodate 800 looms in 1829 – at the time the world's largest. The clock tower and cupola left standing today were originally part of this complex. The Fieldens were Todmorden. Joshua's third son, John, was a philanthropist and so successful that he supported the Ten Hours Bill: his statue is in the park. For the brothers, John Gibson designed the highly correct Dec-style Unitarian Church, 1869, near the town centre: South tower and spire, buttresses, pinnacles and transepts picturesquely set on the hillside above weavers' cottages. Gibson also designed Dobroyd Castle in 1856, which is high on the hillside northwest of the town, for another Fielden. It has a keep-like tower over the entrance with stair turret; its encircling 'curtain wall' is supported by splayed octagonal turrets at the angles and above the generous cornice it is embattled throughout – reminiscent of Armley Prison. The tall round-headed windows have rock-faced stone and ashlar quoins. It stands at the top of Plexwood Road. To reach it cross the canal at the Baccup turning, the road shoots high up the valley giving a car driver the sensation of a plane taking off. Here stone cottages look down on the curving railway below. Although apparently abandoned, permission to approach should be obtained.

The Town Hall (also Gibson), 1875, is a highly ornate classical affair. A rusticated ground floor is the base for an arcade of Corinthian columns and series of statuary niches (never filled), a rich entablature and pediment – with handsome marble relief depicting cotton spinning, industry and agriculture. It is worth looking inside to see the ornately decorated apse with grand staircase and the great ballroom. The Town Hall is built over the (culverted) river and across the original boundary between Lancashire and Yorkshire. In the court room it was held that a person could be tried on one side of the border and jailed on the other. The Parish Church of St Mary opposite, elevated on a corner bluff, is unexciting. The building is of 1770 and has two storeys of Venetian windows like a mill, with a thin embattled classical tower. In 1896 a new chancel was added facing the street with Gothic tracery in round windows. The Rochdale Canal uses this pass through the Pennines; built in 1798, linking the Calder with the Duke of Bridgewater's Canal in Lancashire. As it passes through the middle of the town the tow path provides good views of eighteenth-century stone bridges, locks and canal buildings. In Fielden Square the Golden Lion is a nice Georgian coaching inn with crown-shaped rainwater heads, proud cornice and Venetian window in the gable; and long views down the canal. In the summer it is a good place to sit and muse.

FIREPLACE OVERMANTEL, TODMORDEN HALL.

Opposite: LOBB MILL, TODMORDEN.

When travelling to Blackpool children would take one last gulp of 'good Yorkshire air' before proceeding into Lancashire. Maybe the reverse also applied. [12]

TONG West Yorkshire as it used to be: sixteenth- to eighteenth-century cottages, church and hall in a precious rural oasis of farmland between Bradford and Leeds. Tong Hall, 1704, is a very attractive three-storey Palladian brick mansion with urn decorated pediment and pyramid-roofed wings. Stone quoins, windows and string courses with Baroque carved Tempest Arms over the front door contrast with red brick. Blockish chimneys and effervescent Restoration decoration within, especially the carved stair balusters and overmantels. The garden front has canted stone bays of two storeys which overlook the terrace with its extensive views of Tyersal Beck and Cockersdale. Stained glass sundial over the entrance door where sunbeams hit the hours. Once owned by the council it is now commercially owned and permission must be obtained to visit.

A path leads to St James' Church, 1727, its date over the three-decker pulpit. It is a splendid survival from the eighteenth century with Tuscan piers in the North arcade, round-arched windows, box pews, West gallery and flat plaster ceiling decorated with gold corn ears in geometrical ellipses. Behind the reused Norman chancel arch (with scalloped capitals) is the squire's pew complete with fireplace. In the North chancel wall is a Baroque Victorian monument to Sir Robert and Sir Christom Tempest in alabaster and coloured marble, third and fourth baronets. In the tower – plain with blank parapet and urn finials – is a fragment of a Perp window recast in a round arch. In front of the church are the old stocks and, east, seventeenth-century Lantern Cottage with tiny mullioned windows whose gable used to bear a lantern. The parish pump and cricket field stand next to the seventeenth-century Greyhound Inn with its diamond profile mullions. One mile west down New Lane behind Ryecroft Farm is a modest hall dated 1669 with mullions and a large transomed window in the galleried hall. An estate village whose preservation is a delight. [9]

UPPER DENBY Looks out from the high moors down a prettily wooded valley to Cawthorne with Barnsley in the distance. The tower of St John the Evangelist was built in 1627 but in 1840 Bishop Longly of Ripon declared the nave 'too small and dilapidated' and a new one was built around the old. When the roof was complete the old nave was taken down from within. The

new nave had galleries on iron pillars and box pews but in 1900 they were removed, a chancel and 'false' aisles of four bays with octagonal piers were put in to simulate the English Church in Florence. Rodham Spencer-Stanhope devised this and he was also responsible for the pretty barrel-vaulted ceiling. Against the West wall of the nave is a memorial to Charles Kilner, a professor of music, 1858, with shrouded violin and bow. In the village the George Inn was a three-storeyed seventeenth-century farm with stone mullions, but it is now fronted by a newer wing. At Lower Denby are some pretty weavers' cottages. From here drive east across the major road and along the ridge for good scenery towards Scissett and seventeenth-century Wheatley Hill Farm with its timbered gable. [26]

UPPER HOPTON Overlooking Mirfield from a hillside, Upper Hopton has an old stone-built hall with timber-framed wings showing diagonal struts. The church is an exercise in antiquarianism by the academic architect Ignatius Bonomi, 1846. The windows which are small Perp are, however, not convincing and perhaps show that you cannot objectively reproduce medievalism – true work has a random and more picturesque element which this building lacks. [15]

WAKEFIELD The former County Town of the West Riding sits at the original highest navigable point of the River Calder – the long medieval bridge remains with its own Dec Chapel for the blessing of those who cross, one of only four remaining in the country. Wakefield's wealth was founded on the trade and exchange of wool and cloth, and in the sixteenth to eighteenth centuries its market was the largest in Yorkshire; Defoe said its population was greater than York. Despite being in the midst of the Yorkshire coalfield it did not become an industrial centre and retained its medieval street pattern where, rising above the river, is a splendid medieval church. There are also distinct colonies of Georgian houses and chapels.

The only realistic way to see the town is on foot. Beginning at Wakefield Westgate Station – from platform one, look northwest into the prison where the nineteenth-century blocks have been recased and reroofed, but the fine Regency clock tower remains. The mulberry bush in the nursery rhyme grew in the prison and it remains there today. The railway bisects *Westgate*, one of the ancient entries to the town, which is lined with Georgian mansions and is probably the best street in town. West of the railway bridge are many Georgian

Opposite: Assize Court, 1810, and West Riding County Hall, 1894, Wakefield.

St James, 1727, Tong.

houses with pediments and displaying large blank arches; the orangery to one still stands on Back Lane behind Westgate Chapel. East of the railway, No. 67 has a rusticated arcade on the ground floor, sash windows and, on the first floor, a large central pedimented window; opposite the station is a smaller three-bay Georgian house with a corniced parapet and the curiosity of a Doric-columned oriel window and slotted frieze. Next to it is an early twentieth-century neo-Baroque pub, the Elephant & Castle, a glaze-tiled Jacobean design. Walking further up Westgate to the junction with Smyth Street is Unity Hall, a massive neo-Baroque hall, built over shops.

Over the road is the *Opera House* built in 1894 from designs by Frank Matcham. Its brick front is ornamented with busts of authors and composers. Within are typical Matcham balconies with private boxes and a gallery making good the Matcham claim 'every person will have a full view of the stage'. The plaster decoration tends more to the Rococo than Baroque with an ornate domed ceiling. It is restored once again for performances. Higher up Westgate are more Georgian houses – No. 167 has a projecting bay, Doric columns, garlands, urns and balustrades – like the orangery in Back Lane. The former Wakefield and Barnsley Union Bank is heavy nineteenth-century Italianate. Then another handsome eighteenth-century mansion with a pediment and projecting bays – but its ground floor has been hollowed out for shops.

Westgate becomes Marygate towards the Cathedral where former medieval yards open off the street: Woolpack's Yard, Thompson's Yard and Whitehorse Yard. Next to Thompson's Yard, Cheapside curves interestingly uphill to the north, closed in by unmodernized tenements; on the corner is another Georgian mansion with an eighteenth-century bay window with Doric pilasters and frieze at the first floor. Retrace your steps a little to the east, passing cobbled Bank Street with eighteenth- and nineteenth-century houses and walk south down cobbled Whitehorse Yard to George Street. Here is a handsome independent eighteenth-century brick mansion with beige limestone appointments, bracketed pediments and a Doric porch.

On George Street go east and south, into *South Parade* (via a gennel) to a wonderfully atmospheric terrace of Georgian houses of grand proportions. It is a peaceful enclave on a terrace that still looks over its gardens in the direction of the river – all but cut off from the busy world. You may feel that you are trespassing, but be reassured. Back onto George Street via West Parade is Zion Chapel, a Congregational church of 1844, now offices, but retaining spectacular tall arched windows with cast iron lights. East again on George Street are almshouses by William Shore (railway contractor), 1838, in military Gothic, gabled centre and strange chimneys like thin bobbins. At the end of George Street go into Kirkgate past Wild's Yard and Ship Yard – fine sounding but desultory nineteenth-century development – to the *medieval bridge and chapel*, off Kirkgate over the River Calder with nine arches. The river is broad here but doubtless the banks were the firmest in a marshy area. Built where the river sweeps by the hill shortly after 1342, it has a medieval chapel of some richness. St Mary's is a shrine for travellers and an 'alms point' for safe conduct and upkeep of the bridge. It is the most flamboyant Dec in the county: flowing tracery, crockets and reliefs of, for example, the Nativity and Ascension. This is a copy by George Gilbert Scott as the original was so badly worn. North of the bridge, in an old stable yard with mounting block is an eighteenth-century office of the Aire and Calder Navigation – Doric pillars and a little pediment. These toll offices supervised the working of the canal – there is another at Stanley.

The medieval bridge is now bypassed by a modern concrete one which gives intriguing views over a foaming and cascading weir to a deep section of the river beyond. Here steel barges are repaired, reflecting their image with that of the Hepworth Gallery and stone warehouses. The best warehouse is off Bridge Street, tall, gabled and in stone with stone mullioned openings; early eighteenth century. Off Tootal Street is a Victorian warehouse with polychromatic brick arches known as Rutland Mills, with a good moulded cornice. Also on the river front is the Hepworth Gallery by David Chipperfield, 2011; bold and introspective as one might expect of a gallery, it consists of many interlinked boxes. This broad reach of the river – a historic warehouse quarter with restaurants, offices and gallery of national status – has transformed a formerly rundown area. It has opened a new eye on Wakefield both for visitors and residents.

Returning to town along *Kirkgate* (Kirkgate station is splendid Victorian though dilapidated), keep west to avoid the subways and north on Kirkgate until it turns west, keeping the mighty Cathedral spire of 247ft in view. Dedicated to All Saints this grandly Perp parish church is elevated on a hill and reflects the medieval prosperity of Wakefield. Promoted to cathedral in 1888, J. L. Pearson carried out extensions in 1904. From below the hill you see the chancel extension and transept – with the vestry in the angle – in a slightly ascetic King's College flavour. The 'vestry' is actually an integral part of the new space inside but mellows the assertiveness of the extension, like a kind of architect's remorse. As you climb the hill towards the west of the *Cathedral* you pass Scott's restored South aisle to the tower and spire.

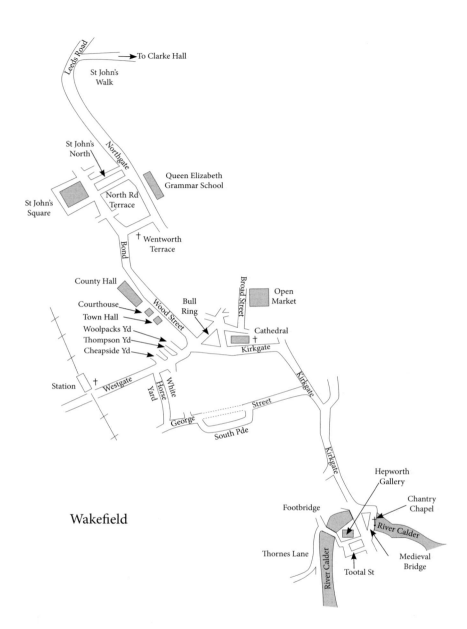

Wakefield

They are the tallest in Yorkshire; the original tower collapsed in 1315 and the present tower was funded by the Archbishop of York selling four-days' indulgence to contributors. The result is the impressive 105ft-high embattled tower with crocketed pinnacles and projecting parapet, Yorkshire fashion. The spire is much crocketed and adds 142ft, but Camden thought it too short. It fell down again in the nineteenth century when the tower was recased by Scott who rendered the style Dec. While the aisle windows are all Perp, that influence is less emphatic inside where arcades of round piers from Norman times (North arcade, West end), octagonal and round from the twelfth century (South arcade) and thirteenth-century quatrefoil piers (North arcade) show the progress of building. There is a good Perp roof in the nave with carved bosses including fleur-de-lis and the Wakefield Arms. The North aisle windows are original Perp but the South aisle tracery was made by Scott from seventeenth-century engravings, the proportions fixed from remaining original openings – authentic and effective. There are good fifteenth-century poppy head carvings of roses and birds in the chancel stalls; a very fine oak Jacobean rood screen; a richly carved eighteenth-century organ case; and over the North doorway a large painting of the Royal Arms dated 1773 in which the lion's face is reputed to be that of George III. The Bishop's throne was given in 1974 by prelate/steam-engine driver Bishop Treacy. Note the fine pedimented marble monument to Sir Lyon Pilkington, 1714. The interior of Pearson's twentieth-century extension is notable for its thin shafting and high lierne vaulting – its proportions signalling Arts and Crafts. The Jacobean oak rood screen is elaborately carved; the 1950 rood above is by Sir Ninian Comper. The pulpit is now chopped down; it was a three decker, made in 1708 from which the preacher could be seen from the galleries (now removed).

The station can be regained via Westgate but the walk now moves to the north of the town. The Cathedral gives on to Northgate which leads to the Bullring; walk via Westmorland Street and Brook Street to the Elizabethan Grammar School. It is at the head of the open market (many degrees less grand than Doncaster), with large mullioned and transomed windows, five lights with two transoms, a stone roof, and the preserved arms of the founders, George Savile and his sons Sir George and Sir John. The father gave the land and stone from a quarry together with 20 trees in 1593. It is a happy survival of quite a grand Elizabethan public building, becoming the Cathedral School when the Grammar School moved to Northgate. Then go north up **Wood Street** where a number of self-conscious public buildings are not entirely comfortable together.

After Chancery Lane see first the *Mechanics Institu-tion*, now a museum. It was built in 1820 as an assembly room for Georgian gentry – chaste Grecian classicism, a plain ground floor but grand saloon on the first with deep sash windows divided by attached Ionic columns. After the Town Hall (which actually comes next) is the Grecian *Court House*, 1810 – bold and proud Doric portico, carved Royal Arms within the deep pediment, and statue of justice at the apex. Reverting to the *Town Hall*, this is like a mini-chateau from northern Europe with three Baroque oriel windows rising above the roof as dormers and a tall thick tower with a mansard visible for miles, for example from the M1. It was designed by Collcutt and built in 1880; it lacks space for appreciation and would look better across a cobbled square. Now after the Court House is *County Hall*, 1898, a rather fey neo-Baroque with exuberant features: a big arched arcade on the first floor, balustrades with transomed windows behind; then above – behind a long balcony – an arcade of smaller arched windows coupled with columns. There is an attitude of joyfulness in the pedimented gable with oriel window and balcony, and on the end of the building a towered dome rises above the roofline on a drum of columns.

Moving north look down Rishworth Street for a Regency terrace with neat iron balconies; the small cenotaph is opposite. The multi-storey car park must be a mistake here. Wentworth Terrace is a nineteenth-century classical terrace with classical Roman Catholic Church and Presbytery enclosed within it. Then comes **Northgate** with more Georgian houses, some grand under a pediment, and a neat pair of small houses at the junction with Cardigan Terrace.

Also on Northgate is Queen Elizabeth Grammar School, institutional Romantic Tudor of 1834 – a gabled and turreted central pavilion with a big transomed Tudor window. Similar big-windowed pavilions at either end are linked by blocks of double-height windows glazed in whitened iron tracery. Shortly, on the west of Northgate is St John's North and North Road Terrace, very complete eighteenth-century terraces. And so to *St John's Square*, a formal Georgian square with a church in the centre; developed by John Lee, a Wakefield solicitor, to provide 'exclusivity' for professionals and merchants. St John's North is a brick terrace with a pedimented central mansion of five bays and stone appointments. They were to provide comfort superior 'to those places exclusively peopled by clothiers'. St John's Square has a greater variety of pediments and Georgian houses but still has unity. In the centre is the classical St John's, 1795, an octagonal tower with a stone dome and two storeys of nave windows – the upper ones round-arched, fenestration divided by twin pilasters rising to urns above the parapet. The interior is quite lavish with a moulded flat

THE BLACK SWAN, WAKEFIELD.

CATHEDRAL SPIRE, WAKEFIELD.

ceiling and arcades of stone Tuscan columns. The chancel arch is Venetian style and leads to a later tunnel-vaulted chancel of 1884 with grand reredos, a lively carved pediment and painting of the Passion.

Too far to walk, to the north up the A642 is a lovely brick sixteenth-century house, *Clarke Hall* on an 'E' plan with cross-transomed windows and a gabled porch. Two further Georgian churches, first *Westgate Chapel* by Northgate Station, brick built in 1751, has a Venetian window and pair of matching pedimented porches. Inside, the late seventeenth-century pulpit has a sound board like a Baroque porch; it was brought from a demolished chapel near the River Calder. Then on the A636, adjacent to Thornes Park, St James, close to the site of a mansion built by John Carr in a design derived from his work at Harewood but now demolished. St James Church by the roadside has big corniced windows and doors, and a dome above the tower.

Outer Wakefield – Little Lake District A pleasant ramble or cycle can be made around the dams and lakes southeast of Wakefield. Begin at Nostell Priory where the Upper Lake is bisected by the elegant estate bridge of five arches built for the Wakefield road to cross it. The valley sides are planted with rhododendron, azaleas and a mature treescape. A National Trust garden ticket is required to walk around these lakes. From Nostell take the road to Ryhill via the B6273, turning immediately right into Swine Lane, second right into Long Dam Lane for extensive areas of water originally dammed for the canal system south of the Dearne – now mostly abandoned. Long Lane leads to Wintersett and the two adjoining Wintersett reservoirs. Paths enable one to walk about their entire shores with rewarding landscapes of willow and plentiful wildlife. There is a Discovery

Opposite, above: SOUTH PARADE, WAKEFIELD; *below*: CLARKE HALL, 1542, WAKEFIELD.

HEPWORTH GALLERY, CHIPPERFIELD, 2011, WAKEFIELD.

Centre at the cul-de-sac of Haw Park Lane where the identity of flora and fauna can be found. Also a sailing HQ for the southerly reservoir, an attractive scene when the club is racing.

From Wintersett take the narrow, tree-lined Ferry Top Lane avoiding Ryhill, along Ryhill Pitts Lane to the smaller Cold Hiendley Reservoir and woods of Haw Park. Following the disused Barnsley Canal you can access Waterton Park with the historic hall on an island (now a hotel). (*See Waterton.*) From there a path takes you to woods and water at Walton Colliery Park – a reminder that this landscape has been transformed since the 1980s. Otherwise, from Cold Hiendley take the Chevet Hill Lane to Lodge Lane and the former estate of the Pilkington baronets at Chevet Park. The house is no more but the romantically wooded estate and dam with Gothic boat-

house are fully accessible from Newmillerdam. Then the old Barnsley road brings you to Pugney's Country Park and reservoir with another sailing club. [16]

WALSDEN Close to the summit of the Rochdale Canal where it crosses the Pennines at 600ft above sea level. The pass is closely confined by high hills bottling up the railway, main road and canal. Stone terraces abut the canal and farmsteads lodge on the sheep-farmed hillsides. St Peter's Walsden has a tapering and buttressed EE-style tower and stone spire with similar Victorian aisles and porch; unusually the nave was faced in stone

Opposite, above and below: EIGHTEENTH-CENTURY WAREHOUSES ON THE CALDER, WAKEFIELD.

crazy paving following a fire in the 1950s. It has pairs of thin lancets with leaded lights. Hollins Mill, 1856, was a cotton mill but is out of use. Built by Ormerods it is a survivor of many cotton mills in the Todmorden area. [West of 12]

WALTON (TADCASTER) A most attractive Permian limestone village in the northeast of the county near Tadcaster. From the north St Peter's Church rises above red pantile-roofed cottages – its Norman tower raised on an eminence looking clear over meadows; the Perp top corbelled out Yorkshire fashion. The church is mostly Dec with fine reticulated East window and doorways with shouldered lintels. The nave is given light by two large Perp windows. The North chancel wall has a big foliated canopy rising to a swaggering ogee arch which stands out against the delicate pink limestone; it contains an effigy of Sir Nicolas Fairfax, a fourteenth-century knight in chainmail. East of the church the old vicarage has mullioned windows and a date stone, 1664. Many handsome cottages are in random limestone. The hall is late Georgian undistinguished by architectural ornament. [5]

WALTON (WAKEFIELD) Just southwest of Wakefield the village is in reality part of its suburbs but liberally planted with blossom trees. A lane known as The Balk leads over a picturesque disused canal arm through Grecian gates to the Georgian hall. It stands on an island within a lake, connected by a fragile cast iron bridge and guarded by formidable iron gates. The hall's plain ashlar front, decorated with a Tuscan porch and Tuscan pilasters under a central pediment, contains the swaggering arms of *Waterton*. On the island an ivy encrusted ruin is fancifully said to be a medieval water gate. The hall itself was the property of Charles Waterton, the nineteenth-century explorer and naturalist; last century it was a hospital; and is now a hotel. [22]

WARLEY TOWN Lodging on the north side of the Calder Valley west of Halifax is St Mary's Church – unremarkable Victorian EE style – South West tower, and a stylistically elevated parapet with pinnacles. The church is some distance from Warley Town (which is a village). In the centre of the village opposite the Maypole Inn is the former Congregational church, institutional Gothic, 1855 – a large transomed window between turrets, pediment and crenellation, now a house. Between Blackwall Lane and the Burnley road south of the village is the former Blackwall Farm, at least seventeenth century, mullions, arched lights with transom – may be seen below the lane side. [13]

WEETWOOD (LEEDS) At the junction of the ring road with the Otley road the former students' hall of residence at Weetwood Hall is now a conference centre. The original hall can still be distinguished among a number of new residence blocks; in the courtyard opposite the stables are mullioned windows from the building of 1625. Although the south and west fronts were Georgianized the original doorway was reinstated – it is flanked by high thin Ionic columns and entablature dated 1625. To the east are other grand houses built or enlarged for Leeds' merchants including Colonel Tetley, the brewer. [9]

WENTBRIDGE Formerly on the A1 this ancient crossing of the River Went has returned to leafy tranquillity while the trunk road rides by high on its viaduct down the valley. Along the bank of the Went north of the village and in an elevated situation is the tall Parish Church of St John, by Arthur Bloomfield, 1878 – Romanesque, pyramid-capped tower with short projecting nave and transepts. Built of local light sandstone it has a rather glaring red-tiled roof with ostentatious ridge tiles like pierced merlons. In the village Wenthill Farmhouse is built of large sandstone blocks, mullioned windows, blockish Jacobean chimneys and has a date stone of 1627. On the tree-clad slopes to the north is an overblown new brick mansion unfairly dominating the village. But Wentbridge House, a modest late Georgian mansion with a canted bay projecting under a central pediment in a leafy garden, is a hotel with a long history of serving travellers on the Great North Road. [23]

WEST ARDSLEY see Woodkirk

WEST BRETTON Displays the educated hand of estate owners in its handsome but self-conscious estate village with houses both in stone and brick, one almost certainly designed by Sir Jeffry Wyattville. On the triangular green is a war memorial obelisk, supported by big consoles. Here is Bretton Lodge, a handsome Georgian brick house – double-cantered bays flank a Doric porch, the broad pediment spans the front with a tripartite attic window.

The main drive leads to *Bretton Hall* where an early Georgian house was added to the old hall in 1720 by Sir William Wentworth, aided by Colonel Moyser, a friend of Lord Burlington. The house looks east rather than directly across the landscaped valley of woods and lakes. The park was made before 1777 when a contemporary note records there took place 'illuminations and fireworks on the Island of Venus'. In 1815 alterations were made by Wyattville for Colonel Beaumont. A full-height bay window was added to the south looking over the

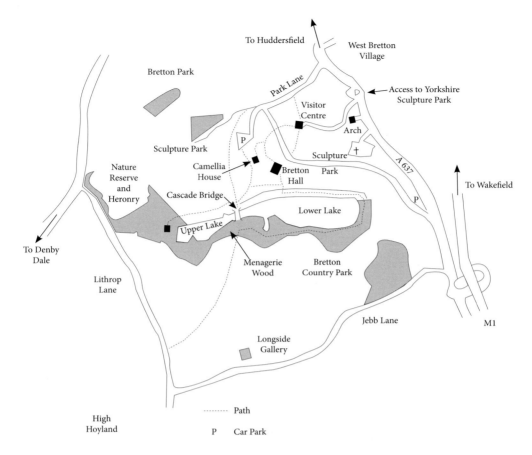

To Huddersfield

West Bretton
Village

Bretton Park

Park Lane

Access to Yorkshire
Sculpture Park

Visitor
Centre

Arch

P

Sculpture Park

Sculpture

Camellia
House

Bretton
Hall

Park

A 637

Nature
Reserve
and
Heronry

Cascade Bridge

Lower Lake

To Wakefield

P

Upper Lake

To Denby
Dale

Menagerie
Wood

Bretton
Country Park

Lithrop
Lane

Jebb Lane

M1

Longside
Gallery

.... Path

High
Hoyland

P   Car Park

Bretton Hall Estate
Yorkshire Sculpture Park

park and lakes; to the plain East elevation was added an austere Greek Doric porch on four massive columns. Wyattville also designed the large Camellia House to the west – south facing with Y-shaped branches, rather plain.

Next to the mansion is the earlier seventeenth-century house – with flat pilasters and squashed capitals and thus not in competition with its bigger neighbour. Further north are the stables of 1830 by George Basevi which are heavy classical, the gatehouse arch flanked by pairs of rusticated columns, the roof has a melon-shaped dome. Up the hill is a long terrace, rhododendroned and balustraded, it looks out over the mansion, park and lakes. Then further to the east is the Georgian chapel built by Sir William Wentworth in 1744 – pedimented

gables on Tuscan pillars; circular turret and dome. It was Sir William's own design. Inside were box pews but they were removed when the church was deconsecrated in 1990. It is now an exhibition theatre. North, near the main road, is a tall triumphal carriage arch flanked by Roman Doric columns, 1807, once the main entrance to the Hall.

The Wentworths of Bretton ceased in the male line in 1792. The estate passed to Sir Thomas's daughter Diana who married Colonel Beaumont. She initiated many of the alterations over the next decades including the grisaille classical medallions in the hall and dining room. John Carr designed the Adam plasterwork, door cases and fireplaces in the dining room and in the library in 1793. In 1815 Wyattville enlarged the stair hall where

Above and right: BRETTON HALL, WEST BRETTON.

WETHERBY TOWN HALL.

there are scenes of classical ruins. Some rooms demonstrate a too-heavy nineteenth-century classicism, as with the heavy plasterwork in the tapestry room.

The house was lived in by the Beaumonts to the full; Diana was ostentatious and known as Madam Beaumont. It was for her that Wyattville created the music room: shallow, elliptical ceiling painted with *trompe l'oeil* musical instruments, apse for her chamber organ, and panels of coloured glass reflecting through gilded mirrors. Henry James visited the Beaumonts in 1878 from Fryston Park (now demolished). He reported trav-

Opposite, above and below: THE SCULPTURE PARK, WEST BRETTON.

elling through the snow by sledge and, with an eye for English manners, noted a 'drawling, lisping fine lady' who was 'enclosed in her great wintry park and her immense, dusky, pictured, luxurious house – with her tea table at one elbow and a table full of novels at the other'.

Today the future of the house is in the balance. After use as a training college and then by the University of Leeds the lease has reverted to Wakefield Council. A combination of educational use for the mansion and funding for the park as a Sculpture Park since 1977 has kept the historic house and grounds in good order, albeit at the cost of some modern residential blocks in the park. It is likely to become a hotel. [21]

LADY IRWIN, DIED 1746, ST MARY, WHITKIRK.

DAUGHTER OF VISCOUNT AND LADY IRWIN, DIED AGED TWO, ST MARY, WHITKIRK.

The main entrance to the *Yorkshire Sculpture Park* in the hall grounds is from the A637 before reaching West Bretton village and takes you to visitors' car parking. From here the mansion grounds, park and outdoor sculptures may be explored. The Henry Moore Foundation runs the Sculpture Park, and has supplied many of the exhibits. He was born nearby in Castleford and was a promoter of the park. By the car park the visitor centre fits easily into the landscape and commands entrance to estate buildings converted to indoor galleries and also a large underground gallery constructed just uphill from the terrace. Across the park at Longside, reached by walking past the mansion and over the Cascade Bridge between the lakes, is an indoor sculpture gallery run jointly by Yorkshire Sculpture Park and the Hayward, whose aim is to circulate Arts Council sculptures. Visitors have free access to the park which is an unspoiled valley of trees, pasture and woods, but the lakes are a heronry and nature reserve. The Park is open every day.

WETHERBY   An old market town standing at the former crossing of the A1 over the Wharfe, many limestone houses with red pantiles. The church of St James (1839–41) known as the 'barn with no pillars' has bulky stepped lancets in the East window, truncated tower pinnacles, and is faintly disagreeable. The classical Town Hall of 1845 has a pediment, rusticated forward-stepped porch, tall arched windows to the side and a low-hipped roof. It stands on the site of a former chapel of ease and was built by J. B. E. W. Atkinson, also architect for St James. The Duke of Devonshire redeveloped the surrounding streets in the early nineteenth century including a covered market of 11 bays opposite the Town Hall. When providing posting on the Great North Road there were 13 inns; the Angel on High Street and Swan and Talbot on North Street may still be visited. Castle Gate is the way out of town and bends interestingly over the widened medieval bridge to the south – six arches with big cutwaters. Below, by the streaming river is Wilderman Gardens where the bandstand is occupied on bank holidays. Castle Garth is an elegant Regency house off High Street whose garden gives onto upstream meadows where the castle used to be. The Great North Road now skirts the town. [5]

WHITKIRK Ancient parish with old brick and stone houses, east of Leeds – not yet entirely overwhelmed. By an understood treaty building has been stopped just down the lane to Temple Newsam Park. Whitkirk was the village for the great house, home of Viscounts Irwin, and the Parish Church of St Mary has their monuments. The building is Perp with a clerestory and an embattled parapet corbelled out like a castle turret on the tower as well as along the aisles; the tower also has a lead-covered spirelet and gold cockerel weathervane. The chancel extension is by G. F. Bodley, 1901. The chancel South chapel was originally a chantry where Sir Robert and Lady Scargill lie in alabaster on a tomb chest; he in sixteenth-century armour and she in a cloak. Viscount Irwin, 1688, is carved in effigy with dapper robes and wig, his wife mourns sitting to his left; to the right is their baby daughter who died in infancy. The Eddystone Lighthouse engineer, John Smeaton, lived in the parish and is commemorated by a marble panel surmounted by a depiction of the lighthouse, 1792.

Up Whitkirk Lane from the parish church to the ring road and then by Austhorpe Lane is Austhorpe Hall, 1694. A transitional William and Mary house of brick with stone dressings, it has mullion-crossed windows in the new shape. The stone roof is hipped with broad soffits on corbels. The two-storey entrance porch projects under a little pediment and the doorway has a broken pediment; it is sheltered by copper beeches and overlooks open country. [10]

WHITWOOD On the river Calder near Castleford, an inland port for stone, and until recently the site of one of the largest collieries in Europe. Developed by Henry Briggs in the nineteenth century, it was famous for its profit-sharing scheme and for having a miner on the board. It was the first colliery to produce one million tons of coal in 1899. The colliery closed in 1968 and the village was demolished apart from the section designed by Charles Voysey for which he was retained by Arthur Briggs in 1904 to build a terrace and Miners Institute. The Arts and Crafts gabled-cottage terrace has mullion-style windows and large dormers with simple large chimney stacks. Big roofs overhang the ground floor on iron brackets. The houses face south or east and windows were purposefully small to prevent heat loss; the ceilings are lower than Victorian houses, and the ventilation is engineered in each room through a grill which

has become an Arts and Crafts monogram. The houses are privately owned but the Terrace is listed to preserve its unity. Voysey also designed the Miners' Institute which has become the Rising Sun pub. Its four-storey tower, small mullioned windows and balustrade is recognizable from afar – a small pyramid roof rises behind the tower crenellation. Behind it is the Memorial Hall, sloping buttresses and semi-circular windows, used for weddings and band practice. It has recently been restored by the proprietor of the Rising Sun. Voysey, an icon of the Edwardian Age and the father of modern suburbia occurs here unexpectedly, although we should recall that he is a son of Hull. [17]

WIKE North of Leeds ring road, and in the country it is the habitat of enwalled commuters. The village has no proper centre. The only building of note is the former school with seventeenth-century cross-transomed windows, now a house. The country is pleasantly undulating – stone buildings and plenty of trees – but the cultivated look is not from farming but the many golf clubs here. [4]

WILSHAW Above Meltham Mills on the B6107. Italianate Victorian church, central tower with pyramid roof rising above a gabled porch. Parades of transomed Venetian windows which are actually almshouses either side and surrounded by big cornice, cast iron railed parapet, 1863. Water Board architecture. [20]

WOODKIRK (and WEST ARDSLEY) On windy heights beside the busy Leeds to Dewsbury main road stands the somewhat isolated church of St Mary. The thirteenth-century tower has a battered base but the embattling and pinnacles are later. The East side of the tower discloses profiles of earlier naves and the present Victorian nave is the third, the lowest, and extends over the chancel without further roof division. In 1831 the nave roof blew off and it was then that the lower nave and chancel were built. The previous church is depicted in a stained glass window with the roof actually blowing off. The windows are odd: there are lancets with nodding lunettes and of intersecting tracery, evidently remnants from the earlier church. Some repairs have been carried out in local stone but some in an alien white limestone which will never assimilate. Within, the flat plastered ceiling dates from 1832 but the choir stalls are old with poppy head sedilia. Over a low arched doorway is a collection of medieval glass. The pulpit stands on nicely carved Jacobean balled feet. The Georgian Royal Arms over the South doorway has a particularly fierce lion wearing a fine crown.

Monastic ruins may be found to the north of the

Above: WHITWOOD ARTS AND CRAFTS. MINERS' HOUSES BY VOYSEY.
Right: WHITWOOD MEMORIAL HALL BY VOYSEY.

church in the churchyard, which is all that remains of a cell for black canons from Nostell Priory. At the demolition of the old church in 1831 the canon's church was revealed, the walls were painted and gilded with 'roses, white and red, tulips, anemones . . . grapes, peaches' but 'rude workmen' tore down the plaster. [15]

WOODSOME HALL (See *Fenay Bridge*)

WOOLLEY St Peter's West tower is hard against the road; it is a Norman foundation but only remnants remain – part of the chancel arch, font and a Norman tympanum carved with a lamb and cross. The tower and aisled nave are fifteenth century. The aisles have octagonal piers and straight-headed or arched foliated windows. The North chapel belonged to the Wentworths of

Woolley Hall, a lengthy right of church way giving access to it. There is a nicely carved sixteenth-century screen to the east of the South aisle, and remnants of a stairway to the rood. In 1869 the badly fractured walls were rebuilt and windows restored; the box pews were taken out and replaced with pine; the pitched roof was removed and replaced with the present barrel-vaulted roof. It was at this time that the 700-year-old font was said to have been found, but to judge by its bulk would have been difficult to lose. Old stained glass lost at this restoration was found broken at the foot of windows in hopeless confusion. It was re-sorted and, unusually, made into new figures. In the West wall of the nave is a window by William Morris. Bell ringers can be seen at work from the nave through the glazed West tower arch.

The village stands round a triangular green with many

Tower, St Mary, thirteenth century, Woodkirk.

attractive old stone houses, for example Old Court House, apparently sixteenth century with finial-topped gables and stone-mullioned windows. In fact it is a successful amalgam of salvaged materials. Next door, west is the old farmyard with a range of buildings, including a Venetian windowed pigeon tower, now converted to houses and flats. To the west, Mount Farm is an unusual early eighteenth-century building (1719) – tall stone-sash windows, ashlar faced but the truncated gables (with robust twin chimney stacks) accommodate an additional half storey. Opposite is a farm cottage with mullions and, unusually, an arched window to match the doorway. Also in the village are many good new commuter houses mostly in stone of an attractive appearance and low density.

Just a little to the south of the village through octagonal lodges lies the entrance to Woolley Hall, the earliest part of which dates from 1635. The present house was built by Michael Wentworth, a kinsman of Thomas Viscount Wentworth, and dates from 1796 after fire destroyed the old hall. He added new wings north and south, stepped forward, with stone sashes, embattling and shaped gables. He remodelled the house inserting a central canted bay with three arched windows on the ground floor for the ballroom. It also has an Adam ceiling, Grecian overdoors and Grecian alabaster mantelpiece. The staircase is not central but is in the West wing through a Doric screen; it rises singly before dividing; the balustrading is of serpentine wrought iron foliage. [22]

WOOLLEY EDGE A high ridge south of Wakefield above the River Dearne which provides spectacular views west to the 1,884ft transmitting tower at Emley Moor, and east over rural pasture towards Barnsley in a scene now untrammelled by the mining industry. [22]

WRAGBY Estate village to *Nostell Priory*. The late Perp church was built in 1533 by the penultimate Prior of Nostell and dedicated within the Church of England (as opposed to Rome) from the start. It has an embattled tower, octagonal piers, straight-headed clerestory windows, and a tall West arch into the tower with nicely carved oak screen. The quality of the stone walls and piers is the result of their preservation under plaster – they have been revealed only recently. The chancel follows the dimensions of the nave and there is no choir as such, therefore the chancel is exceptionally spacious.

The private Winn family pews are on the North side where there is a monument to Sir Roland Winn, 1765. In the chancel are funeral hatchments for Winns. The stained glass is Swiss and was collected by a Winn. A primitive carving of St Michael carrying Our Lady's body to heaven was brought from an ancient crossroads, then in the forest where it showed the way to the Priory. Four panels of the pulpit carved in high relief depict episodes in the life of Christ. The organ is a music room item from the Priory. Electric lamps are chandeliers made of torchères – rather Art Nouveau. The very fine Norman font with substantial zigzag decoration comes from Bridlington. St Michael and All Angels is heavily enclosed by trees which give it a too gloomy ambience. It may be defensiveness against the recent heavy presence of a colliery across the main road with its huge bulk, light and noise. It is hard to believe that it has gone. (See *Nostell Priory*.) [23]

WYKE Between Brighouse and Bradford, Wyke holds the hill between the two. Of particular interest in Lower Wyke (south of the A58) is Manor Farm, the former Manor House on a lane gently sloping south among sturdy stone farms and trees. The Manor is a little private from the road but can easily be seen as a clothier's mansion of 1614. It has a black-stone roof, stone gables and stone-mullioned windows whose lights have round heads. Of at least theoretical interest is the Moravian Chapel, a little lower down, of 1755. It is austere, rendered, with arched windows and lantern on the roof. [14]

YEADON The nineteenth-century stone-built High Street and Town Hall indicate the beginning of Yeadon's prosperity. The Town Hall standing in a little cobbled square is fortissimo Gothic – big arched windows with shafting. The entrance arch has quadruple shafting. Above it a central tower rises to a large clock stage; the clock is within another large arch; and then above that is a tapered French mansard. The roof line is exciting – where windows rise above the roof level into little towers they are capped with ogee spires. It is a distinguished, balanced and adventurous piece. At Nether Yeadon, across the A65 southwest, is Low Hall of the seventeenth century – seven-light hall window. The two-storeyed porch was re-erected from Esholt Priory and has the date 1658. The regional airport for Leeds and Bradford is nearby. [3]

Glossary

Ambulatory Semicircle enclosing an apse.

Arabesque Decoration of flowing lines, e.g. of vegetation tendrils interspersed with e.g. vases.

Arcade A range of arches, e.g. the supports for a nave enabling it to open into a north or south aisle.

Arch Bridge in a wall supporting masonry or bricks above to allow passage through the wall or a window. The Romans bridged with round arches; Gothic arches began tall and narrow but over time broadened to an ellipse. Georgian windows bridged by a rubbed brick arch are also arched, albeit flat.

Architrave The decorative support for doors and windows, strictly the lowest parts of an entablature.

Ashlar Blocks of masonry fashioned with an even face and square edges.

Attached (or engaged) column a column that is part of a wall, not freestanding.

Attic Topmost storey of a house.

Bailey Courtyard of a castle.

Baldacchino Classical canopy on columns.

Baluster Small column or pillar alongside a staircase or forming a balustrade, e.g. to a balcony.

Balustrade A series of balusters with coping.

Bastion A fortification projected out at an angle.

Battered A wall with an inclined face.

Battlement Parapet with raised portions called merlons or crenellations.

Bays The external divisions of a building by fenestration.

Bay window A projection of a house usually fenestrated. If projecting on an upper floor it is an oriel.

Beakhead Norman ornamentation showing bird or beast heads with beaks.

Belcote Gabled housing from which to hang bells on a roof.

Billet frieze Norman ornamentation of short raised rectangles.

Block capital A cube fashioned on its lower parts so as to match a rounded column – sometimes called a cushion capital.

Boss A projection usually found at the intersection of ribs in a vault but also in timber intersections in e.g. a Perpendicular roof.

Box pew Enclosed pew usually with its own door.

Bracket Stone support projecting from wall, e.g. to carry a beam.

Bressumer Beam in a timbered building supporting a projection, e.g. an oversailing storey.

Buttress A projecting wall of masonry designed to give additional vertical support.

Angle buttress At the angles of a tower each wall projects, slightly tapering to the top of the tower.

Diagonal buttress Flies off each corner at 135°.

Set back buttress Angle buttress set back from the corner, i.e. not the continuation of a wall.

Flying buttress An arch typically supporting the upper part of a wall or roof from a structure distant from that supported. It enabled medieval builders to engineer lighter storeys than the weight of the building or roof would otherwise allow.

Cable moulding Norman moulding with the appearance of twisted rope.

Campanile An independent bell tower.

Canopy A projection over e.g. a pulpit, niche or statue.

Capital The top part of a column where it expands to bear the weight of other members. See 'block', 'crocket', 'scalloped', 'waterleaf'.

Cartouche Ornate frame surrounding e.g. coat of arms or inscription.

Caryatid Female or male figure supporting an entablature or e.g. fireplace mantel.

Castellated Usually artificial battlements for decorative purposes.

Chamfer Mitigation of a 90° angle in wood or stone by planing off 45°.

Chancel The east part of the church, usually narrower than the nave before the sanctuary and where the choir sings.

Chancel arch The arch towards the chancel and sanctuary at the east end of the nave.

Chantry chapel   An independent chapel either attached to or within a church formally endowed for mass to be said for the soul of its founder.

Chevron   Norman moulding in the shape of a series of arrow heads.

Choir   The designated part of a church where services are sung.

Clapper bridge   One made of large slabs of stone.

Classical   Greek and Roman architecture together with subsequent revivals of it.

Clerestory   An upper storey of windows in the nave walls above the line of the aisles permitting more light to enter the church.

Coffering   Ceiling decoration of sunken square or polygonal panels.

Colonnade   A range of columns.

Console   A bracket with a sinuous decorative outline.

Coping   The top cap to a wall.

Corbel   A stone projection (or bracket) designed to support another feature.

Corbel table   A series of corbels designed to support the roof eaves, often in Norman buildings.

Cornice   Decorative moulded feature at the top of a wall abutting the ceiling; or the top section of the entablature in classical architecture.

Cove or coving   A moulding between the top of a wall and the ceiling, now popularly called the cornice also.

Crocket   In Gothic architecture where spires and pinnacles regularly sprout a leaf shape as a spikey protrusion.

Crocket capital   A capital made up of a horizontal series of leaf shaped projections.

Crossing   Intersection of the nave, chancel and transepts, often with tower over.

Cross-window   Window divided by one mullion and one transom.

Cupola   A small domed roof turret.

Curtain wall   Connects the towers of a castle.

Cusp   Where an arch is foliated it is the peninsular dividing the leaf-like foils.

Dado   Decoration to the lower part of a wall, it may be a moulding.

Dagger   In Decorated Gothic architecture it is a tracery design like a lancet.

Dec   Decorated style, the architecture of the English Gothic period, 1290–1350.

Demi-column   One half of a column only projecting from a wall.

Diaper   Surface decoration achieved by the use of different materials, typically different coloured bricks.

Dogtooth   EE ornamentation of four-cornered stars placed diagonally and which rise pyramidally.

Dormer   An attic window placed on the slope of a roof.

Dripstone   Projecting moulding designed to deflect water from the face of a wall.

Drum   The circular wall of a dome or cupola.

EE   Early English, period of English Gothic architecture, 1200–1300.

Easter sepulchre   Recess in a chancel wall like a tomb designed for the placement of an effigy of Christ at Easter.

Eaves   Beneath the sloping overhang of a roof.

Encaustic tiles   Decorated and glazed earthenware tiles used as paving.

Engaged column   An attached column.

Entablature   In a classical building the whole of the edifice supported on the columns, e.g. architrave, frieze and cornice.

Fillet   Part of a shaft or roll moulding which is flat.

Finial   Decorative pinnacle, e.g. on a gable.

Foil   The leaf shape within a window head or roundel commonly divided by three, four or five, called trefoil, quatrefoil, cinquefoil – the divisions forming the shapes are 'cusps'.

Foliated   Leaf-like carvings.

Gable   Commonly triangular as fronting the roof truss to an Elizabethan house.

  Dutch gable   Where the flanks make an ogee shape surmounted by a triangular pediment.

  Shaped gable   A gable displaying steps and curves, particularly in Elizabethan and Jacobean buildings.

Gadroon   A moulding consisting of oblique ridges.

Gallery   Additional internal open storey in a church or in a theatre.

Garderobe   Medieval chute for disposal of faeces.

Gargoyle   Spout whose purpose is to direct roof water away from a building, often in a grotesque shape.

Gazebo   Summerhouse.

Gibbs surround   Door or window whose architrave consists of quoins, i.e. long and short block work often showing an architrave band on the short verticals.

Groin   Where the legs of cross vaulting meet.

Herringbone   Building work in brick or stone laid diagonally rather than flat, each course in an opposite direction. Often found in Roman or Saxon work.

Hill fort   An iron age fortification achieved by earthworks, i.e. earth banks and ditch, to assist a naturally defensive area. The addition of timbered fencing was likely.

Hood mould or drip mould   A moulding that projects over a door or window to throw off rain from the walls. Often connected along the sides of a building by a string course.

Impost   Bracket like a capital projecting from a wall carrying the ends of an arch.

Inglenook   A seat inside the chimneybreast of a large fire for resort in times of extreme cold.

Iron age   Shortly before the Romans came to Britain, i.e. 600 BC onwards, but also used in relation to the ancient Britons until the Saxon invasion.

Jamb   Window or door casing.

Keel moulding   Its section looks like the keel of a ship.

Keep   The central and most secure fortification built as a strong tower in a castle.

Keystone   Central component in an arch which meets the pressure from either side equally.

Kneeler   Bracket at the base of a gable cornice allowing water to drain off clear of the wall.

Knob   Decorative finial, giving e.g. seventeenth-century box pews a picturesque effect.

Label   Decorative end to a moulding.

Lancet   Slender window with pointed arch.

Lantern   Fenestrated turret on the roof of e.g. seventeenth-century building, or maybe a short storey in the roof with fenestration, the latter also sometimes called a clerestory.

Linenfold   Tudor panelling carved to represent linen folded vertically.

Lintel   A single beam carrying the weight over a window or doorway.

Loggia   Part of a building protected by an upper storey built on columns yet open to the weather.

Long and short work   Characteristic Saxon stonework, the uprights unusually high.

Louvre   Horizontal vanes set in e.g. bell openings of a tower to deflect the weather but also to let out the sound.

Lucarne   Elaborate decorative dormer-like opening in a spire.

Lunette   A semicircular opening.

Lychgate   Wooden gate to a churchyard with roof, where a coffin might be received.

Machicolation   Corbelled out fortification from a castle or church tower.

Misericord   Church seat that is hinged so as to provide support when the occupant is standing.

Modillion   Usually a series of brackets beneath a cornice, e.g. supporting the soffit of a Regency projecting roof.

Motte-and-bailey   Primitive castle made from erecting a wooden tower on an earth mound, usually surrounded by a wooden palisade.

Mouchette   Motif in window tracery like a curvilinear dagger.

Mullions   Stone or wooden uprights dividing a window.

Nail-head   EE moulding ornament of tiny pyramids.

Narthex   An enclosed porch.

Neolithic   Between 3500 BC until the bronze age when the first farming communities were established.

Newel   The principal posts in a staircase railing, the lesser uprights are balusters.

Obelisk   Independent square pillar tapering at the top.

Ogee   Where the foundation for a curved arch reverses half way up to rise to a pointed arch.

Orders of columns

   Greek Doric   Fat, fluted, tapering towards the top with plain capital – its **Roman** equivalent more slender and elegant.

   Tuscan   A plain unembellished column.

   Ionic   Fluted column with horned device in the capital.

   Corinthian   Fluted column with capital embellished with acanthus leaf devices.

   Composite   A combination of the latter two types of capital, often on a fluted column.

Oversailing   Where an upper storey or course of stonework projects out from the one below.

Ovolo   A plain rounded convex moulding.

Palladian   Classical ideas as formulated by Andrea Palladio.

Pantile   Interlocking S-shaped roof tile.

Pargetting   Patterned plasterwork.

Pediment   Triangular device set over e.g. an individual window or series of windows maybe alternating over windows with a segmental or elliptical shape.

Pendant   Decorative device at the intersection of e.g. ceiling plasterwork, where the boss hangs down.

Perp   Perpendicular period in Gothic architecture, 1350–1530.

Piano nobile   The main living storey of a grand house on the first floor.

Piazza   A deliberate space between buildings especially when the buildings are colonnaded.

Pier   A support, maybe a pillar.

Pilaster   Pier-shaped architrave.

Pinnacle   Conical or pyramidal decoration protruding from a tower parapet, spire or a gable.

Piscina   Stone basin in a church for washing Communion vessels.

Plinth   Protective base of a wall, possibly moulded like a skirting.

Poppyhead   Where the tops of benches or stalls are carved with leaves and flowers.

Portcullis   Castle gateway which may be hauled up vertically.

Portico   The columned centrepiece of a house.

Priory   Monastic house.

Quadrangle   Courtyard of a building.

Quarry   Diamond or square-shaped glass set in lead.

Quoin   Larger cornerstone often alternately wide and narrow.

Rampart Wall of earth or stone fortifying a castle or city.

Reeding Long parallel convex mouldings.

Refectory Dining hall.

Reredos Decorative screening behind an altar.

Respond A half pier projecting from a wall which carries part of an arch.

Reveal The door casing as far as the window or door.

Rococo More delicate later Baroque style.

Roll moulding Moulding aping a shaft perhaps in series.

Romanesque Usually called Norman and typified by round arched windows and doorways of the eleventh and twelfth centuries.

Rood A screen at the entrance to the chancel perhaps carrying a crucifix.

Roofs

   Hipped Sloping rather than vertical roof end.

   Mansard Roof as an additional storey with steeply sloping sides.

   Kingpost Roof construction in which the ridge of the roof is supported by a single post rising from a beam lying across the summit of its walls.

   Queenpost Similar with two struts.

   Hammer beam Extra support for the roof from large brackets projecting from the wall summits, the hammer beams, i.e. brackets are supported on arched braces.

Rose window or wheel window Circular window with spokes of tracery.

Rubble Building stone laid in courses of differing stone sizes.

Rustication Deliberate rough-facing on stone, the opposite of ashlar, it may be contrived, e.g. vermiculation.

Sanctuary The part of a church where the altar is placed.

Scalloped Like the block capital but subdivided into e.g. three cones rather than a cushion.

Screen Decorative separation between chapels.

Screen's passage Area between the hall and kitchen in a medieval house.

Soffit The ceiling beneath a projecting roof or arch.

Solar Upper living room of a medieval house usually on the south side.

Sounding board or tester Board over a pulpit to project sound.

Spandrel The part left from a rectangle when an arch is deployed within it.

Stiff-leaf capital EE capital decorated with leaves.

Strapwork Formal interlaced banding imitating leatherwork, often deployed on Elizabethan screens.

String course A projecting horizontal band following an external wall marking the storeys.

Stucco Plasterwork.

Swag Plaster festoon like a suspended piece of cloth.

Tracery The decorative divisions within a window which developed as wider windows became possible. First were single or double lancets maybe with a quatrefoil at the head, or Y-shaped with a third diamond light at the head, 1250–1310.

   Intersecting tracery i.e. three or more lights, whose mullions intersect at the top.

   Reticulated tracery Like intersecting tracery this comes within the Dec period, 1290–1350, the tracery captures (usually) quatrefoils between interweaving tracery in a curvilinear pattern often displaying great elegance.

   Perp tracery Within a wider and flatter arch, the arch flattening even more in Tudor times and involving:

   Panel tracery A window head made up of a series of panel shapes, sometimes with other patterns superimposed.

Transept Wings of a church protruding north and south from the crossing, rendering the church in the shape of a cross.

Transom Horizontal glazing bar in wood or stone, the opposite of a mullion.

Turret Small round tower.

Tympanum Arch holding the stone or brick over the top of a doorway, often decorated with carving e.g. in Norman times.

Vault Construction of stone roof springing from the walls of the building.

   Fan vault Where the ribs radiate springing from single points – evoking a sense of lightness and strength.

   Tunnel vault or barrel vault A semicircular or pointed section, usually Norman.

   Groin vault When two tunnel vaults meet at right angles.

   Rib vault Vault of diagonal ribs.

   Lierne vault Occurs where the principal or transverse rib springs to the centre from corners or along the wall, but intermediate ribs are constructed perhaps in the form of a star, i.e. they do not spring from the walls.

Venetian window Three windows in series with the central larger than the outside two. A popular eighteenth-century feature.

Villa In the nineteenth century it was a country house for the residence of an opulent person but has come to mean a substantial urban house.

Volute Spiral scroll sometimes in the shape of a bracket.

Waterleaf Capital decorated with a tapering leaf.

Weepers Carved figures showing desolation in the niches of a tomb, perhaps little people.

Houses and Parks Open

Bankfield House, Halifax
Italianate Mansion. The former home of Colonel Akroyd, industrialist, now a museum.
www.calderdale.gov.uk

Bramham Hall
Early classical house, important Louis XIV garden. Home of the Lane Fox family.
www.bramhampark.co.uk

Bolling Hall, Bradford
Medieval and Elizabethan house and museum.
www.bradfordmuseums.org

Bretton Hall (YSP)
House not open but sculptures in the park and visitor centre.
www.ysp.co.uk

Cliffe Castle, Keighley
Industrialist's Gothic mansion and museum.
www.bradfordmuseums.org

East Riddlesden House, Keighley
Jacobean hall. NT.
www.nationaltrust.org.uk/main/w-eastriddlesdenhall

Harewood House, Leeds
Magnificent eighteenth-century palace. Home of the Earls of Harewood.
www.harewood.org

Kirkstall Abbey and House
Substantial Romanesque ruins including Norman gatehouse converted to museum.
www.leeds.gov.uk/abbeyhouse

Manor House, Ilkley Museum
www.bradfordmuseums.org

Nostell Priory
Eighteenth-century mansion. NT, and home of Lord St Oswald
www.nationaltrust.org.uk/nostell-priory

Oakwood Hall
Elizabethan manor house and museum.
www.calderdale.gov.uk

The Parsonage, Haworth
Eighteenth-century house and museum.
www.bronte.org.uk

Shibden Hall, Halifax
Substantial timbered hall of seventeenth century.
www.calderdale.gov.uk

Temple Newsam House, Leeds
Large Tudor and Jacobean mansion. Former home of Viscount Irwin.
www.leeds.gov.uk/templenewsamhouse

Industrial Archaeology

Railways

The Keighley and Worth Valley Railway
www.kwvr.co.uk

Kirklees Light Railway
www.kirkleeslightrailway.com

Middleton Railway, Leeds
www.middletonrailway.org.uk

Mine

Caphouse Colliery
www.ncm.org.uk

Mills

Armley Mills, Leeds
www.leeds.gov.uk/armleymills

Gibson Mill, Hebden Bridge
Phone 01422 841023 (NT)

Moorside Mills, Bradford
www.bradfordmuseums.org

Thwaite Mill, Leeds
www.leeds.gov.uk/thwaitemills

Markets

Batley	Friday, Saturday	Hemsworth	Tuesday, Friday, Saturday
Bingley	Wednesday, Friday, Saturday	Holmfirth	Thursday
Birstall	Thursday	Holmfirth Farmers	Third Sunday in month
Brighouse	Wednesday, Saturday	Huddersfield Farmers	Second Sunday in month
Cleckheaton Farmers	First Saturday in month	Normanton	Saturday
Dewsbury	Wednesday, Saturday	Ossett	Tuesday, Friday
Elland	Friday	Ossett Farmers	Fourth Saturday in month
Featherstone	Thursday	Otley	Tuesday, Friday, Saturday
Halifax Farmers	Third Saturday in month	Otley Farmers	Last Sunday in month
Halifax Piece Hall	Saturday	Pontefract	Wednesday, Saturday
Headingley Farmers	Second Saturday in month	Pontefract Farmers	Friday
Hebden Bridge	Thursday	Pudsey	Tuesday, Friday, Saturday
Hebden Bridge Farmers	First, third Sunday in month	Pudsey Farmers	Last Thursday in month
Heckmondwike	Tuesday, Saturday		

Acknowledgements of Sources

John Betjeman, 'The Licorice Fields of Pontefract', John Murray. Used by permission.

Colour photographs

The Hall (by Robert Kay), the Gallery, the Yellow Drawing Room and the State Bedroom at Harewood House. Reproduced by the kind permission of the Earl and Countess of Harewood and Trustees of the Harewood House Trust.

Three paintings of Calderdale: *Halifax No. 2* by John Piper; *Bowling Dyke* by Claude Muncaster; and *New Bank* by Tom Whitehead. Used by permission of Calderdale Council, Halifax.

Pontefract Castle by Alexander Keirinx (c.1620–40). Used by permission of Wakefield Council.

Wakefield Bridge and *Chantry Chapel* (1793) by Philip Reinagle. Used by permission of The Hepworth Gallery Wakefield Council.

Map of West Yorkshire used by permission of Bartholomew Collins.

Photographs by William Glossop: Dewsbury Minster: Medieval glass showing farming; Bolling Hall, Bradford: the Ghost room; Halifax Minstry: 'Old Tristram' poor box; Halifax: Gothic cast-iron North Bridge, 1871, by J & J Fraser; Halifax Minster: the East Window by Hedgeland; Junction of Rochdale Canal; Welcome to Batley; Bargee and boy statue at the Lock Beam, Sowerby Bridge, Halifax.

Photographs by Harland Walshaw: Bankfield House, Halifax: the Saloon ceiling and fireplace; Cliffe Castle, Keighley, Pre-Raphaelite glass: Tristram and Isoude drinking the potion by Dante Gabriel Rossetti; Tristram and the Harp, and Recognition of Tristram by la Belle Isoude, both by Edward Burne-Jones; Weaving and dying at Roberts Mill, Keighley.

Index of Names

Old Market, Halifax